HARVARD HISTORICAL STUDIES

PUBLISHED UNDER THE DIRECTION
OF THE DEPARTMENT OF HISTORY

FROM THE INCOME OF
THE HENRY WARREN TORREY FUND

VOLUME LIX

Georges Sorel

Prophet Without Honor

A STUDY IN ANTI-INTELLECTUALISM

by

RICHARD HUMPHREY

1971

OCTAGON BOOKS

New York

Copyright, 1951 by the President and Fellows of Harvard College

Reprinted 1971
by special arrangement with Harvard University Press

OCTAGON BOOKS
A DIVISION OF FARRAR, STRAUS & GIROUX, INC.
19 Union Square West
New York, N. Y. 10003

LIBRARY OF CONGRESS CATALOG CARD NUMBER: 72-159195

ISBN 0-374-94037-1

Manufactured by Braun-Brumfield, Inc.
Ann Arbor, Michigan

Printed in the United States of America

PREFACE

This study assumes that the part of the work of Georges Sorel that has permanent value is his analysis of social dynamics and his development of a series of hypotheses leading to a greater understanding of behavior in modern politics. I have not been particularly concerned with his position in the factional struggles of sects and parties of the early twentieth century. I have not thought it necessary to labor the errors and inconsistencies and obscurities of his writings since they must surely be evident to even the superficial reader. My intention has been to present as clearly as may be such of his ideas and observations as should be taken into account in arriving at a judgment of his contribution to the study of social forces in the modern world. For this reason I have used his own words wherever possible.

Sorel's interests were wide; he wrote as other men might talk—unguardedly and as ideas occurred to him. He published principally in periodicals, which gave him the freedom he required. Many of his books, in fact, are collections of such periodical articles. A very full bibliography of his works, compiled by Paul Delesalle, is to be found in the *International Review for Social History*, Volume IV (1939). The translations of quoted passages are my own except for the *Reflections on Violence* where I sometimes used the English version of T. E. Hulme.

I am particularly grateful to Professor Crane Brinton for his assistance and encouragement at all stages of this project and to Professor Shepard Clough for his friendly interest and advice. My colleagues Professor Melvin Kranzberg, Professor Herbert Dinerstein, and Professor Philip Campbell have been most kind in reading the manuscript and suggesting improvements in the presentation. The views expressed are, of course, only my own.

R.D.H.

Hoboken, New Jersey
October 8, 1950

CONTENTS

Woe to the crown of pride, to the drunkards of Ephraim, whose glorious beauty is a fading flower . . . The crown of pride, the drunkards of Ephraim, shall be trodden under feet.

—Isaiah. Quoted by Sorel in Contribution à l'étude profane de la Bible.

CHAPTER I

INTRODUCTION

C'est une loi générale de l'histoire: une doctrine ne peut conquérir le monde qu'en perdant tout lien personnel avec le fondateur: L'exemple agit pour maintenir quelques groupes peu étendus de disciples qui s'évanouissent;—la masse adapte l'invention à ses conditions de vie, la fait sienne et la rend parfois méconnaissable.

—*Georges Sorel*, Sociologie de la suggestion

GEORGES SOREL is one of the most provocative and baffling figures of modern thought. It is strange that his reputation should be so great and, in another sense, strange, too, that it should not be greater. To the world he is known as the author of one book, the *Reflections on Violence* and, more vaguely, as a man who influenced the ideologies of fascism and communism. He has been called on to play the role of a modern Machiavelli: praised for his flashes of insight on the basic forces of politics but damned for the methods he seemed to condone in the fulfillment of his purpose. Actually his first preoccupation was always with problems of ethics.[1] However his overwhelming concern to find an honest basis for new values in the modern world led him so far from conventional and accepted attitudes that both his admirers and detractors have often fallen into the error of judging him too narrowly within the frame of their own ethical preconceptions. He is too subtle to be dismissed so cavalierly. Benedetto Croce has said that he and Marx are the only truly original thinkers socialism has had; there is much to justify this opinion—particularly if his work is viewed as a whole and his many apparent inconsistencies related to the inner purpose that dominated all his thought. Such an effort of understanding depends on an acquaintance with the character of the man and with the development of his ideas as he continuously drew conclusions throughout his career from history and from events of the world around him.

Sorel was truly what the French call a *moraliste*. The causes that interested him and the support he gave to some of them were wholly secondary to his personal need for an active expression of constructive social wishes. He was not a reformer in the conventional sense, nor was he a dogmatist with a plan: he was a searcher; he valued more highly the means than the end. His most outstanding characteristic, in the eyes of his friend Croce, was his very marked consciousness of moral problems.[2] This consciousness is evident in his first published book, *Le Procès de Socrate*, and it continues unblunted through the flood of writing that followed. Without a recognition of this impelling interest his career would be meaningless and his ideas a chaos.

Sorel's intellectual production and his quiet personal life provide very little direct evidence of the primary experiences out of which grew the structure of his moral ideas. They do give us, though, a clear picture of a complex character; they tell us the kind of man he was; they set for us the pattern of the personality by which he valued and judged the experiences of the world he worked in. An appreciation of the tone and inflection of this personality is particularly important to an unraveling of the obscurities and contradictions that mark his written word.

E. Georges Sorel was born on November 2, 1847, at Cherbourg of an old Catholic family in moderate circumstances. He had the blue eyes and ruddy complexion of the Norse stock of his land. It later years his sturdy frame and white beard gave his appearance a rather heroic touch which his friends thought singularly appropriate in this man whom they regarded as a kind of modern Viking. Nothing more eventful is recorded of his early years than the expeditions and visits to relatives usual for a boy in his position. One of his close boyhood friends was a cousin Albert Sorel who was to become the well-known historian of the Revolution. Family friendships remained important to him all his life and he came to rely on them especially after the death of his wife. One of his nieces cared for him in the several years of heart trouble that made him a semi-invalid before his death on August 28, 1922.

His early education was at a private school in Cherbourg and, for a brief period, at the Collège Rollin in Paris. At seventeen he entered the Ecole polytechnique where he distinguished himself for his mathematical ability. Two years later he took his degree and found a place in the Department of Bridges and Roads of the French government. He served there with distinction for twenty-five years and rose to the position of Chief Engineer. In 1891 he offered his resignation, which was regretfully accepted. He refused the pension to which he was entitled because he did not wish to be bound by any official obligations. However he did accept the Ribbon of the Legion of Honor as a recognition of his work, and it is characteristic of his pride in the kind of practical achievement for which the award stood that he should wear the Ribbon the rest of his life through all the fluctuations of his feelings toward the government and institutions of his country.

During the period of his service in the government Sorel was seldom in Paris, his duties taking him into the provinces and through the colonies. It was then that he laid the foundations, through omnivorous reading, of the encyclopedic knowledge that astonished his friends later. As he himself put it: "During twenty years I worked to deliver myself from what I retained of an education; I read books, not so much to learn as to efface from my memory the ideas that had been thrust upon it."[3]

When he retired he was able to settle in a modest house at Boulogne-sur-Seine, a suburb of Paris, where he could put on an old straw hat and carpet slippers and dig comfortably in the garden. He remarked once that men ought to have only one house as they have only one mother. As a matter of fact there was a very real relationship between the two in his own life since it was a legacy that came to him on the death of his mother that provided him with the small but comfortable income he lived on after his early retirement.

In 1875 Sorel married a girl of peasant stock to whom he remained devoted the rest of his life. Several of his books bear affectionate dedications to her and on her death in 1897 he wrote to his friends of his loss in moving terms. She was "the companion of twenty-two years of work" to whom he still felt bound by "la forza del primo amore."[4] It is clear that these phrases were not conventional tributes but represented a deep feeling of obligation and gratitude to a woman who had supported him with her love and had taught him that justice is not an abstract thing but is based on the actual relationships of human beings. It was she who had first turned his attention to the potentialities of the working people and it was to her memory that he sought in his remaining years to erect a philosophical monument. She had revealed to him his genius. "It is thus that our intellectual life depends in large part on the chance of a meeting."[5]

Sorel's intellectual life was an intense and disciplined one. He spent a good deal of time after his retirement in the Bibliothèque nationale where he collected, and stored in his memory, an extraordinary diversity of facts and references. He might be seen in syndicalist circles, at the Bourse du Travail, the Société de Philosophie, the courses of Henri Bergson, or at the Ecole des Hautes Etudes sociales, a kind of free peoples' school, of which he was an administrator for a number of years. He was quite aware of the schools and tendencies of art, music, and the theatre in Paris, although, especially in his later years, he became impatient with the sterility or ineffectiveness of contemporary culture expressed in these forms and withdrew from them.

The place where he was most regularly to be seen in the decade before the First World War, and where he was to be seen in the most characteristic light, was on Tuesdays in the tiny front office of the *Cahiers de la quinzaine*, which had been founded by his friend Charles Péguy. This was the modern gymnasium, the Stoa, where he found listeners for the provocative and always original conversation in which he clarified and expressed the ideas that had arisen from his current reading and thought. There was never any doubt about who was master of the little circle that gathered in the shop of the *Cahiers*: Sorel by prescriptive right sat on the only chair in the room; to him questions were directed and from him came the firm grip that held the talk to a line of consistent development. His assertion of authority in the circle was unforced and was as naturally accepted. However strong his own opinions on a subject, he never brushed aside an opposing view without fair consideration of its possibilities. Unlike many famous conversationalists, he was not so much concerned with creating an impression as he was in testing his ideas on the minds of his friends. Often he would return after considering some intellectual position for a week and admit that it had been too hastily taken or that it required serious modification. He pursued these questions with a tenacious zeal that sometimes astonished and amused his friends. He might accept the company of one of the circle as far as the corner where he was accustomed to board the streetcar to Boulogne-sur-Seine and, if the car did not appear immediately, walk his friend, absorbed in conversation, all the way out. He might turn up at a friend's house, knock heavily on the door and, after a perfunctory greeting, resume a topic of conversation of the week before as if there had been no interruption or as if he had been preoccupied all his waking hours since with a reconsideration of the arguments then advanced. On one occasion a mutual friend of Sorel and Maurice Barrès decided to bring together at lunch these two men who criticized severely each other's work but who had never actually met. Plans were carefully laid and the principals greeted each other most amicably in an atmosphere of the best behavior. Each of them was so anxious not to offend that Barrès talked nothing but sociology and Sorel nothing but literary criticism. The conversation was a ludicrous dodging of each other's susceptibilities so that each left with serious doubts of the other's intelligence.

Sorel loved good conversation; his taste in this art, as in other respects, showed him to be a man of Old France. One day he confided to a friend that, despite his fondness for talking about the most abstract ideas, he found writing exceedingly hard. He wished that he could communicate his ideas by phonograph recordings instead of by books. Often, indeed, his writing is actually a kind of conversational monologue with all the charm, the allusiveness and the lack of orderly, balanced exposition of that form of expression. Sorel was too impatient to bother filling the spaces between his ideas. He wrote for those few interested thinkers capable of filling the gaps themselves from a sympathetic understanding of his purpose. This style, free from the obligations of consistency and cautious moderation, was well suited to his bold and searching personality and to the fluidity of his philosophical mind; but it has prevented his works from becoming popular and it has promoted misunderstanding. Many of his commentators have wasted their ingenuity in a sterile accounting of his attitudes and judgments instead of in trying to reach beneath the surface to the feelings and images that alone give life to the work.

In a letter to his friend Daniel Halévy which prefaces the *Reflections on Violence* Sorel very frankly states the problems he found in communicating his ideas. He speaks of the *ready-made* kind of knowledge, convenient for students who need formulas for practical life, and then dissociates himself from that approach:

"My own method of work is entirely opposed to this, for I put before my readers the actual struggle with which thought seeks to escape from the confines of a structure already made for the world at large so as to reveal the part of it that is personal to me. The only things I find it worthwhile entering in my notebooks are those I have not met elsewhere; I readily skip the transitions between these things, because they nearly always come under the heading of commonplaces.

"The communication of thought is always very difficult for anyone who has strong metaphysical preoccupations; he thinks that speech will spoil the most fundamental parts of his thought, those that are very near to the moving force of the mind, those that appear so natural to him that he never seeks to express them. The reader has great difficulty grasping the thought of an inventor because he can only arrive at its meaning by finding again the path that first led to it. Verbal communication is much easier than written communication because spoken words act on the feelings in a mysterious way and easily establish a sympathetic bond between people; it is in this manner that an orator is able to convince listeners by arguments that are hard to appreciate when read later by someone else."[6]

As he went on to say, one great virtue of his method was that he was in no danger of becoming his own disciple, of becoming a slave to his own system or, even, of becoming the founder of a school to which he might find himself bound. His ambition was to be the awakener, the one who stirs the ashes and makes the flames leap up in the minds of others so as to kindle in them, too, the spirit of invention.[7]

Although his work covers a truly encyclopedic range of subjects, Sorel never gave a formal and systematic exposition to any one of them—not even to his famous theory of syndicalism. One reason for this lack of organization was that, finding writing extremely difficult, he nearly always chose to maintain his bearings by choosing as subject for discussion some book by a good author rather than to look for initiative entirely within himself.[8] This practice of making discursive notes on other men's works had certain drawbacks that are obvious to any reader, but it had at least one very great advantage: it allowed Sorel to use his remarkable critical faculty in the development and emendation of hypotheses latent in the methods of many different systems of thought. The fruitfulness of his criticism was, in fact, due to the very qualities that led him to this method of composition; instead of criticizing a philosophy by comparing it to some external system, he sought to understand its virtues and its shortcomings on the basis of its own procedures. As he says: "The true method to follow in order to understand the faults, the insufficiencies and the errors of a philosophy of any importance, consists in criticizing it after its own principles."[9] There could be no better rule of criticism for judging the significance of Sorel's work than that which he himself followed; consequently the various explanatory hypotheses that he developed in the course of his studies may be profitably applied to his own theories just as those theories were applied by him to others.

Chief among these hypotheses is that of the *myth*, a conception evolved by him to account for the expressions of will that have given a dynamic force to the manifestations of all great social beliefs. In using this theory to throw light on the social forces animating such historical phenomena as Christian faith or Revolutionary idealism, Sorel seems to show an attitude of scientific detachment and skepticism towards them; but when, in his enthusiastic advocacy of a philosophy of syndicalism, he declares that the success of this ideology too is dependent on a myth, on an implicit belief in the achievement of a general strike that is never actually going to be attained, such a skepticism takes on a paradoxical appearance. It would almost seem that his critical exposition of the theory of the myth must necessarily have provided a fundamental obstacle to his own acceptance of it as a valid instrument for shaping proletarian aspirations. Such, however, was not the case: although he was never an active participant in the proletarian movement he was by no means simply a disinterested and objective observer of it. The passionate fervor and sincerity of purpose that he brought to his study of proletarian tactics could not have been the product of a purely skeptical spirit; they must evidently have had as basis some profound sympathy with the underlying motives of the syndicalist movement. The proper explanation of this zeal, however, must be sought not in the ideals or myths of the proletariat as such, but in the convictions, the aspirations, the personal myths of the man himself.

The real unity of Sorel's work, and its real impetus, are to be found in his unremitting search for some new ethical principle that might bring about a rejuvenation of modern society. Many of the paradoxes in his work and career that prove so baffling to the casual reader may be explained by the fact that he was not interested for their own sake in the program and proposals of any particular sect or party but only in the possibilities that such groups might offer of providing a moral stimulus to society. "It is hardly worth while," he says, "to know what is the best morality, but only to determine if there is *a mechanism in existence capable of guaranteeing the development of morality.*"[1v]

Some attempt will be made elsewhere to show in a general way what Sorel meant by *morality*; but such an exposition can hardly hope to reach any satisfactory conclusion since Sorel himself never felt obliged to give to the word a precise or scientific definition. To him morality was not a system that might be described, but was the outcome of action, of an expression of will. "It must be recognized," he says, "that all the discussions of metaphysicians on morality are not able to affect the production of action, because they do not bring the feelings into play: by these methods one can find only formal laws." Sorel's own advocacy of morality certainly did not lack such an appeal to feeling; as he says, a morality of autonomy demands that we should be *"the worshippers of our own faith."* In his way of thinking, however, a faith of this sort does not necessarily imply the subjection of the individual to external authority—it is, on the contrary, an expression of the fullest internal liberty; the individual can act only when the consequences of that act are completed in his imagination by a process of faith that allows him to see the act, not disjunctively, but as a fully accomplished state. "When we act," says Sorel, "it is because we have created an entirely artificial world, placed in advance of the present, formed of movements that depend on ourselves."[11]

It was the creation of just such an artificial world or myth that supplied a lifelong stimulus to Sorel's moral aspirations. Filled as he was with a deep pessimism, a pessimism reminiscent of many of the great figures in Christianity, he looked on nature with distrust and fear. To him nature was a blind and arbitrary and fatal force that threatened always to overwhelm the small conquest of liberty won from it by man in his bitter struggle to become civilized and human. It was moreover a decadent force: the recurrent renewal of life and the multiplication of seed meant to Sorel not prodigality but dissipation; the true aspect of nature to him was to be seen in the second law of thermodynamics. But just as with physical phenomena it is possible by the extravagant expenditure of energy to create apparent individual exceptions to this general rule of degeneration, so in the history of civilization a similar effect occurs when man asserts himself to control and modify the forces of nature. Such an event, Sorel thought, ought properly to be regarded as only an episode, a temporary check in the normal tendency of human nature "to escape toward decadence";[12] but, to him, it represented, nonetheless, the only possible basis for human grandeur, since it proclaimed the victory of man, in however limited and tentative a way, over the dominance of an arbitrary nature. The whole meaning of Sorel's life is contained in this conception of a struggle of liberation, or, as he calls it, in the striving for *deliverance*. His conviction in the necessity of this struggle is the one uncompromising principle from which he never deviated; it is the key to all the changes and apparent inconsistencies of his conceptions; it is, in short, the *myth* that provided the inner meaning and dynamic force to all his thought and work.

Sorel's conception of a clear-cut struggle between the two opposing forces of man and nature is, like all myths, an artificial creation. In reality no such distinction can be made: man is himself simply a part of nature; he cannot divorce himself from it and consequently cannot conquer it. In fact the whole basis of the myth when viewed as a rational exposition of reality becomes palpably absurd. The question of its validity, however, is of no particular importance in understanding the significance of the theories to which it gave rise: it is useless to analyze the ends postulated by a myth and to attempt to judge the success or the efficacy of it by the possibility of attaining those ends. As has already been explained, the myth is an expression of will, and the ends are significant not in themselves but only because action is governed by them *as if* they were a true representation of reality. It was of no particular concern to Sorel whether or not man could actually be distinguished from nature, or whether the mysterious powers of nature could ever be conquered by human reason. These myths were merely artificial worlds created by the will as an explanation and completion of its own action. Their significant aspect is to be found, therefore, not in a simple representation of action but in the actual tendency of the will manifesting itself through the creation of that representation.

In Sorel this tendency arose from a highly developed feeling of individuality that showed itself at once in a constant effort to maintain the integrity of his self from the encroachment of outside forces and in an almost equally powerful desire to assert that self through a common struggle with other men against the dominance of circumstances and environment. The unquestioned postulate of his action, the faith that could not be questioned, was that man must win his freedom through ceaseless struggle for the preservation of his self as expressed in the common aspirations of a human society. To Sorel progress was a purely dynamic conception; it could not rest on the fruits of past victories or on the accomplishments of other struggles. Grandeur is possible only through a moment of action and, when that action ceases, the forces of decadence once more resume their course. As he says: "Chance favors some epochs that are prolific in superior men: when one compares times that have preceded grandeur and those that have followed, one is forced to affirm that some striking analogies exist between them; although the ways of presenting things may be very much changed, it is a like spirit of mediocrity that animates the two periods. The law of apparent regression is therefore not without foundation; but it has a quite different import from that which its promoters have attributed to it; it signifies that humanity sometimes departs from mediocrity under the pressure of certain constraints, but that it returns when it is abandoned to its own tendencies; it would not be impossible then that the future of societies, refined and fallen into full decadence, would resemble a distant savage past."[13]

Far from being free, the natural man, Sorel thought, must inevitably be enslaved by the arbitrary forces of physical necessity of which he is a part and in which he is submerged. He can rise above them and emancipate himself, paradoxically enough, "only under the pressure of certain constraints"—that is to say, only by creating an artificial world of order within which he can confine his strivings and within which he can hope for mastery. The most obvious example of such constraint is in the artificial world created by modern scientists, a world that has been extraordinarily successful in providing the means for controlling physical phenomena, but one that makes no pretense of being necessarily an actual representation of reality. Although this man-made creation demands a rigid adherence to a complicated system of laws and conventions—rules that sometimes are so purely mathematical as to be quite beyond the scope of common-sense comprehension—it is nevertheless through science that man has been provided with his most powerful instruments for the conquest of nature. Social action, Sorel thought, must be bound by similar constraints; a hypothetical form must be envisaged before action can be taken and it is the struggle to fulfill the purpose of this form, within its self-imposed limitations, that constitutes "the way of deliverance." In his opinion man is free only in action, and the sterility of modern civilization, the impotence of modern man, is due to lack of forms or myths suitable for the expression of a common will. The belief that this "decadence" could be overcome, that man could free and redeem himself only through a participation in moments of fervor and grandeur, was the dominating principle of his thought; it was the criterion by which he judged the usefulness of all social theories and systems; it was the motive of his life-long search for a new social myth that might serve to revitalize the morality of contemporary civilization.

Many of the apparent shifts and inconsistencies in his
point of view that might appear to show a certain fickleness
or instability of mind are, in fact, simply the result of his
honesty and his singleness of purpose in pursuing this
search. Consequently he sometimes felt obliged, almost in
spite of himself, to evolve theories that seem to be at complete variance with his earlier thought and at variance even
with the ends he proposed to achieve through them. One of
the most characteristic aspects of this way of thought was
his refusal to bind himself by any system, either his own or
that of others. As Ascoli says in an excellent little essay on
him: "Few authors have found it possible to attain a similar
degree of fluidity."[14] The secret of this fluidity lies in the
fact that Sorel was interested not in epistemology but in
action, and consequently could abandon, without impairing
his very real consistency of spirit, any theory that did not
promise to forward the ends of his personal myth. He himself gives a clear expression of this attitude in a reply he
made to an interpretation of his work by a contemporary.
"I myself," he says, "have never sought to determine what
would be the synthesis of my various writings. I write from
day to day according to the need of the moment."[15] The
common mistake of many of Sorel's commentators has been
to analyze the various phases of these day to day writings
as if they were separately formulated philosophical systems
capable of being dissociated from the strivings and convictions that animated all his work. The important thing to
observe, however, is not the manifestations of his thoughts
in themselves, but the conflict between principles and needs
of the moment that made those manifestations necessary.

At the beginning of his career as a writer, Sorel published
almost simultaneously two books: the *Contribution à l'étude
profane de la Bible* and the *Procès de Socrate*. In the first of
these, which was primarily a work of Biblical exegesis, he
deplored the deleterious spread of utilitarianism among the

middle and lower classes, a corruption that might be
checked, he thought, by a return to "the heroic life" whose
principles are embodied in the Christian scriptures. "The
Book of the people exists," he says; "it is the Bible."[16] In
the second work, a treatise on the decay of Greek democracy, he denounces the irresponsible demagogy and cosmo-
politanism that followed Athens' imperialist ventures and
shows a strong sympathy for such representatives of the
Old Guard as Aristophanes and Xenophon in their stand
against the corruption of civic virtue by the Sophists,
aesthetes, and Eastern mystics. Although unconventional
and in some ways decidedly audacious, neither of these
books would have led a contemporary to suppose that its
author was more than a somewhat original disciple of Renan
or possibly an admirer of Nietzsche. Both works show a
rather aristocratic disdain for vulgar opinion and a puritanical disapproval of self-indulgence—attitudes that could
hardly have provided grounds for a surmise that the ideas
of this same man were soon to be strongly influenced by
Marxian socialism and that he was later to be the foremost
exponent of a purely proletarian ideology. With the advantage of knowing the subsequent development of his
thought, however, and knowing from his own statements
that these two studies were consciously undertaken as a
part of that "self-education" by which he hoped to prepare
himself for an original investigation of social problems, it
is possible to see even this early in his career the conflict
of feeling and circumstances that was to carry him from a
defence of traditional conservatism to the support of intransigent radicalism.

The patriotic virtues of heroic Greece and the militant
zeal of early Christianity were to Sorel outstanding examples of myths that succeeded in raising civilization from
mediocrity to a moment of grandeur; it was to them that
he turned in order to understand the dynamics of a process

that he hoped might serve a similar purpose in the modern world. The strength of Greece and the strength of the Church, he concluded, lay in the dominance of a moral aristocracy, a dominance that was in the end undermined by the very success of their ideologies and by their spread. "It is necessary," he writes, "that laws adapt themselves to the least troublesome, the strongest and the most general tendencies of the human spirit; however, in proportion as we have investigated regions in which our intelligence manifests itself most freely, we have recognized that mediocrity holds a more complete sway. What is called in this study by the pejorative name of *mediocrity* is, by political writers, called *democracy*; thus it is shown that history demands the reintroduction of democracy."[17]

The relationship that Sorel established early in his career between democracy and mediocrity, and between mediocrity and decadence, was never to be abandoned. In modern France as in ancient Greece, he felt, the demagogues recklessly squandered the spiritual heritage laid up by the moral aristocracy of former days. In the decadence of Hellenistic times, however, a new faith had arisen and a new aristocracy pledged to the service of Christ offered a way of deliverance. The great question in Sorel's mind was whether there might not be found in the modern world a similar force capable of bringing about a *ricorso*, a revitalization of moral principles by which it would be possible to check the decadence, the mediocrity, the democracy of the time.

Following his preliminary studies of former cultures, Sorel turned his attention to the movement that seemed to be replacing the Church as the champion of moral values, to socialism and in particular to Marxian socialism. This interest in Marx can be understood, however, only in the light of a much earlier, more profound, and more enduring attachment to the philosophy of Proudhon—an attachment due not to any essential similarity of their theoretical systematizations but to a common agreement of feelings on the ethical basis of society. The rather naïve faith that Proudhon had in the ideals of the Revolution. could not be accepted by Sorel. It was, in fact, Marx's attack on this Revolutionary ideology that led Sorel to adopt his theories with so much enthusiasm; they were, he believed, a truer representation of actual social forces, and hence a more adequate vehicle for the expression of Proudhon's ethical aspirations, than were Proudhon's own. Sorel's synthesis of these two thinkers was not a simple process, however, and was evolved only gradually as a development of his own thought. Although he says of Proudhon, "No philosopher of the nineteenth century was, more than he, the victim of rationalist prejudices"; and although of himself he declares, "It seems to me that I have never had a great veneration for the men of the French Revolution";[18] yet he did, nonetheless, cling for some time to certain intellectualist illusions, as he himself later called them.[19] In 1899 he had convinced himself that "in France socialism is becoming more and more a *labor movement in a democracy.*"[20] At the time the statement was made, Sorel believed that this tendency was a necessary and desirable step in the progress of socialism; it represented a transition, he thought, from abstract speculation to real life; it raised socialism from a sect to a political party and gave it the place of an organ in an organism.[21]

The basis of this democratic illusion, as he himself subsequently confessed, was a confusion of the traditional philosophical utopia of democracy with the reality of the actual democratic regime instituted by demagogues.[22] Encouraged by the common enthusiasm that had united men of the most diverse beliefs in the cause of Dreyfus, Sorel was led to believe that a similar sort of coöperation might be possible for the accomplishment of particular reforms in the future. At the beginning of the "Affaire" it appeared that the triumph of the popular front movement over the corrupt regime of Church and Army would result in the institution of a government truly interested in social questions; but this triumph had quite other consequences. Instead of producing a socially responsible republican aristocracy, it undermined the whole basis of social authority on which alone a parliamentary regime can successfully function; instead of implementing a philosophy of solidarity it resulted only in hypocritical evasions and in the satisfaction of sordid ambitions. Although his name had been at the head of the list of intellectuals who first came to the support of Dreyfus,[23] the ignominious outcome of this great struggle for justice so embittered Sorel that he turned with fury on his former comrades and renounced forever his illusion that proletarian socialism could be achieved through political tactics.[24] The Dreyfusian Revolution which he considered so significant in the history of French politics was also very significant to him personally, since it crystallized once for all the as yet imprecise ideas that he had on questions that were later to form the principal concern of the *Reflections on Violence.* As he himself declared subsequently: "The liquidation of the Dreyfusian Revolution obliged me to recognize that proletarian socialism or syndicalism realizes its nature fully only if it is by its own will a labor movement directed against the demagogues."[25]

Forced by circumstances to abandon Proudhon's hope that the problems of social justice would be solved by a republican aristocracy asserting a new morality through the channels of democratic institutions, Sorel now returned to that study of purely proletarian institutions that he had begun as early as 1897 in the *Avenir socialiste des syndicats,* but which had been interrupted by the false hopes of the Dreyfus Affair. Disillusioned in the leadership of intellectuals, he thought to find in the growth of workers' *syndicats* the necessary stabilizing basis, the source of *social authorities* that could alone permit an autonomous development of a disciplined labor movement; it was a study of the possibilities inherent in such a development that led him to evolve his famous philosophy of syndicalism in the best known of all his works, the *Reflections on Violence.* It is interesting and significant that this period of fully developed syndicalism lasted with Sorel less than five years. The *Reflections* was written in 1905–1906, but by 1910 its author had already abandoned hope in the ideology he had expounded with so much zeal.[26] Instead of producing a distinctively proletarian ideology, the syndicalist movement tended more and more to become simply a convenient stepping stone for aspiring politicians; instead of developing a new aristocracy and a new morality, the syndicats were rapidly abandoning intransigent principles and were sinking to the level of the opportunist politicians with whom they bargained. Since Sorel's original interest in them was due almost entirely to the role he expected them to play as exponents of a vigorous ideology opposed to bourgeois culture, and since they had obviously failed to fulfill this ethical purpose, he abandoned them without any hesitation. Feeling that socialism was dead, he turned once again to his studies of the early Church. In a letter to Croce he says: "Socialism is becoming a demagogy, in the syndicats as well as in political factions. Consequently it no longer offers anything of interest to philosophers; that is why I am resolved never again to write on this subject."[27]

Although he did not altogether succeed in renouncing his interest in socialism, it is undoubtedly true that the high point of his enthusiasm was now passed; never again was he able to find in any social movement the same possibilities of a *ricorso,* the same hopes of an ethical rejuvenation that he had once looked for in syndicalism. The twelve years from 1910 to his death were years of increasing bitterness and of increasing isolation from the struggles and the aspira-

tions of the world about him. Having renounced the workers' movement to which he had given a theory and an
international fame, he was left without a cause; but the
principles that had carried him through so many vicissi-
tudes remained as clear and as firmly planted as they had
ever been. His so-called alliance with the royalist Action
française before the First World War, and his interest in
Fascism and enthusiasm for Bolshevism after it, represent
no fundamental change in his beliefs; they are simply the
attempts of his spirit to find, wherever it might, some concrete expression for the personal myth that never ceased to
urge him on from thought to action.

No period in his life has raised so much controversy
among his followers as these last years when he was, as a
matter of fact, most retired from the world and from polemical questions. The proponents of various political creeds
have maintained with heat and citations that the record
of these years shows him to be the true father of their
movement and of no other; but the controversy is largely
an academic one based on forms rather than principles.
The very fact that there should be such a disagreement
among his would-be apostles is sign enough that Sorel did
not hold or express any convictions profound enough to
commit him to any single one of the various conventional
categories into which politicians and zealous believers like
to classify mankind. If there was any appreciable change in
his fundamental point of view it was simply a deepening of
his life-long distrust of demagogic democracy; but this
tendency in itself was a negative one and its manifestations
prove nothing more than that he sympathized to a greater
or less extent with various movements that promised a
rejuvenation of morality through the creation of new social
authorities. It is true that in 1910 Sorel and his principal
disciple Edouard Berth, joined with Jean Variot, Pierre
Gilbert, and Georges Valois in a project to edit an anti-

democratic, traditionalist, and nationalist journal to be called *La Cité française*; but the fact that the project was abandoned because of too great a disparity in the ideals and interests of the collaborators is a significant illustration of the true relationship between Sorel and the Action française group.[28] However much he may have favored authoritarian principles, Sorel was never willing to accept the means that his royalist friends offered for implementing them. Although he did not disapprove of monarchy as such, he felt that it was dependent for the proper exercise of its authority on tradition and that when the tradition was broken, as it had been in France, the revival of the institution could result only in Bonapartism.[29]

His nationalism too, from the standpoint of the Action française, was of an equally unsatisfactory sort; when he spoke of following "the noble ways opened by the masters of national thought,"[30] he did not mean to assert a supremacy of French culture over all other, but was simply advocating a return to the solid virtues and duties of Old France. The foreign influences that he deplored were not those of his country's potential enemies and cultural rivals, but were rather those that have now been given the generic name of Americanization. In fact one of the bitterest blows that he suffered in the whole course of his career was the outbreak of war with Germany, a land whose culture and institutions he had often praised to the disadvantage of his own. Any sympathy that he had with the Nationalists now vanished; throughout the war he deplored the revolt against everything German,[31] and at its close when Germany was crushed, and Italy, in his opinion, betrayed, he turned on the victors with the bitterness of his disillusionment. "I am only an old man," he says, "whose life is at the mercy of the smallest accident; but may I, before descending into the grave, witness the humiliation of the arrogant bourgeois democracies today so cynically triumphant!"[32]

As early as 1906 Sorel had predicted that a foreign war might reinvigorate the waning energies of the bourgeoisie, but, as he says, "in any case it would, without doubt, bring into power men having the will to govern."[33] This prediction, reminiscent as it is of Burke's famous foreboding of the Napoleonic dictatorship, is even more remarkable in that he recognized as early as 1912 the very person who was to become the agent of the Fascist *coup d'état* in Italy. "Our Mussolini," he said, "is not an ordinary socialist. Believe me: you will see him one day perhaps at the head of a sacred batallion saluting the Italian banner with the sword. He is an Italian of the fifteenth century, a condottiere! The world does not know him yet, but he is the only energetic man capable of redressing the feeblenesses of the government."[34]

Sorel died a few weeks before the March on Rome so the world will never know just what his reactions would have been to the spectacle of a Fascist state in action. It is significant, however, that the writings of his last years gave relatively little attention to the movements in Italy and that he reserved the last sparks of his enthusiasm for another postwar upheaval, for a revolt that many people have thought of as based on principles completely at variance with those of Mussolini's totalitarian state.

In Russia another strong-man had succeeded in ousting the would-be democrats and liberals from their newly won position. The situation and the methods were by no means those outlined by Sorel in his theory of syndicalism; but in accordance with his conception of himself as the interpreter, not the creator, of socialism, he welcomed Lenin as a new Messiah. "I have no reason to suppose," he says, "that Lenin may have accepted any ideas in my books; but if that were so, I should be proud in no small degree of having contributed to the intellectual formation of a man who seems to be at once the greatest theorist that socialism has had since Marx and a head of the State whose genius recalls that of Peter the Great."[35] Although he deplored the bloody repression and the terrorist methods that marked the Bolshevik Revolution, Sorel explained them as necessary consequences of the foreign intervention attempted by the Allies, and even more, perhaps, as a consequence of the centuries of brutal rule by which the tsars had maintained their autocratic power in a barbarous country. As he says, Lenin "ought to be measured by the standards of the great tsars and not by those of a president of the United States."[36] It was, he thought, greatly to the credit of the Bolshevik leaders that the number of victims of the Russian Revolution should be hardly a tenth of that found necessary by the followers of the French Revolution who talked so loudly of democratic justice.[37] "In any case," he insisted, "Lenin is not a candidate for the prize of virtue that the French Academy bestows; he can be judged only in the light of Russian history. The only truly important question that the philosopher should have to discuss is that of knowing whether he contributes to the task of orienting Russia towards the constitution of a republic of producers, capable of encompassing an economy as progressive as that of our capitalist democracies."[38] On the basis of knowledge at his disposal Sorel decided this question in favor of Lenin; the institution of the Russian Soviets seemed to him to provide the essential framework of social authorities that he had hoped to find in the syndicats; it provided also the possibility of developing a new *suppletory justice*, a justice exercised by men placed close to the facts and in a position of intimate understanding with the accused.[39] Envisaging the war of the Red Guard against the interventionist forces of the Entente as a heroic struggle of the Russian proletariat against the corrupt forces of bourgeois democracy, Sorel renewed his hope that civilization might yet be revitalized by the virtues engendered in the sacrifices of the Bolshevik soldiers. Just as in the ancient world decadence was overcome by the fresh energies of the Roman legions, so in the future, he thought, if the world is to attain a strong and progressive culture, "new Carthages must not prevail over what is now the Rome of the proletariat."[40]

In a certain sense, the rise of the Soviet Union was a justification of Sorel's prophecy that, despite the apparent collapse of syndicalism in France, the principles he had expounded in the *Reflections on Violence* were not dead but merely driven underground, and would in due course reappear as the basis of a new ideology.[41] The fact that these principles found an expression in Russian Communism is a tribute to Sorel's powers of perception and analysis, but it does not necessarily imply, as many commentators would have it, that he is the "father" of Bolshevism or that he is in some mysterious way "responsible" for it. If there were any real influence of this sort, it could have been exerted only through the medium of ideas; but the testimony of Lenin, the great ideologue of the Russian Revolution, is available to show that he considered Sorel a mischief-making spirit "capable only of thinking the absurd."[42] Since his books were never widely read, even by the working-men themselves,[43] it is difficult to see how Sorel can be given any share of the glory or the shame that belongs to those who replaced the Romanovs with the Dictatorship of the Proletariat.

It is ironic enough that Sorel, who so often ridiculed the intellectualists for their pretensions of being able to alter the course of events through the simple statement of theories, should in his turn be credited with the legendary powers of a lawgiver, and should find that posterity had endowed the publication of a single book of his with a world-shaking significance comparable, almost, to the opening of the mythical Pandora's box. Although he certainly hoped to influence or to guide socialism in its development along certain lines, yet he never expected or desired to impose a private theory of his own on the forces of social unrest. Indeed he insisted throughout his life that his social theories were not original but were simply formulations of actual tendencies at work in the world about him: his function to socialism, as he saw it, was not that of a father but of a midwife.

It is true that he was sometimes mistaken about the actual facts of a situation; but it must be recognized that many times when the disparity between fact and theory became apparent, he abandoned the theory without hesitation. There is, indeed, considerable justification for his claims to a pragmatic method: he was not, of course, a detached or unbiased observer, but the very strength of his passions and prejudices, by giving him a penetrating insight into the basis of contemporary social forces, resulted in the elaboration of a system of scientific observations whose application can be extended far beyond the field of syndicalism in which they were made. In an appreciation of his place in the world of ideas Vilfredo Pareto admits that Sorel's personal taste would find neither Fascism nor Communism acceptable, both movements pursuing ends quite different from those he envisaged, but that they, nonetheless, offer a splendid confirmation of the experimental uniformities (laws) noted by him in his studies. "It has been said of Sorel," Pareto continues, "that he was the 'theorist' of syndicalism, just as of me that I was the 'theorist' of nationalism. I note the resemblance in order to be able to note also the difference in the two concepts, a difference that lies in this: that Sorel in the same breath states a faith and notes interdependences of facts, whereas the disciple of the experimental method accepts only this second category of considerations. Thus also, in the *Reflections on Violence* of Sorel there is one part that expresses wishes for the social future, and another that treats of experimental uniformities. One can accept the former and reject the latter, or vice versa, or even accept them both together, according to the relative influence brought to bear by feeling and reasoning."[44]

Whether or not it be believed that Sorel would have given his support to Fascism or continued his enthusiasm for Communism after observing the actual practices of these regimes, at least it can be stated that on a number of crucial points the particular "wishes for the social future" arising out of his myth are irreconcilable with the real aims and results of both of these forms of dictatorship, and most particularly of Fascism.[45] Even though it is true that Mussolini hailed him as the principal apologist of violence, it is difficult to see how Sorel was any more "responsible" for the activities of the Black Shirts than was Machiavelli for the tactics of the Borgias. Mussolini's seizure of power in Italy did not need a theory of violence any more than did the similar action of countless other tyrants who have troubled the serenity of existing institutions in all ages; indeed one of the most remarkable characteristics of the Fascist movement, a characteristic that Mussolini himself was at pains to emphasize both in words and deed, was that it had no theory.[46] The justification that Sorel gave to violence in syndicalism was a justification of certain ways of acting for certain specific ends, ends that were certainly not those of *squadrismo*. Violence in itself is not a theory, nor was it ever advocated by Sorel for its own sake. Although he described and analyzed some of the forces that lay back of Fascism and Communism, he can hardly be called the creator of them; in so far as his observations and analysis were accurate, he was simply a good scientist and not, as the intellectualists would have it, the author of such forces and hence responsible for their consequences. As a matter of fact, the nonrational use that Sorel sought to make of the experimental uniformities that he uncovered was explicitly intended to forestall the development of many of the political and social practices later to be exemplified in the totalitarian state. In a certain sense of that much abused word it is quite possible to say, indeed, that he was a liberal. Although he was one of the bitterest and most caustic critics of the variety of liberalism that stemmed from the eighteenth-century proponents of perfectibility and progress, yet his greatest objection to them was based on the ground that they failed in their promises, that instead of freedom they produced intolerance and that they stifled individual expression under a blanket of mediocrity. In condemning these men he also condemned democracy; but, as so distinguished an authority as Aristotle pointed out long ago, there is no necessary connection between liberty and democracy—often, in fact, the reverse.

Sorel was never an optimist about human nature and he never trusted the ability of the common man to choose wisely for himself or for his fellows. Even his advocacy of a proletarian socialism was based on the conception—or misconception as it turned out—of the syndicats as "social authorities" that would assume the functions of an aristocracy by embodying "a passionate feeling of the duties imposed by tradition."[47] The part to be played by the syndicats in relationship to socialism as a whole should be, as he himself said, analogous to that formerly played by the monasteries in preserving and reinvigorating the strict doctrine of the Church.[48] When it became obvious to him, however, that the syndicats were failing in this function of leadership and control, when they abandoned their early intransigence and adopted the demagogic tactics of political compromise, then he felt that socialism had lost all hope of becoming the agent of an ethical *ricorso* and he renounced it.[49] So much importance, indeed, did he give to the necessity of developing an aristocracy of workers in the syndicats, who could act as guides and custodians of the socialist ideology, that it would almost be fair to say he did not believe in the proletarians at all, but merely in the desirability of attaining certain ethical qualities through them. It is true, of course, that he looked to the proletariat as the most likely agent for the development of these qualities, but only on condition that it undergo a training and discipline such as he had described in his theory of syndicalism.[50] Although he admired certain individuals of the proletariat, and looked on certain tendencies in it as anticipations of a new morality, Sorel was under few illusions as to the actual moral level of the working class. He never tired of ridiculing the sentimentalists for their naïve belief in the natural virtues of the common man, and no one realized more fully than he the disasters and oppression that would ensue if an undisciplined proletariat should impose its "slave morality" on a conquered state. Unlike the utopians, Sorel was not interested in the proletarians because he admired their present moral qualities, but simply because he saw in them the only hope of a *ricorso* strong enough not only to sweep away the corruption of bourgeois society but also to provide an entirely new outlook for the workingman himself. Such a transformation, he thought, could be effected only by the spontaneous rise from among the workers themselves of a group of disciplined men who, by their sacrifice and devotion, would be an exemplification of the virtues of socialism just as the monastic orders were, from time to time, an exemplification of the virtues of Christianity. In both cases the individual feels himself to be participating in a heroic struggle for the attainment of his myth, and it is in this expression of the will that he realizes his freedom; the individual, moreover, does not feel any infringement on his personal liberty, because his discipline is self-imposed and so is regarded by him simply as a part of his "struggle for deliverance."

It is important to distinguish this principle of the myth from the quite different conception of the propaganda lie, familiar in the practice of the totalitarian state. Sorel did not suggest that myths be created and imposed on a guileless proletariat by their overlords; rather he sought to recognize appropriate images of conflict and movement already in existence so that they might be made to function in a process of heroic action springing from the workers themselves.

Some interpreters of Sorel might agree that the observations of experimental uniformities that comprise the scientific aspect of his work, and even the metaphysical postulates that he combined with them, do not in themselves provide sufficient grounds for the claim that he should be held responsible for the theory of modern totalitarian government. But, they might say, there is another side to his thought, a mystical, religious side, that led him to deify the proletariat; and it was the propagation of this faith, with all its emotional overtones, that truly makes him the father of communist socialism and even, in a somewhat different way, of national socialism. Such a point of view would be strengthened if an analysis of him by Pareto should be accepted as valid.

"It is necessary to distinguish three personages in this author," said Pareto: the first is "a believer in the divinity of the proletariat," the second is "a metaphysician," and the third "an adept at the experimental sciences."[51] Although it is often useful and illuminating to consider a man's work from various aspects, there is always a danger of mistaking this kind of diremption, which is at best only an artificial technique of analysis, for an explanation of the actual processes at work in the production of thought. Psychologists have long since given up the attempt to make a clear-cut distinction between *intellect* and *emotions* in their description of mental functions; similarly, if the realities are to be observed, the theory that a man's personality can be divided into a number of distinct personages must be recognized as an abstraction of no experimental value. It is true that for certain purposes it may be useful to make a rough distinction between qualities in a man that would seem to tend toward metaphysical conclusions and others whose conclusions would be scientific—just as it may be useful to speak of the blackness or whiteness of grey, even though that grey be originally composed of red, yellow, and blue—but such a distinction is based on the relatively simple principle of opposites; or, as the Hegelians would put it, on the assumption that everything has its own other. When a third factor is introduced, however, and particularly so intangible a one as religion, the whole basis of the distinction is changed, and it then becomes necessary to recognize strict categories among which all phenomena have to be distributed by more or less arbitrary definitions.

It is not unreasonable to suppose that a certain general agreement might be obtained on what is metaphysical and what is scientific in Sorel's work; but a similar distinction between metaphysical and religious, for example, would demand a definition of religion on which there could be no approach to a general agreement and which, consequently, could lead only to the hopeless confusion that ensues whenever an attempt is made to use a word already charged with powerful emotional associations in a special and limited sense. This difficulty becomes very apparent when an examination is made of Pareto's assertion that Sorel believed in the "divinity of the Proletariat."

If he was truly a celebrant in such a cult, it might be said that Sorel went through a novitiate of several years before taking the vows, which solemn step occurred, presumably, on the publication of the *Reflections on Violence*. For five years thereafter he was a priest—or rather, a pope, since he almost always spoke ex cathedra—but in 1910 he must most certainly have been unfrocked by any standards of religious orthodoxy or dogma. A man who states that socialism has fallen to the ground and that he intends to have nothing more to do with it, can hardly be called a worshipper of the Proletariat—hardly even a heretic. It is true there was something like a death-bed repentance, but like most such spiritual returns there is considerable doubt as to its actuality, and even more as to its significance.

In view of the many doubts and qualifications and conditions in his work that have been noted elsewhere in discussing the various periods of his thought—even the period of high syndicalism—it is very difficult to see how Sorel could justly be said to have believed in the divinity of the Proletariat. He was, of course, animated by a faith in his own myth; but that myth had no necessary connection with socialism, as the events of his life so clearly show. For a time he hoped that the proletarians would be the agents of a *ricorso*, that they would engender in themselves a new morality; but to say that he had hopes in them is something quite different from saying that he was willing to accept their dogmas with unquestioning faith, or that he was ever able to abandon his individuality in the contemplation of a higher power emanating from them. If he were indeed a true devotee, his period of communion must have been one of the shortest in history. It is inconceivable that a man like Sorel should have undergone a real conversion, such as is implied in the acceptance of any system of religious belief, and should have lost that faith in less than five years, not because of any new spiritual crisis, but simply because it did not correspond with experience.

Fortunately Sorel has left his own opinions on this question of the relationship between religion and socialism; they are interesting not only for the personal views they present on the subject, but also as an elaboration of some of the basic postulates of his philosophy. One of the most important of these postulates was that general terms, such as "religion," must be understood pragmatically as descriptions of the actual phenomena that experience has come to associate with them; attempts to reduce all these implications to a simple formula, he thought, cannot but do violence to the historical meaning of the term, and when the new definition, which has been thus arbitrarily obtained, comes to be used as if it were a description of a reality, then appears that besetting sin of all intellectualists: the intolerant use of abstractions. "The true conclusion that the philosopher should draw from these polemics," says Sorel, "is that one sets out on a course without issue when one pretends to determine *in abstracto* general characters of this sort; in order to be useful, the study of religions ought always to remain historical, thus demanding a strict contact with the concrete; this rule banishes all possibility of finding dialectically any analogies between the profound psychological reasons that explain socialism and those that animate Christian belief."[52] It is almost a commonplace to speak of certain militant socialists as "mystics" who believe that they possess a social Truth, just as in another time they would have acknowledged a religious Truth; but Sorel believed that there is no way of establishing a real psychological correspondence in these states. The qualities observed in the socialists might be expected of any disinterested, enthusiastic individual prepared to sacrifice his life for a cause; whereas those customarily attributed by theologians to the religious mystics involve such peculiar phenomena as ecstatic states of prayer, visions, and other evidences of miraculous powers.[53]

Although he denied the validity of tracing socialism and religion to the same psychological forces, Sorel believed that the evolution of both these movements produced effects in society that might quite legitimately be made the basis of certain interesting comparisons. "In a good many cases," he says, "it is possible for religious and socialist institutions to have reactions on the world similar enough for it to be profitable to make use of the now long experience of Catholicism in order to illuminate the quite youthful experience of the proletariat; but from these comparisons established between realizations of ideas it is necessary to guard against inferring the identity of inner forces."[54] Socialism, as such, is not concerned with reflections on the final ends of man; so that when conceptions of this sort are introduced by its theorists, they can usually be identified as adventitious growths derived from the outward forms of some system of faith.[55] An example of such an influence is the "quasi-ecclesiastical docility" of the working classes that has contributed so much to the success of political socialism. Such clerical characteristics, Sorel thought, were simply a legacy from the forms of democracy that did little more than reproduce, in their worship of the General Will, in their superstitious reverence for the peculiar powers attributed to representatives elected by popular vote, in the doctrine of progress by which they sanctified all the decrees of its legislatures, the outward administration of the Church—without, however, adopting in any way its inner spirit or meaning.[56]

The reason for much of this confusion on the relationship of socialism and religion—and the reason, too, for the illuminating analogies to be found in a study of their reactions on society—lies in the fact, according to Sorel, that they both depend on the activities of a common force, on what Hegel calls "the free spirit." This free spirit, however, manifests itself not only in religion but in art, so that its presence in socialism is no more a sign of one approach than of the other. In fact, says Sorel, in the history of art may be found most of the supposedly religious characteristics of socialism: good taste, like the theses of socialism, is incapable of demonstration; many great artists in judging the work of schools remote from their own technique have shown a fanaticism unsurpassed by the most dogmatic reformer; the blind hatred shown by the restorers of the medieval cathedrals in their desire to destroy the accretions of the eighteenth century was quite as real as that of a convinced proletarian toward the evidences of bourgeois culture.[57] If it be said, however, that these characteristics of art are in their turn simply a manifestation of the religious spirit, then religion must be admitted as an element so wide-spread, so all-pervading, that it is hardly worth pointing out.

The trouble with nearly all definitions of religion is that they end in just such an unsatisfactory way: either they are too narrow, and so fail to include many of the more prominent characteristics of known religions, or they are so broad that they lose all particular meaning, thus vitiating the only reason for their creation, which is the establishment of exact distinctions. If there is any real difference between religion and art—and most people would agree that there is—it is more likely to be found, as Sorel suggests, in the qualities of mind that experience has shown to be associated with these manifestations of the spirit, than in abstract formulations of dogma or systems of belief. Nothing could be more sterile than a discussion of whether Sorel did or did not attribute to the proletariat an importance great enough to constitute a "deification" of it; the only really significant question is whether his outlook and his aspirations were sufficiently similar to those of great religious spirits in the past to justify the assertion that he, like them, was a member of a Church and a communicant in a Faith.

One of the fundamental characteristics of all great religions has been submission before the gods, in whom the worshipper sees a personification of all the unknown and arbitrary powers that interfere with the free exercise of man's will in the world. The worship of these gods is not intended to give man an understanding of their mysterious powers or an ability to control them; but is meant, rather, as an acknowledgment of his helplessness, so that the gods may be led to feel compassion and to do for him what he himself cannot do. In humbling himself at the altar, the worshipper acknowledges his inability to create unaided the forms of his own existence; and he seeks through spiritual communion to abandon the unreal world of matter in order to blend his soul in the mysterious, external soul that is God's will, a will that to him represents the only real truth.

There are, however, very few of these qualities of submission and humility and longing for the infinite to be found in Sorel. He was, as one of his circle described him, "a practical Norman, who did not have the least desire to escape towards heaven."[58] It is true that he looked on nature—or as he called it, "natural nature"—as a great indeterminate force that must forever escape the control of man and that he believed in the necessity of man's deliverance, but these conceptions must be understood in the special sense that he gave them: nature, to him, was not a deity to be propitiated, but a force to be conquered, and deliverance, consequently, was to be found not in submission to the power of the unknown, but in the attempts by man to assert his own will on that power through the creation of *artificial* forms of human usefulness and validity. It was for this very reason that Sorel rejected the Bergsonian philosophy of flux and the Marxist doctrine of strict economic determinism; both conceptions, he thought, failed to recognize man's role as the conscious creator of his own realities; both of them were denials of the Greek conception of human dignity and of human responsibility that was the core of all his philosophy.[59]

As Pirou has emphasized, Sorel was a technician,[60] and one of the reasons he admired the Greeks was that they too were technicians in their incomparable ability to reduce refractory stone to the shape of their wish. This quality permeated their whole culture; they were a race of artisans and they found in their daily victories over brute matter a solid basis for the belief that man can fashion for himself the forms of his own existence. Sorel, too, was a respecter of the concrete and the tangible; his whole life, in fact, might be summed up as a search for some solid, resisting element, external to man, that would challenge him to develop the qualities of self-discipline and restraint that are as necessary to morality as they are to good craftsmanship. This conception is analogous to art rather than religion: the creative expression of the "free spirit" is based on human needs and it fulfills a human purpose; the myths that move men to action are *artificial*—that is, they are man-made—and they are successful only when based on the necessities that rise out of human society. The fact that Sorel was so often disappointed in his hopes, that all the expected *ricorsi* came to nothing, proves only that society makes its own conditions and that no man can say when a new Greece will appear, or a new Christianity or a new Risorgimento.

· If the ultimate judgment on Sorel be that he was an intellectualist in misjudging the possibilities of the proletariat, and a decadent in his introspective probing of the basis of moral action, it is because his age was in these respects sterile and decadent. Sorel was a militant spirit who longed for the epic qualities produced in the great heroic periods of the past; all the changes in his outlook and theories must be understood as a part of his constant search for principles or myths that might once more give man the opportunity of taking part in noble action. The search, however, proved barren: one after another his various enthusiasms had died out and in the end he was left a lonely figure without a cause and without, even, the consolation of a hope. In 1921, a year before his death, he gave in the following words a

·final expression of the pessimism that had always lain back of his thought and now was left bare: "What a sad future we have before us! It is true that I am now 74 and that . . . I cannot have many more years to live; I shall not see the worst days."[61]

CHAPTER II

THE WORLD OF IDEAS

Science demands the believing spirit also . . . The pure materialist has no place here.

—*Max Planck*, Where is Science Going?

SOREL SPENT A LIFETIME probing and discussing ideas and attitudes of men, but he belongs to no school and acknowledges no master. The human mind, or at least the mind of the intellectual, is somehow comforted when it succeeds in assigning a thinker to a system. An illusion of understanding is achieved when a tag colored white, red, or black is pinned on the subject of investigation to mark him as belonging in some established category. Sorel defies such classification: he was greatly interested in Marxian theory but he was no Marxist; he felt deeply the national spirit of France but he dissociated himself from the Action française; he watched with interest the birth of Fascism and Communism but he accepted the working principles of neither; most disconcerting of all, the father of syndicalism in the end abandoned his own child and so demonstrated that he cannot even be classed as a syndicalist.

The more general categories of liberal, conservative, and radical are equally unsatisfactory when applied to him. He was all of them—and at the same time. He resists even the usual attributions of influences. A game can be played by assembling references in his work to the ideas of Renan, Bergson, Proudhon, Hegel, Marx, Nietzsche, Le Play, Poincaré, Newman, William James, and a host of others, but it leads to no more profound conclusion than that he read widely and critically examined the speculations of his contemporaries. No one of these men was accepted by him without major critical reservations. Moreover, those to whom he refers most frequently do not seem to show any particular resemblances among themselves in their systems of ideas: he respected Renan and Marx; he respected Proudhon and Bergson.

The thought of a man of consequence can never be understood simply as a patchwork of other men's ideas. It is to be assumed, however, that the ideas of his time are the currency of any individual's thinking. It is to be assumed, too, that he will select from among them those that best suit his particular uses. To acknowledge sound perceptions in another thinker does not necessarily imply an acceptance of the validity of his system or its purpose. The fact is that men pick their intellectual associates as they pick their friends—because they already have something in common; this *something* is much more likely to lie in the realm of common experiences and common attitudes than in the intellectual abstractions that outwardly frame a system of ideas.

Sorel was very much a man of his time; he clearly reflects attitudes sympathetic or unsympathetic to his contemporaries; he takes sides, often violently, in the conflicts of men and ideas around him, but his ground of judgment is not *doctrine*, it is *method*. It was in method that he made his real contribution to the world of ideas by enlarging the body of useful hypotheses that constitutes the technique of the social sciences. He was in spirit a scientist above all else; that is why he could never become a disciple of his own system of ideas any more than of another's. The intellectual company he chose, and the company that chooses him, may be expected, then, to have some common agreement in attitude, approach, method—but not necessarily in system.

An approach that could always be counted on to provoke Sorel's disapproval was that of the intellectualists. He himself uses the term "intellectualism" throughout his works and by it he means a kind of abstract rationalism that fails to deal with reality. In his turn he, and others like-minded, have been called "anti-intellectualists" and by this is often meant that he somehow opposes the role of the intellect in determining action, that he is antirational and therefore an advocate of intuitive, mystical, and emotional responses of the personality to the environment. These charges and countercharges bear on some of the most fundamental parts of Sorel's work and of his philosophy of history, so it will be worth while to review the intellectual currents of the nineteenth century that form the background of the controversies he was concerned with.

Many of the most characteristic conceptions that distinguish the nineteenth century from the period that preceded it were the product of its latter half; but even before the eighteenth century had ended, strong opposition was rising to those of its theorists who wished to apply the Cartesian scientific method to social problems. The dramatic events of the French Revolution appeared to many of its contemporaries as a practical expression of the difference in point of view between the apostles of Reason, who wished to see the old restrictions of a feudal regime replaced by a more natural order, and the advocates of Tradition, who clung to precedent and to custom as the only safeguards of civilization against chaos. Although at the outset the rationalists seemed to be winning an overwhelming victory, it was not long before it became apparent that the Age of Reason had not yet arrived, that the power of Natural Reason, from which so much had been hoped, was as ineffective or at least just as difficult to understand and just as contradictory in its manifestations, as the old God of the despised Church. In order to give an explanation for this anomalous outcome, and an explanation also for the objections raised by the traditionalists, it is necessary to understand the particular meaning attached to rationalism by the men of the Enlightenment.

Raison is a word that seems to have a peculiar association with the eighteenth century; to define it with all its overtones would almost be to write a history of eighteenth-century thought. Not only did rational mean the intellectual, the logical as against the mystical-intuitive, in the sense of the medieval distinction, but, most important, it came to mean the *right*, because the rational, the reasonable is *natural*, and Nature was now supplanting God as the norm of philosophic truth. In this lies the great distinction between the eighteenth and the thirteenth centuries: both were rational, both regarded reason with the highest respect—indeed, on this point Thomas Aquinas would not have yielded an inch to Voltaire[1]—but where the thirteenth century consciously and freely admitted the supernatural to its cosmology, the eighteenth century audaciously attempted to elaborate an almost self-contained system governed by Laws of Nature alone, whose actions, unlike those of God, could become knowable and once known, predictable.

Although it is true that each of the two ages claimed reason as the basic instrument of its thought system, and though in each case the instrument so lost contact with reality that a scholasticism developed; yet between them had occurred a momentous change in man's outlook on the world. The movement that was marked by the rise of the bourgeoisie, by the decline of the medieval church, produced, in the Protestant Reformation, a return to primitive Christianity and, in the new scientific movement, a reliance on the direct observation of nature; these were the principal elements in a far-reaching revolt against the overdeveloped subtleties of the Schoolmen, who had pushed logical synthesis to absurd lengths.[2] Galileo and Bacon in their remarkable applications of the inductive method forecast the revolution that was to come; the rarefied atmosphere of medieval philosophic disputation was now to be enriched by what William James calls "irreducible and stubborn facts"; the way was opened for a renaissance of thought.

The widespread acceptance and far-reaching effects of this new scientific cosmology are a striking manifestation of the relief felt by the world on its emancipation from the irksome limits of the scholastic method. Direct practical applications seemed to establish its principles incontestably; but in this optimistic assurance there lay a new danger. Descartes, Newton, and after them, Locke and the French *Encyclopédistes*, tended to develop a mechanistic scheme of the universe; they were, in this, products of the same impulse that led to the invention of the steam engine and of the factory system. The great and obvious extension of man's knowledge and power led to a general belief that he had at length conquered his environment. As Whitehead says: "The success of their ultimate ideas confirmed scientists in their refusal to modify them as the result of an enquiry into their rationality."[3] Thinkers were not satisfied with establishing scientific laws of force, mass, and velocity, but sought also to treat human beings in a similar mechanical fashion. The feeling that man is the master of his environment, that he has only to discover the combination in order to succeed in unlocking all the secret vaults of Nature, is the basis of the cult of Progress; a faith which is one of the most interesting intellectual outcomes of these modern scientific conceptions since it has had implications in nearly all succeeding thought up to the present day.

The greatest technological derivative of the new science-philosophy was the steam engine and, in a sense, the steam engine is the best pragmatic proof of the validity of scientific conclusions.[4] Although technological development has been one of the most brilliant achievements of this outlook, yet, ironically enough, the success of machines, independent and self-contained in the sense that they are controllable at will, has destroyed the grand monistic theory of the closed, immutable Newtonian world system; through the construction and operation of machines, man is able to assert his particular will over the forces of nature and hence is provided with a pragmatic refutation of the concept of strict determinism inherent in the doctrine of a mechanistic universe that lay back of much eighteenth-century thought. Applications of this pluralist view will be found in Chapters V and VI.

Although the physics of Descartes and Newton had at least a pragmatic success, the psychology based on the same principles by Locke and the philosophes came off much less happily. In place of an absolute belief in original sin, the men of the Enlightenment substituted an equally firm belief in original virtue, so that the transposition from religion to mathematics was not as radical a change as might at first be imagined; they both deal in absolutes and they both promise certainty.[5] The eighteenth century struggled valiantly against the dogmatism and obscurantism of the Church only to fall into a dogmatism of a different sort, into an attitude that is sometimes called intellectualism.

Like romanticism, the term intellectualism has been bandied about in so many polemics and applied in such a variety of ways, that its use is almost suspect. However, again like romanticism, its use is often indispensable; and back of all its seeming contradictions there is a real meaning. Among the principal reasons for lack of clarity in its use are the common assumptions of critics that the charge of intellectualism must be leveled at some particular system or systems of thought, at Positivist or Platonic or mechanistic philosophies; and that anti-intellectualism is necessarily antirational, so that if it seeks to use rational weapons in its attack, it is denying its own essence. These assumptions all stem from the fundamental error of regarding the terms "intellectualism" and "anti-intellectualism" as dichotomous and mutually exclusive. It is unfortunate, perhaps, that language gave such names to these two sets of ideas; but the misfortune is one common enough in philosophy: Bergson and James, the two best known philosophic exponents of anti-intellectualism, both deny precisely and emphatically that their doctrines imply any abandonment of reason as an instrument of thought.[6] What they do try to do is to set limits to the flight of reason and to recognize the intuitive and nonrational element always present in man's thought. Both anti-intellectualism and intellectualism accept rationalism: the difference lies only in their respective conceptions of its use and form. To put the opposition as simply as possible, the intellectualist starting from a given set of axioms constructs a logically coherent system without feeling any great need for objective verification: the anti-intellectualist, on the other hand, accepts logic and accepts reason but insists on constant reference to the "irreducible and stubborn facts"; and since these facts are often intractable in their apparent contradictions, he is, as a rule, much less certain of his conclusions. This uncertainty, however, is in some ways a very great advantage to him: the logician, being bound by the necessity of maintaining the symmetry of his system, often finds it difficult to abandon any part of it for fear of spoiling the whole; but the anti-intellectualist can readily remodel the rambling structure of pragmatism without seriously altering its original purpose. The feeling of certitude induced by a logical demonstration may therefore be a very dangerous condition for the development of the true interests of science, since it tends to create intolerance towards all facts that do not fall readily into its preconceived pattern.

Although anti-intellectualism may be negatively described as a protest against this assumption that man can fashion, out of pure logic, the order and form of reality; in no sense does it act to intellectualism as a mere antithesis. This place would be given rather to pure antirational materialism, using the word materialism in the sense of an objective enumeration of objects and sensations. As a matter of fact, of course, such objectivity is impossible in practice, unless one conceives of an omniscient, pantheistic god who *knows* everything because he *is* everything and so by the direct perception and feeling of objects no longer needs to form conceptions; a human epistemology must be content with a much more limited direct perception of reality and must rely to a greater or less extent on abstract concepts. The mistake of Descartes and of the eighteenth century was in thinking that their mathematical philosophy had some necessary and immediate relation to universal reality, whereas in fact it was a highly artificial and abstract system based on some limited parts of it. William James was careful to point out the danger of such a confusion and the need of constant verification by experience: "To be helped to anticipate consequences is always a gain, and such being the help that abstract concepts give us, it is obvious that their use is fulfilled only when we get back again into concrete particulars by their means, bearing the consequences in our minds, and enriching our notion of the original objects therewithal." The failure of the Cartesian philosophers to return to concrete particulars led them often to mistake the word for the thing, the concept for the object, and they fell into a new kind of scholasticism which James describes as exaggerated rationalism: "*The viciously privative employment of abstract characters and class names is*, I am persuaded, one of the great original sins of the rationalistic mind." This "sin" also impressed Whitehead, and in words very similar to those of James he provides what might serve as an excellent definition of "intellectualism": "Thought is abstract, and the intolerant use of abstractions is the major vice of the intellect."[7] If a man is to obtain any meaning from the physical world about him he must rationalize, he must make abstractions, but it is in the *intolerant* use of abstractions that the danger lies.

The word "intolerant" here obviously means "intolerant of reality" as James' phrase "viciously privative" does likewise. In this meaning lies an implication that rational process may lead to false conclusions. This implication has troubled thinkers through the whole history of Western thought from Plato to Freud. It was sensed by Glaucon and Adeimantus when they squirmed under the word twisting of Socrates, helpless to refute his logic but unconvinced of his conclusions; however it is only since Freud's work of investigation and synthesis that it has been possible to make a formal statement of the relationship of the thought process to the response of the whole personality. The key to the differences between intellectualists and anti-intellectualists is to be found in their different conceptions of this relationship.

Nietzsche anticipated Freud in recognizing the great significance of unconscious motivation in human decision. This anticipation has been widely recognized; in fact Freud himself has spoken of the stimulus to his thinking that came from Nietzsche's work. Less well known is the place of Sorel in the same field of anti-intellectualist speculation. When he said that it took him twenty years to unlearn what he had been taught at the Ecole polytechnique he is referring, primarily, to the Cartesian method that in his youth still colored the attitude of scientists and is exemplified in the mathematical disciplines. He was later to say that the mathematical mind, accustomed to the certainty of a logical demonstration, was peculiarly susceptible to a blind acceptance of dogmatic beliefs in metaphysics and religion since these, too, promised certitude. Sorel could never permit himself the intellectual indulgence of such dogmatic finality, implying, as it does, a quantitative and static view of reality. To him reality was a process of coming into being, of action toward an end—not the end itself. The role of the rational faculty is to detach certain moments from this unceasing flow of universal experience and to arrange them in a self-justifying system—to create, as he called it, an "artificial nature" as an instrument for the control of specific parts of that experience, the ultimate reality of which must nonetheless escape all systems.

In making his distinction between artificial and natural nature Sorel did not intend to derogate the usefulness of rational systems—in fact he placed a high value on them—but he did insist on the need of caution in accepting them, on the necessity of taking constant soundings to check any calculated course against the empirical reality of the charts. The failure of the medieval scholastics to test their logical development of system against empirical observation resulted in notorious inadequacies in their representations of the physical world. The eighteenth century was so preoccupied with the removal or subordination of the supernatural element of the medieval cosmology that it failed to realize sufficiently that reason without pragmatic validation may still lead to quite unrealistic conclusions. The ease with which the physical sciences were able to develop experimental techniques had lulled the social scientists into a deceptive confidence in the primary role played by reason in the new scientific formulations. Lacking explicit data for experiment in their own broad field of observations, they fell into the habit of a narcissistic detachment from reality not very different from that of the medieval scholastics whom they so much disdained. In terms of the individual personality such a detachment manifests itself pathologically in the fantasy world of the schizophrenic—a world logical beyond the dreams even of the mathematician, since its constructions need not be impeded in the least by the hard facts of reality. Unchecked rationalization, then, does not necessarily lead to realistic conclusions. The reasoning faculty of man provides him with an instrument of great power in regulating his actions to the world around him, but it is an instrument that can be used just as effectively for self-deception if the defensive needs of the personality so dictate.

The pragmatic success of rational systems of scientific hypothesis in the modern world has almost universally led to an overvaluation of this particular faculty in the personality. However the discovery by Freud of the enormous extent and significance of the unconscious in relation to the conscious, where the rational faculty operates, has had a very chastening effect on those who have admitted its significance. Freud himself was quite pessimistic about man's prospects of success in controlling through reason the great destructive forces of his personality. In fact he seems to regard these forces as operating in a determined, inevitable, and fatal way analogous to the process of entropy in the physical world. Perhaps, indeed, they are an actual expression of the entropic process of the universe which represents a tendency toward the reduction of potential energy, toward randomness, and consequently, toward a diminution of system and orderliness, as stated by the second law of thermodynamics. In human affairs the order, the systems, the predictability of events and actions, necessary to a man's sense of control over his environment, were viewed by Sorel as temporary and *artificial* positions standing like islands in the eroding flow of a fatal process that tends always to a degeneration of order, to a diminution of potential or differences, to inertia.

The intellectualists may be thought of historically as thinkers who presumed to believe from the striking successes of the scientific method that the universe not only can be understood through rational analysis but that its forces can be controlled by the application of essentially quantitative laws derived from such an analysis. Although the roots of this attitude can certainly be found as far back as the Greek Sophists—especially in Socrates, the greatest of them—the intellectualists were not far wrong in taking to themselves the title of "modernists." Like the physical scientists they were nonhistorical, optimistic, and most significantly, confined by a demand for clarity to that part of experience that lies within the realm of consciousness.

These were truly radical innovations and were clearly recognized from the beginning as threats to established ways and institutions, to Church and State, to the whole pattern of accepted social behavior. The traditional, being rooted in the unconscious, was not susceptible to explanation or justification in terms of the new rationalism. As long as *reason* remained the test of truth, arguments from tradition necessarily appeared defensive; but with the gradual clouding of the initial naïve confidence in the power of reason alone that came as the nineteenth century wore on, there came a change in the test of truth and a change, therefore, in the roles of attacker and defender in this conflict between intellectualist and anti-intellectualist. A useful way to demonstrate the extent of this shift of values is to apply to several characteristic thinkers of the time a fruitful hypothesis developed by Freud a century later from his analysis of the dynamics of the personality.

This hypothesis is based on the observation that only a small part of an individual's total experience is accessible to conscious recognition but that none of it is lost and all of it is significant in determining decision and action. Lying in the unconscious sphere are the great instinctual life drives and, possibly, conflicting tendencies toward death and destruction; it is the sphere, primarily, of the *id*, or, very roughly, of what used to be called "the passions." Largely in consciousness is the *ego*, the self-cognizant aspect of the personality that is capable, within limits, of regulating the relationship of the instinctual drives to the demands of reality. It is in the ego that rationality plays a role; so it may be thought of, again very roughly, as corresponding to what used to be called "the reason." Lying between the ego and the id, partly conscious and partly unconscious, is the *superego* formed from the injunctions of parents and other authorities; it is the judge of what is permissible or safe in terms of those injunctions and corresponds, roughly, to what used to be called "the moral sense" or "the conscience."

Freud's hypothesis is that any decision of an individual involves a dynamic relationship of these aspects of the personality and that the quality of the decision depends on the particular capacities and experiences of the individual. There is no rule to establish the *rightness* of any one kind of decision for mankind at large nor is there any rule to determine that the primacy in a decision of one aspect of the personality is *better* than another. The test of a decision is the extent of the mutual accommodation achieved between individual and group and of both with their general environment. Failure is measured by the degree of tension arising from needs left unfulfilled in the adjustment: success is marked by a feeling of ease or freedom ensuing on the relaxation of tensions through some adequate expression of the needs. Any theory that discounts the significance of the passions or the reason or the conscience or that fails to recognize the role played by unconscious motivation can result only in a partial and distorted explanation of human conduct, if the postulates of Freud's theory are accepted. When this criterion is applied to the ideas of Burke, Maistre, Condorcet, and Bentham, as examples of the variety of nineteenth-century thought, curious differences of emphasis emerge that throw an interesting light on the intellectual currents of their time and on the particular strengths and weaknesses of their theories as useful instruments for dealing with reality.

Of these four thinkers Burke and Maistre fall in the category of the anti-intellectualists and Condorcet and Bentham in that of the intellectualists. Each of them, though, has his own particular attitude and emphasis. Both Burke and Maistre were traditionalist and conservative but not in the same way or for the same reasons. Government, to Burke, was not based on natural rights either of the governors or the governed, but was a contrivance of human wisdom to provide for human wants. There can be no legal contract between the state and the individual because between the two no distinction can be drawn. Society itself, however, is a kind of universal contract uniting all beings according to their natures in an organic relationship. Man's advantage is to take his place in the organism of society even though his will may seem at times to be opposed to this interest. Burke had a deep and fearful distrust of man's passions and particularly of man freed from authority and acting in society. "We are afraid," he says, "to put men to live and trade each on his own stock of reason; because we suspect that the stock in each man is small, and that the individuals would do better to avail themselves of the general bank and capital of nations and of ages." Government is only possible by an appeal to *prejudices*, to various feelings that, through the painful struggle of civilization, have become imbedded as tradition in the consciousness of society. The aims of the Revolution were avowedly to destroy prejudice, to *free* mankind; but Burke had no belief in the noble savage, in the natural goodness of man. To him freedom meant license and license is not the interest of man as a social being. Prejudice is a sort of magnetic force that holds society to its shape; it "renders a man's virtue his habit, and not a series of unconnected acts";[8] it is the means by which society becomes an organism; it is the explanation of why the sum of political wisdom is greater than its parts.

Burke's political theory shows a remarkably accurate anticipation of Freud's hypothesis of personality structure. He clearly recognizes the three aspects: the passions or the id, the reason or the ego and the prejudices or the superego. He recognizes, too, the essential irrationality of the passions and, consequently, the futility of looking to the reason as an effective control of them; he sees that prejudices are the key to the social relationships of men: that it is through injunctions imposed from without that the individual becomes socialized and that they are, therefore, the means by which the interests of society actually become an integral part of the interests of the mature personality of the individual. Burke's anti-intellectualism does not rest on a denial of reason, but rather on the emphasis he gives to the essentially irrational force of prejudices or social injunctions in directing the drives of the passions. A very important consequence of this view is that he places *within the individual* the whole drama of free wishing and repression instead of conceiving, as did the rationalists, of the wishing as being an expression of an internal individual *right* exposed to infringement or repression by the external laws of society. In short he obviated the problem, which gave John Stuart Mill so much trouble, of trying to reconcile the freedom of the individual with the needs of society. To Burke they were indistinguishable since the individual is necessarily a part of society and society a part of the individual expressed through the moral code or prejudices voiced by his conscience. The rationalist saw the individual as an atom, a bit of discrete matter, subject to external influences called forces. Burke saw him as an element of a field of forces and inseparable from that field. The psychology of today, as does today's physics, tends toward a conception of reality as process: this is favorable to anti-intellectualism. Eighteenth-century psychology, as its physics, tended toward a discrete, quantitative conception: this is favorable to intellectualism.

The fear that Burke expressed of the irrational drives in man was felt in an exaggerated degree by Comte Joseph de Maistre, the theorist of Catholic authoritarianism. His work presents a picture of the personality as a field on which is fought the unending battle between good and evil. In this struggle the reason plays so small a role as to be practically negligible. To Maistre "individual reason is only a brute beast all of whose powers in the end lead only to destruction." Reason is powerless to control human conduct, "for few indeed can reason well on everything; so that in general it is well, whatever one may say about it, to begin with authority."[9] The great danger of individual reason, evidently, is its threat to the beliefs, the dogmas, the prejudices with which society "properly" surrounds the cradle of the young. Reason, eliciting a feeling of self-identity, separates the individual from the social complex. By questioning social traditions and authorities it prevents the individual from finding his proper and "natural" expression in worship, morals, and government. Maistre, in fact, gave so much weight to the demands of society that he almost came to believe that individual reason must *necessarily* be antisocial in its working. The explanation of this curious assumption is to be found in his failure to distinguish clearly the respective roles of the id and the ego; consequently he came to regard the reason as little more than a mechanism used to rationalize the passions, the libidinal drives, by giving to them a spurious justification. He was quite right in thinking that the rational faculty can be so used, but he failed to recognize that such a situation is not representative of the ordinary operation of a well-balanced personality; it occurs when a too restrictive super-ego forces the ego to abandon in part its characteristic role of intermediary between the id and reality; it represents a disfunction rather than a function of the ego. In so far as Maistre accepts this pathological state as universal and inevitable, he limits and distorts the conception of human nature that he derives from it.

Having dismissed reason as untrustworthy and powerless, Maistre is left with the picture of a dualistic conflict between the passions, conceived of as bad, and the conscience, which is good. Actually he did not deny that some individual wishes can be good or that some of the prejudices implanted in the conscience by the authority of society may be bad. His position was that this world is imperfect and that authority vested absolutely in the state may well present "grave inconveniences" but that "we find ourselves between two abysms."[10] The choice to him was clear: the individual must submit his will to the higher purpose of the state; he must act as if the injunctions of society are good and as if the expression of individual will is bad.

Maistre, like Burke, recognizes the paramount importance of the irrational forces in human nature but, unlike Burke, he so reduces the role of the reason as almost to dismiss it completely. The resulting distortion of human motives and needs led him to serious difficulties in providing a justification for the authority of society on some other basis than pure force. This justification he found in God's will expressed through revelation and enforced by a theocratic state. Maistre's anti-intellectualism is religious; it denies the right—or the possibility—of an expression of individual needs in the creation or maintenance of a social organization. At best the individual is no more than the instrument by which God, in his grace, manifests his mysterious will: at worst the individual is a compound of evil passions, an agent of the devil. Submission to the dogmas of the Church and to the authority of national traditions, as embodied in a Christian prince, are the only safeguards,

Maistre thought, against the arbitrary and irrational impulses of individual man.

The theory of individualism, of individual rationality and individual right that both Burke and Maistre took such great exception to had its characteristic expression among the philosophes of the eighteenth century. Their view of human nature was simple, naïve, and superficial in many ways, but it has the virtue of a clarity that was later lost by their more sophisticated and disillusioned followers in the century following. The ideas of Concorcet and of Bentham are an illustration of two ways that eighteenth-century rationalism showed itself before more critical reservations were introduced to cloud the expression of its early enthusiasm. Their systems of thought are something of a caricature of the position taken by rationalists and liberals of the later nineteenth century, but for that very reason they show the more clearly the basic tendencies of the intellectualist approach that marked a good deal of the thinking on social problems not only of the eighteenth but of the nineteenth and twentieth centuries as well.

The Marquis de Condorcet states in his *Historical Sketch of Progress* that his purpose is "to show by reasoning and by facts that nature has set no bounds to the improvement of human faculties; that the perfectibility of man is really unlimited; that the progress of this perfectibility, henceforth independent of all forces that should stand in its way, has for a limit only the duration of the world in which nature has placed us. Without doubt, this progress can proceed with more or less rapidity; but it will never retrogress, so long as the earth, at least, occupies the same place in the world system; and so long as the general laws of this system produce on this globe neither a general catastrophe, nor such alterations as would no longer permit mankind to survive, to exercise the same faculties, and to have command of the same resources."[11]

The optimism of this statement depends on the conception of the future as a fair white page on which may be written what man wishes. Condorcet believed that man wishes for happiness, for beauty, for justice; he believed that these wishes could be realized if man were only free; he believed he knew the key to that freedom—it was a key that had only recently come into the hands of men as a consequence of the progress of civilization; it was the key that had already unlocked the secrets of the physical universe; it was the power of the human intellect applied rationally to the classification of the facts of experience. These facts Condorcet proposed to find in a study of history. What he found there was a record of misery and ugliness and injustice. He concluded that these errors must be the result of irrational prejudice, of superstition and oppression. The remedy, obvious to him, was to throw the bright light of reason on the dark jungles of institutions, laws, and customs that still held man in serfdom. As he says, "there exists no religious system nor any supernatural extravagance that is not founded on ignorance of the laws of nature"; and of these laws, those with particular application to the Rights of Man may all be deduced from "this single truth, that he is a being capable of perceptions, of forming rationalizations and of acquiring moral ideas."[12]

Although Condorcet proposed to collect and classify the facts of history as the basis for a rational derivation of social laws he was, in fact, completely unhistorical in his attitude. To him the past was not viewed as a rich complex of human experience but rather as a gothic record of human error. He was very little concerned with experience in any form except as it demonstrated the need for reform; he readily abandoned the discouraging task of contemplating concrete reality and allowed his mind to soar away on the wings of fantasy; he was intolerant in his use of abstractions.

To the extent that Maistre dismissed reason as effective

in governing social relationships, Condorcet accepted it; as Maistre distrusted the individual will, Condorcet placed in it supreme confidence. Each of them seriously distorts the dynamic relationship of the various aspects of the personality. Condorcet attributes the obvious irrationality of human conduct to the restrictions imposed by a bad social environment. He completely ignores the existence of the unconscious; he denies, too, the existence of the superego— or at least that part of it that is irrational or unconscious. The moral sense to him is purely a matter of right reason. In fact he impatiently dismisses all the irrational part of the personality as cavalierly as he dismisses the superstitions of the ignorant past. His definition of freedom takes into account only the ego aspect of the personality. It is not surprising, therefore, that freedom, to him, means freedom of the individual *from* society rather than freedom of the individual *in* society as it meant to Burke. Here is the explanation of his unquestioning assumption that once man is capable of reasoning he will always choose to be directed by it rather than by other nonrational urges: to reason is to be free and all men want freedom.

The difficulty with the kind of freedom Condorcet sought was that it attempted a detachment of the ego, and of the rational faculty, from the other parts of the personality through which reality is perceived; it thereby introduced all the dangers of unchecked abstraction and made easy the kind of flight from reality that is said by its critics to be a common characteristic of intellectualism. No clearer statement of this kind of escapism could be made than that to be found in the actual words of Condorcet himself: "This contemplation of progress is for him [the philosopher] a refuge, where the remembrance of his persecutors is no more able to pursue him; there he lives with his kind, in a paradise that his reason has known how to create, and that his love for humanity embellishes with the purest joys."[13]

Not all rationalists and optimists, however, attempt to escape in a flight from reality or, if they do flee, it is not from quite the same realities. Jeremy Bentham, for example, had a supreme contempt for the tender-minded; he prided himself on his courage in facing brute facts: he recognized that all men are essentially selfish, self-regarding; that benevolence itself is selfishness with a twist. On this basis he wished to codify laws that would frankly recognize the egoism of the individual and would use it to promote the general utility of society. "Nature," he says, "has placed mankind under the governance of two sovereign masters, *pain* and *pleasure*. It is for them alone to point out what we ought to do, as well as to determine what we shall do. On the one hand the standard of right and wrong, on the other the claim of causes and effects, are fastened to their throne. They govern us in all we do, in all we say, in all we think; every effort we can make to throw off our subjection, will serve but to demonstrate and confirm it. In words a man may pretend to abjure their empire, but in reality he will remain subject to it all the while. The *principle of utility* recognizes this subjection, and assumes it for foundation of that system, the object of which is to rear the fabric of felicity by the hands of reason and of law. Systems which attempt to question it, deal in sounds instead of sense, in caprice instead of reason, in darkness instead of light."[14]

Burke had believed in the Duties of Man and Condorcet in the Rights of Man; but Bentham would have no truck with either of them. He refused to set up any abstract criteria of morality: "The greatest happiness of the greatest number is the measure of right and wrong."[15] This maxim is not based on any principle of democratic idealism; but is merely an expedient to assure to each individual the maximum opportunity for self-aggrandizement which, in turn, will promote the greatest possible social good since, as he says: "The interest of the community then, is what?—the sum of the interests of the several members who compose it."[16] Burke regarded government as a trust, Condorcet as the organ for expressing the people's opinions, but Bentham thought of it as a system of unfortunately necessary restrictions on individual pleasure-seeking. "For taken by itself," he says, "government is in itself one vast evil."[17] Since there must be a government, however, it should be a democratic form, because the governors of a state invariably turn power to their own advantage; so that the only way of protecting "the greatest number" from the exploitation of the few is to make everyone a governor. Hence, in a democracy the "pains" of governmental restriction are lighter and more evenly distributed than under any other form.

Bentham prided himself on being tough-minded and in certain respects he was so to a degree remarkable in his time. His work was an excellent antidote to the sentimental rhapsodizing of the noble-savage school—it served admirably as a weapon against much that was extravagant, and sometimes even dishonest, in the idealism of the early nineteenth century; but it suffered from several serious misconceptions. The most fundamental of these was his failure to recognize the role of the unconscious in human motivation. His emphasis on the primary urge of man to seek pleasure and to avoid pain expresses a hedonistic attitude not dissimilar to Freud's theory of libidinal energy, but it lacked Freud's understanding of the unconscious source of this energy. It led him, therefore, into two important errors: the first of these was that the libidinal wishes can be identified by the ego and the second is that, once identified, they are susceptible to a rational control by it.

By a different route from that of Condorcet, Bentham arrived at a similar conclusion: man is capable of testing right and wrong—or pain and pleasure—by an exercise of his rational faculty. Because of the supremacy that both gave to the ego, the seat of the self-identifying part of the personality, they both tended to regard men as social atoms, discrete and self-sufficient, and sought without much success for an explanation of the binding force that held them in society. Bentham's theory, particularly, suffers from this defect; he never really succeeded in reconciling the individual and the group. On the one hand he states the claims of the *felicific calculus,* his humorless and mechanical attempt to provide a scale of measurement for individual happiness, and, on the other, the mysterious "identification of interests" necessary for social coöperation—which is to be arrived at by means of legislation. To resolve his dilemma he is forced to recall the ghost of the General Will that he has already condemned in his rational world.

Bentham's errors were the errors of other rationalists and, despite his hard-headedness, led him to the unreal abstractions characteristic of other forms of intellectualism. By ignoring the unconscious and by dismissing with disdain the part played by the superego in the dynamics of the personality he made it impossible to relate the individual organically to society or to relate his picture of the possibilities of the future with the experience of the past. It was Sir Henry Maine who said of him: "No geniuses of equally high order so completely divorced themselves from history as Hobbes and Bentham."[18] Instead of being, as he thought, the most practical of men, he is the classical type of cabinet philosopher. He had an almost childish ignorance of the ways of the world and of men's real motives; yet, as Leslie Stephen says: "Bentham's position is in one respect unique. There have been many greater thinkers; but there has been hardly anyone whose abstract theory has become in the same degree the platform of an active political party."[19]

Bentham's thought, as such, is very limited and not at all profound. Karl Marx, indeed, has called him "the arch-philistine . . . the insipid pedantic, leather-tongued oracle of the commonplace bourgeois intelligence of the nineteenth century";[20] but these very defects of philosophy were virtues for the popular acceptance of his ideas. It is significant that although he had been writing since 1776, Bentham was practically unknown as an influential thinker until the nineteenth century was well under way. Utilitarianism, it is true, was in existence long before he took it up, but only after his death did it become a really important current in popular thought.

The world of ideas of the nineteenth century reflected complicated crosscurrents of social and economic change that had to be fitted somehow into a pattern of new explanations and new faiths. Democracy was spreading, the belief in Progress, the Rights of Man, humanitarianism, and utilitarianism were all inextricably confused and combined to form the axioms of politics. These axioms can be seen as an aspect of the emergence into the forefront of politics of an industrial and commercial class newly conscious of its power. The factory system, the capitalist, needed a justification and this justification was found in the theory of enlightened self-interest. The appeal that utilitarianism made to *common sense* and to the bourgeois virtues, and its apparent solution of the problem of the "identification of interests," gave to it a plausibility that was soon converted into a certainty by the optimistic self-assurance characterizing the outlook of the new manufacturing class. The physical world each day seemed to become more tractable under the hand of man; communications drew distant parts close and machines stamped out new forms with demonic speed. It is not surprising that many people spoke of "conquering nature" and thought of man as master of his environment. There seemed to be progress, and not only progress in material things, but also in things spiritual: *Humanité* became a religion and rival armies fought for the souls of the heathen. Almost as quickly as machines, beliefs became obsolete; but always men hastened onward and upward, so they thought, toward better things.

The coal-owning noble and the factory foreman, as well as the entrepreneur himself, constituted the powerful middle class that dominated the value system of the nineteenth century and was the chief support of the political, economic, and social dogmas included in the term "liberalism." Even socialism, for the first half of the century at least, was a typical development of this point of view; it was a socialism of the bourgeoisie, idealistic, utopian, and impractical. The conception of a purely proletarian movement, based on existing class characteristics, was hardly recognized as a possibility; during the Revolution of 1848, in fact, when some elements of revolutionary communism did appear, they attained so little success that their effect was chiefly to discredit such tactics for several years to come. So generally accepted were the ideas of economic reform and peaceful progress that Louis Reybaud shocked no one when he said in 1854: "Socialism is dead; to speak of it is to make its funeral oration."[21]

The rapid industrialization of the economic structure that had brought so many changes in England first became prominent in France during the period of the Second Empire. The concentration of capital in the hands of a few bankers and the concentration of workers in large factories and at Paris had provided the groundwork for a real feeling of class-consciousness; but the development of this feeling was retarded by the policy of the government and, more particularly, by the tendency of the proletarians to seek redress of their grievances through coöperation with the republican party. It was not until 1876 that the syndicats began to assert themselves as an independent force with aims frankly opposed to the vague program of social amelioration that had been for so long the stock-in-trade of the radical politicians; the vague formulas and optimistic hopes of the utopians had by now lost all real influence and were being replaced by the more realistic and more brutal doctrines of Marxism. Socialism was no longer simply a pleasant form of philosophic speculation but had become a real movement with real power in determining the policy of the state.[22]

Although the history of the Third Republic is in many ways one of great activity and great change, it is not one to which the words "grand" or "inspiring" could readily be applied. With the increased privileges of suffrage came an increase in demagogic skill; the men who preserved the Republic in the crises of the Sixteenth of May and of the Boulanger Affair took their reward in the dispensation of tariff concessions and, even more directly, in the opportunities that offered in such enterprises as the Panama Canal project. The conduct of foreign affairs was hardly less depressing; although France joined the race for a world empire, she was rebuffed and humiliated by the stronger power of Britain, a humiliation dramatized in the famous Fashoda Incident. Finally, at the end of the century, the bitterness and dissension stirred up by the Dreyfus Affair seemed to show a weakness of purpose and a political ineptitude in the governing classes that threatened the stability of the state and advertised its moral debasement. It was in this world that Georges Sorel came to maturity and it was with its problems that his work was primarily concerned.

CHAPTER III

THE MORAL CRITERION:
SOREL THE MORALIST

La France a perdu ses moeurs . . . Quand je dit que la France a perdu ses moeurs, j'entends . . . qu'elle a cessé de croire à ses principes. Elle n'a plus ni intelligence ni conscience morale, elle a perdu jusqu'à la notion de moeurs . . . Pour tout dire d'un mot, le scepticisme, après avoir devasté religion et politique, s'est abattu sur la morale: c'est en cela que consiste la dissolution moderne.

—*P. J. Proudhon*, De la justice dans la révolution et dans l'Eglise

IT IS NOT WITHOUT SIGNIFICANCE that Sorel, the *moraliste*, should have begun his career as an engineer. His approach to the world was factual; he respected the concrete and the tangible; he sought always to comprehend reality in clear-cut forms. Like the engineer he accepted abstract theory of any kind only with considerable reserve. His epistemology might well be described as prehensile: the way of perception he most trusted was through the hand; the kind of people he most trusted were those who used their hands to deal with the world—working people and artists. It was this respect for *makers* and *doers* that evoked a sympathy in him for the philosophy of Vico and that led him later to a formal statement of pragmatism in anticipation of William James.

It is not surprising, either, to find that he looked on architecture as the highest of the arts: there, form and structure are most evidently displayed; there, most clearly, the marks of man's will are made on a resisting element; there, a certain part of the eternal flow, of the chaotic and incomprehensible reality of the universe is caught momentarily by columns and walls and made subject to a human purpose and a human understanding. It is in such moments of creation that man is truly free. "We are free in this sense," he says, "that we are able to construct apparatus that has no model in the cosmic sphere; we in no way change the laws of nature, but we are masters in the creation of sequences having an arrangement suited to ourselves."[1]

Sorel's epistemology is thoroughly pragmatic. He never made much distinction between the means of knowing and the means of acting. In fact, in his view, knowing is primarily a function of acting. As he said: "I have already had occasion to say several times that I look on the problem of knowing in the Greek manner: I assume that reality impresses itself on us by penetrating from the outside."[2] Man, then, is not an observer detached from the world either through his own individual powers or through divine knowledge; but he is himself a part of the world, attached by the hooks and bonds that are his senses. Moreover, since reality is process and change, man's knowledge cannot rest at a point of static perception but must flow in action corresponding to the flow of the forces around him.

Sorel respected the artist because his function was to deal with concrete things, to recognize the possibilities of materials, and to mold them through his sensitive perception into significant form. To achieve his purpose he must be at the same time a seer and a doer. It is because of this intimate touch with reality that the products of the artist provide so penetrating a commentary on the culture in which they were made. The great artist sees more than his fellows; he goes beyond accepted types to the invention of new forms; he is truly creative. In this characteristic he differs from the artisan whose task it is simply to reproduce the forms created by others.

Corresponding to the hold exercised by the artist on the real world around him, and often in fact indistinguishable from it, is the relationship of the worker to his environment. Sorel says of Marx with approval that he "looked on production from a metaphysical point of view. Man sets himself in a practical relationship with nature by means of his technical tools (which form a prolongation of his natural organism) and effects the transformation of the objects of his work." In another passage he again refers to the views of Marx: "We should not be astonished to see him borrow so many examples from mechanics; we know from the teachings of the master that this tendency arises from the importance he attached to the use of tools in the transformation of the environment. In order to understand man, it is always necessary to take him whole, as worker, and never to separate him from the apparatus with which he gets his living."[3]

Although most workers are artisans who will never get beyond conformity to the accepted views of the world, there are some, corresponding to the great artists, who create anew and so keep alive the organism of which they are a part. In a sense, Sorel thought, art is an *anticipation* of the highest forms of production and the motives and attitudes of great artists may throw light on the creative forces latent in industrial organization. Both the artist and the worker at their best have a respect for the materials and the medium in which they work that goes beyond all expectation of material reward or even of public recognition. They seek to express their creative wishes directly, without tricks and evasions; they establish themselves in an honest relationship with the reality around them; they provide a common basis of understanding and action for society at large; they operate, in a fundamental sense, on moral principles.[4]

Sorel considered the machine, through which the worker handles reality, to be a prime social instrumentality: "If there is something that is most specifically social in human activity, it is the machine; it is more social than language itself." The machine is the ultimate expression of man's ability to understand and control the forces of nature. "It might be said, "he states, "that the machine is a reasoned representation of material forces since it requires these energies to manifest themselves according to predetermined movements."[5] The construction of artificial mechanical systems that serve to control material forces is an expression of man's freedom and it is an expression that can be understood and participated in by everyone that has to do with machines. On this common basis of mechanical rationalization must rest not only the theory of the abstract sciences but also the understanding of social organization in general. As the world becomes more industrialized, more people come directly under those influences of the workshop that bind them one to the other in a common creative effort. Industrial production is the common ground of science and art. Through it man's triumph over arbitrary forces of nature can be made evident; through it the constructive, creative, socializing forces of man can be uncovered and brought to mature expression; through it man can find the means of moral action.

The socializing tendency of industrial practice seemed to Sorel to be a fundamental fact of the historical development of society and the principal key to the problem of creating more adequate forms for the expression of social action in the present. Industrial practices are the ground out of which grows the abstract formulations of scientific knowledge, but this knowledge must never become detached from the soil that feeds its roots. As Sorel says: "Science gains nothing by being relegated to ethereal spheres; to grow and prosper it needs to derive its principles from industrial practice; all classes should collaborate in its progress." A science thus derived is in little danger of being warped to the personal advantage of the individual seeking his own selfish interest and pleasure. "In so far as it is a social expression," he points out, "science acts in a never ceasing and enormously powerful way for the well-being of the whole community."[6]

The ancient conception of the inventor as being in some sense divinely inspired has led to an emphasis on the role of special talents in the world and on a special reward for talent. With the advent of modern technology, however, such a conception is no longer appropriate or even tenable. The improvements and refinements of industrial processes have come largely from anonymous workers who neither sought nor received a reward for them. Even the great inventions are products of the time rather than the revelations of geniuses or prophets in a class apart. Industrial development, Sorel says, resembles the growth of a plant. It is a kind of process that has its own laws of development, laws that are often quite unrecognized by men at the time and that often run counter to their expectations and wishes. The claims for a special reward for talent are, then, pre-scientific; they fail to recognize the new kind of equality, completely different from the conceptions of the philosophers, that rises out of the mechanical workshop of the present. "This equality," he says, "is not the former equality of conditions; it is able to admit of differences in pay that are sometimes very considerable; it is *proportional* and consequently, in a quantitative scale, it is an inequality. But what will become of the *thinkers*, the men who have no place in the line of production? They show themselves as auxiliaries—or more often as parasites—that society should expel as energetically as possible so that it may reach a clearer idea of the nature of work. *Nothing, in short, should be claimed as a right that does not correspond with work*; and work, from the socialist point of view, is something of a man that is incorporated in the product, in the inception of which this man has *directly* collaborated."[7]

Sorel's anti-intellectualism is very evident in the force with which he denounces thinkers, or intellectuals, who claim a special privilege in directing society. They are not makers, they are exploiters; they do not produce, they consume; they are not agents of morality but of social disintegration and chaos. "The real vocation of the intellectual is the exploitation of politics; the role of the politician is strongly analogous to that of the courtesan and it requires no industrial aptitude."[8] Not only are such intellectuals exploiters of society but, through their role as parasites, they bring about a demoralization of their own values as well as those of society. Sorel felt this was an inevitable consequence of their detachment from the world of productive work. As he says: "The essential vice of Greek society lay in slavery: this diabolical institution destroys every society that practices it; it corrupts the master still more, perhaps, than the slave. . . In classes that do not work, in those, notably, that live in the Athenian manner on power, the demoralization is extreme. This has been so in all centuries and it is a law of human nature."[9]

To Sorel moral action is always structural or, to make an analogy with physics, it is disentropic: it creates order, form, and difference of potential; implied in it, therefore, is energy and implied also is the possibility of a human determination of the events of the world. It runs counter to the fundamental disintegrative forces of the universe, disclosed by the process of entropy, that must forever seem to man to be blind, arbitrary, and fatal. By the creation of useful forms man frees himself momentarily and to an extent from the tyranny of nature. Such a freedom must be distinguished from the pseudo-freedom of the rationalist mind which takes no account of the demands of tangible reality in its flights of unchecked wish-fulfillment. In political terms Sorel sees this as a contrast between a society based on functional groups of workers and a society that postulates a classical democracy. "The organization [of the syndicats]," he wrote, "is the passage from an order mechanical, blind, dominated from the outside to a differentiation organic, intelligent, and fully accepted; in short it is a moral development. . . Social institutions are not the outcome of the decisions of great statesmen, no more than of the calculations of the learned. They are arrived at by accepting and condensing all the elements of life."[10] In contrast, he believed that:

"Government by all the citizens has never been anything but a fiction; but this fiction was the last word of democratic science. No one has ever been able to justify this singular paradox according to which the vote of a *chaotic majority* is made to appear to be what Rousseau calls the general will which cannot err. In spite of their distrust of the utopians of the eighteenth century, socialist writers often reproduce Rousseau's idea: they say that the state will no longer exist because, classes having disappeared, there will no longer be oppression in society and that then the public administration will truly represent the whole of the citizens. These affirmations are without a vestige of proof. Rousseau, moreover, posed as a condition of his paradox the disappearance of all intrigues and factions: but this is a terribly improbable hypothesis. . . Groups of former times were above all political, that is to say, constituted principally for the conquest of power; they gathered together all the bold men who had only a mediocre aptitude for making a living through work. The new groups are professional: they have as a basis the mode of production of material life and they have in view industrial interests; they are capable then, according to the principles of historical materialism, of giving support to the socialist structure. . . For an equality purely ideal and utopian they would substitute a just and real organized equality."[11]

When Sorel speaks of the intellectual in politics as a courtesan it is not an accidental comparison used without deliberation. To him, both the intellectual and the courtesan are parasites: they take without giving; they are the exploiters of human needs; they live on the very failures of society to achieve truly satisfactory solutions to problems in the two fundamental areas of human relationships, work and the family. Just as the intellectual who loses touch with the real world of work becomes an agent of social demoralization, so also the prostitute, by threatening the stability of the family, represents a different aspect of the disintegrative forces of nature which the institutions of civilization seek with so much difficulty to control. Sorel believed that a proper understanding of social organization must take into account not only work as a moral agency but, underlying it and influencing it in many ways, the constitution of family relationships also. He felt, for example, that one of the greatest deficiencies of Marx's theory was his failure to deal adequately with the family: "Morality depends in so intimate a way on sexual relationships that we have the right to say that a class that has no clear idea about the family has none either about morality. It seems that Marx has never gone deeply into such questions."[12]

Sorel followed Proudhon in taking a great interest in the processes by which the individual learns through his emotional relationships with others the constructive attitudes that make of society a going concern. He was fortunate, it is very clear, in his own relationship with his wife and he undoubtedly had that in mind when he said: "Woman is the great educator of mankind, less perhaps of children than of man; love transforms man and disciplines his instincts; it is woman who moralizes us; thus the respect for woman is a very essential element in the advance towards socialism."[13] In another place he speaks of the significance of youth and infancy in setting character and says that sexual influences are very important in this process.[14] Again, in more general terms, he notes the significance of sexual customs on the structure of morality: "This question of customs is of the highest importance for social reforms: all philosophers, since antiquity, have, more or less specifically, noted the influence that sexual usages exercise on the prog- ress of society; our whole psychology centers itself, in some way, on these usages; there is for the social observer no law more fruitful in results than the psycho-erotic law. This is why the statesman should always ask, when he studies a legislative reform touching in some way on a family statute, what bearing it will have on the conduct of man and on his respect for the dignity of woman. We are able to assert that the world will become more just to the extent that it becomes more chaste."[15]

Although he never approached the subject with a medical interest or with a concern for pathology, Sorel's views on sex are not unlike those later advanced by Freud. At least they contain little that does not fit into the general scope of Freudian theory and they show in certain particulars a rather remarkable anticipation of some of the findings of modern psychology. Sorel, like Freud, recognized the dom- inance of unconscious forces in most human decisions, and the dominance of sexual drives in the unconscious. Like Freud, too, he had personally a kind of puritanical reserve about sexual matters. Both of them were pessimistic about the possibility of channeling all the libidinal drives in a socially constructive way. Freud in his later theory speaks of the "death wish," embodying the forces of hate and destructiveness, as an inherent and inevitable part of the human personality: Sorel looks on sex, in its primitive expression, as the enemy of social constructiveness and, to the extent it is arbitrary, as an uncontrollable force that represents in this sphere the universal process of entropy. It is the essential formlessness and unpredictability of sexual feelings and of their emotional derivations that aroused Sorel's distrust of impulsive actions growing out of them. To him an adequate control of natural forces can only be achieved through the conscious application of the mind or, where that is not possible, by a reliance on the established customs and institutions of society. "Indeterminism," he says, "expresses itself as emotional action in life; I have already explained that every serious study of man should be based on the impossibility of representing feeling states; for when these states intervene the logical course of representations is broken and the illusion of free choice is produced."[16] It should be noted that this free choice is an illusion and is not to be confused with the feeling of freedom that was earlier shown to rise from man's structural activity. The apparent free choice in the emotional sphere is due to the fact that consequences cannot be predicted, even though determinism in reality be complete. The opposite is true of structural activity: there the consequences may be calculated, so that man is master of the situation in the sense that he can direct his actions assured in the knowledge of their outcome. In this sense he determines his destiny; in this sense he is free.

Sorel's anti-intellectualism implied no lack of respect for the use of the conscious mind in areas where its processes are valid. When he questioned its ability to control human behavior he was not suggesting that it had no value or that its effect was undesirable; rather, he meant that it was limited and that no clear-cut victory in the unending struggle with the great irrational and emotional driving forces of life could be expected. "The sexual obsession," he states, "is a very clear manifestation of intellectual powerlessness and ought to be studied in all its forms, because it permits us to analyze (if not to explain) all the phenomena of the unconscious."[17]

The intellect is notoriously weak as an instrument for the control of the emotions. It has its place and it has its importance, but for the most part the direction of the feelings along socially constructive lines must be effected by agencies more closely related to the unconscious forces with which they have to deal. The sense of right and wrong, of the desirable and the undesirable, is not something that man works out primarily by rational process; it is a consequence of a long history of learning in which he models his attitudes on those of people close to him and on those of the society in which he lives. According to Sorel:

"Education has as its object so to direct our lives as to cause us to find certain acts agreeable or attractive, certain others disagreeable or repulsive; this is the end that Aristotle assigned to it formally in the *Ethics*; it acts to superimpose on our natural sense of feelings moral habitudes which are, in some sort, the impression on us of the moral systems received as good in our environment.

"This work of education would be impossible if the educator did not possess a method for studying *individually* the characters of each of his students and such a method can only be furnished by experimental psychology. This subject has, then, a great role to play: instead of aping physics, of losing itself in abstractions and of constituting a false science of activities it ought to become a critical science of accurate methods suited to the education of the will."[18]

All moralists agree on the necessity of educating the will, but they differ widely in the methods by which they propose to achieve this end. Some think this process of moral education should be one of rational conviction, others that it can only be attained through a threat of punishment for transgressors. Sorel dismissed the first of these methods as largely ineffectual and proposed a fundamental modification of the second that quite altered its characteristics. Instead of trying to block or deny expression to the human feelings that manifest themselves in an undesirable or antisocial way, he suggested a careful study of the mechanics of the personality to see if such feelings could not find adequate expression in some more acceptable way, or even better, to see if the constructive and positive aspects of the emotional drives could not be capitalized for the good of society. The first of these suggestions, the process now called sublimation by psychologists, he saw illustrated in certain religious practices. For example, he says: "The great discovery of Christianity has been the means of making use of factors of eroticism by diverting them towards mysticism." The second suggestion, involving the process now called transference, he illustrates with the following example: "If sexual influences truly play so great a role in our moral life would not the answer be to use normal love to develop in us the feelings of gentleness and good-will? Might we not find in woman an educator who would teach us to see our brothers in the disinherited?"[19]

These speculations of Sorel can be readily reduced to the conventional terms of modern psychology. He felt that most human decision was strongly, though unconsciously, influenced by the libidinal drives of the id and so was not open to conscious control through the rational faculty of the ego. The true manager of man's feelings is his superego, the part of the personality that learns its rules from the social authorities who surround the individual. In the training of the superego, therefore, lies the key to man's moral development. This is the focal point of Sorel's anti-intellectualism. Human actions, he believed, do not result simply from innate impulses toward good and evil; they cannot be understood, either, as the result of a rational process detached in cold logic from the emotional substratum of human life. The superego operates in a zone that is partly conscious and partly unconscious; its processes are not so much logical as paralogical; it has its own dynamic pattern, its own laws of relatedness. The basis of Sorel's anti-intellectualism is his recognition that much of the action of individuals or societies can be understood and predicted only through an exploration of this twilight zone of the personality. When he attacked the intellectualists it was not on the grounds that the rational approach is in itself bad or dangerous, but rather that it is not applicable to certain very important areas of human decision. As a matter of fact the whole tone of his personality, his pragmatism, and his almost passionate desire to see order in the world around him indicate clearly enough how much he valued the kind of control over things that reason can sometimes give. The task he set for himself, essentially, was to widen the sphere of the intellect by extending its analytical power and control into the partly unconscious and irrational realm of the superego. He had too much respect for the power over things that man's mind gives him to leave unexplored the vast realm of the unconscious where the reputable laws of logic do not seem to apply. He had too much intellect to remain content with being simply an intellectual.

It is not by chance that the first two books Sorel published were *Le Procès de Socrate* and the *Contributions à l'étude profane de la Bible*. They were the result of a conscious plan of study, as he himself says, that was intended to expand his knowledge of the two great foundation periods of Western civilization, the Classical World and the World of the Christian Church. The object of his investigation was to find the secret of the driving force that held these societies together and gave them their significance. He expected to find in the past the record of human limitations and of failures, but he hoped to find also the story of triumphs in the growth of civilization and occasionally, perhaps, to glimpse tendencies that might be anticipations of solutions yet to come. Sorel's mind was fundamentally historical: he viewed the past and the present as organically related in a developing process. Social ideas and institutions, he thought, unfolded and matured in much the same way as does the life of the individual. The biologists have noted, and more lately the psychologists, that ontogeny recapitulates phylogeny, that the individual grows through stages of development analogous to those through which the species has passed. In this sense, then, it is possible to think of the infancy, the youth, and the maturity of civilization in terms of the process of growth of the individual in modern society from the child to the adult. Although Sorel did not state this idea explicitly he presents the material for an interesting example of how it might be applied to an analysis of the development of systems of morality.

He distinguished three main types of moral systems in Western civilization. In the first of them sanctions are imposed by society on the individual who violates its code. Among primitive people, "man is given to understand that he would expose himself to the greatest dangers if he violated the rules, and the whole tribe is persuaded that it too would be threatened if it did not purify itself and punish the guilty one. To this morality of terror a morality of interest may later be added: profits are assured to those who follow certain precepts. Under its grossest form this system manifests itself in the taboos of savages; but it ends by becoming more refined and turns into a largely utilitarian conception sustained by the approbation and blame of reputable citizens; this is rather close to the stage that classical Greek morality reached."

The second type of morality is characteristic of religions like Christianity, "where the ideal of sanctity requires one to profess allegiance, to be the disciple of the master; where one must follow the life of the master without balking at dangers to be run and without expecting any recompense."

The third type is "the morality of autonomy in which our conscience becomes a severe and watchful judge of ourselves; we seek to build high structures of ideals in order to judge not only our own acts but even our most secret

intentions. There is no longer an external judge, no longer
a master to imitate: it might be said that God is truly
descended into our hearts; we protest against evil because
we have a horror of it; we cry aloud what we believe to be
the truth because we are the *devotees of our own faith* and
because we judge the truth worthy of humanity. This morality has found its most complete expression in Kantism."[20]

These characteristic stages of moral development in society have a strong resemblance to the characteristic stages
in the development of the superego of an individual in the
present world. The small child, like primitive man, conforms
to the dictates of authority in the fear of punishment or
the hope of reward. If the authority is removed, and with it
the fear or the hope, there is no longer a restraint on the
child's expression. As he grows older the child begins to
identify himself with his parents: he tries to model himself
on them, to do as they do. This is the stage of allegiance or
discipleship described by Sorel. It is a necessary preliminary
to the final development in the adult of an independent self-
discipline when he will look no longer to "an external
judge," to "a master to imitate." The superego, if it is
soundly formed, now fulfills its function of protecting the
personality from conflict and damage by permitting an
expression of the libido along socially acceptable lines. The
individual is mature.

In actual fact, of course, no individual is mature in the
sense that he has shaken off all influences of the previous
stages of his development: everyone at times bows to authority or demonstrates allegiance to a leader. Similarly
a society in the third stage may be expected to contain
within itself reminders of the forms through which it grew.
There will be claims and conflicts rising out of previous
experiences that will trouble the equanimity of society as
they do of the individual; there may be regressions, too,
as there are with individuals, when problems become too

complex to be readily solved. In short the whole moral history of society is latent in every immediate decision.

Sorel began his study of European morality with the civilization of Greece. It was a subject that fascinated him. His admiration, however, was not directed to the earnest figures of the Academy or to the disputative crowds of the Agora. He looked, rather, to the more primitive society of sailors and pirates and shepherds, to "the poor warlike tribes living in the mountains, who were filled with an enormous aristocratic pride, but whose material conditions were correspondingly poor."[21] He praises the creative energy of the Homeric hero: "No people has felt as strongly as the Greek people the grandeur and the beauty of creation. . . . The Greek hero loves life; nature is wholly animated by his happy genius and he is in communion with her."[22] This admiration, however, is not to be confused with the conventional eulogizing of the noble savage by nineteenth-century sentimentalists. Sorel pictures the Greek hero as violent and amoral. He quotes Nietzsche in describing the Achilles of the Iliad as having "the terrible gaiety and the profound joy that [the heroes] taste in all destruction, in all the voluptuousness of victory and cruelty." Again he quotes from Nietzsche: "The value judgments of the warlike aristocracy are founded on a powerful bodily constitution, on a flourishing health, not forgetting what is necessary to the support of this overflowing vigor: war, adventure, the hunt, the dance, games and physical exercises and in general everything that is implied in an activity robust, free and joyous."[23]

The picture here drawn is hardly that of a being inhibited by the morals of civilization; it is not even a probable picture of the actual life of any real person; but it is a picture all men recognize because it corresponds to the fantasies with which the weak and undeveloped child must content himself when he finds his gargantuan wishes frustrated by the world of things and people around him. Nietzsche's hero-ideal is the primitive man—or the child— who feels more directly the great libidinal drives of the id and responds to them more directly than he will later do when he is civilized—or mature. Sorel's admiration for the type was the admiration he might have for the boundless energy and curiosity and quick response of a child. He did not make the mistake adults so often do of judging the child by their own standards and condemning him. He knew that the sometimes misdirected exuberance of youth is the source adult action must later draw on. He observed with a sympathetic interest the attempts of the young and inexperienced to work out the complex problems of human relationships—knowing full well that a certain loss of naturalness would be the price of their success.

The great poetic examples of heroism are almost all from the small group of tribal states around the Greek peninsula. Whether Achilles lived or Hector died is in itself of no great importance; but it is of inestimable significance that for several centuries Greek youth was indoctrinated with the stories of Homer, so that the epic characters were almost a part of their own existence and the epic *prejudices*, as Burke would call them, a personal inheritance. "These Athenians of the old school," says Sorel, "are vastly superior to our envious, ignorant, and epicurean bourgeoisie: the Jacobin type has no existence among them. Their citizens are not merchants, demanding the security of their exchanges, the protection of their industry, soliciting government favors. They are soldiers whose existence is bound to the grandeur of the city. The least weakness would put the state in peril."[24]

The mainspring of Greek life was war; on this foundation stood the whole elaborate social structure of the city-state. Under the stimulus of "images of battle" they were bound together by a conception of sacrifice that produced the community of interests they called *koinonia*. As long as this community could be maintained reasonably intact the citizen body was able to preserve its freedom—that is to say, the independence of the state—against constant threats and dangers from without.

Ironically enough the Greek states were not conquered by the obvious danger from without but by a more insidious threat working from within. They did meet the Persians and they defeated them; but the real enemy, against which they were powerless, was a new spirit of individualism that undermined the old loyalties radiating from the family to the tribe and to the state. This crumbling of the old customs and the old ideals showed itself in many aspects of life. The peculiarly rigid conception of family integrity that had dominated the heroic age of the city-state changed rapidly before the new conceptions represented by the increasing influence of the *hetaira* and by the general demands for the emancipation of women that show themselves so clearly in the contemporary plays of Aristophanes and Euripedes. The Greece that had defied the Great King now accepted a third-rate Roman conqueror as god.

There is no doubt that Sorel would agree completely with the famous opinion of Grote that the Eastern religions were a greater menace to Greek life than the Persian invasions. Because their doctrines led to individualism and universalism they attacked the core of Greek society, the family, and affected radically the traditional role of women. "In what way," he asks, "was ancient society menaced by the existence of oratories where women gathered together for prayer? . . . The difficulty cannot be avoided by saying simply that according to primitive laws prayers ought to be monopolized for the benefit of the God of the city: this is an exaggeration. It was not the city that was directly in danger, but the family, a question of quite different significance in ancient society." The danger was significant not because of any immediate effects it might have on the personal life of the individual, but because it involved a challenging of the very basis of the unwritten and sacred private law through which tradition had hitherto governed the conjugal relationship. It has already been seen how much importance Sorel attached to marriage as a training in the ethics necessary for man's coöperation in society; to him, therefore, a weakening of this relationship must mean a weakening of the institutions resting on it. "The statesmen of ancient times," he goes on to say, "did not understand the question at all like those of the present. Our law, wishing to be completely laic, has altogether disfigured the principle of marriage. This institution has become a contract, of a particular though ill enough defined type. Among the ancients it depended on sacred private law. Our fathers, filled with the Revolutionary idea, have not understood the nature of marriage; one of the great contemporary questions is the reform of their misconceived ideas."[25]

It is no coincidence that the question of the emancipation of woman should become so vital a problem in Greek drama about the same time that the *universal* tendencies appeared in the new cults and in the popular philosophies. Many of the Sophists, like the later Stoics, deliberately assaulted the family as a barrier to the broad world outlook. "These philosophers," says Sorel, "were like her [Aspasia], they had no fatherland; before long they will be declaring that their fatherland is the world. Like the *hetaira* they had no hearth, no national cult, no ancestral tombs to preserve, no relics to protect from the barbarian."[26]

It has been customary to except Socrates from such accusations as these and to consider him as altogether above and apart from the itinerant Sophists. The well-known stories of his fortitude and endurance in military service, his aphorisms on the citizen's duty to the state, the ultimate death accepted by him in respect for the law, these things do not outweigh, in Sorel's judgment, the fact that Socrates' appeal to his *inner voice* was an appeal to an individual, arbitrary, and religious conviction that could not be reconciled with the old conception of *koinonia* and which Socrates did not succeed even in reconciling with himself. "Aristophanes," says Sorel, "was not mistaken in having very clearly pointed out the religious and quasi-prophetic character of the master's teaching. After the developments that we have given, it is easy to understand how the accusation of impiety was much more easily raised against Socrates than against any other. . . We have said that two things were odious to the people, and here we mean the upright and patriotic part of the population of Athens. These things were, on the one hand, Socrates' pretensions to prophetic inspiration, and, on the other, his life of renunciation. It was in this that the philosopher wounded the most intimate and the most noble feelings of his fellow citizens, in this that he most resembled, in their eyes, those Asiatics so odious to the plebian conservatives."[27]

The mystical side of Socrates' thought, that side on which Aristophanes insisted in *The Clouds*, and that which Socrates himself never sought to conceal from his contemporaries, has been too much neglected by the overly enthusiastic advocates of modern rationalism. Sorel did not believe that Socrates was essentially a mystic, as the term might be applied to such figures as Saint Augustine, or that he was consciously iconoclastic in attacking the accepted ideals of the city-state. The fundamental tragedy of Socrates' life and death, in fact, was his struggle, unsuccessful in the end, to remain a good citizen and at the same time to emancipate himself from the prejudices of the past. Socrates' fame is based on a recognition of his contribution to the development of an ideal of individual excellence different from and perhaps abstractly superior to the social ideal of his day. The price to be paid for this development, however, was a bewildering complexity of new problems as the old social forms crumbled and the individual became more and more isolated from the group. "Socrates," Sorel states, "worked hard to break the chains that enclosed the citizen in the city of antiquity. These chains were those of military discipline. The citizen was a soldier, closely watched over and controlled; it was demanded that he submit to a system of education destined to inspirit him and to prepare him as well as possible for war. . . The Socratic state is *ecclesiastical*. The child, taken from his family, is transformed into a novice. His masters' duty is to mold his spirit in such a way that he will never forget their lessons."[28]

In Western society, one of the critical periods in the growing up of children is adolescence. It is a time when the passive state of belonging to the family group is broken in on by the new demands and responsibilities of personal independence. The child looks to a parent as a model, as an object of allegiance. He finds himself in conflict, often, with other members of his family whom he now observes with a new kind of detachment. He has not yet become mature and truly independent nor has he lost the need of living through the family; he is between two worlds and his feelings are often in stormy conflict.

The crumbling of the ancient world and the growth of new religions—especially of Christianity—might be thought of as an analogous stage in the history of civilization. Many of the great figures of this age of transition, some of them fathers of the new Church, looked back with nostalgic regret to the security of the old days when the responsibility of man for individual decisions was less. There could be no turning back in the process of development, but there was to be much floundering and many failures before the increasingly self-conscious individual could find a new kind of security appropriate to an adult. Christian ideology, says Sorel, "has cut the ties that existed between the soul and social life; it has sown on all sides the seeds of quietism, of hopelessness and death. This mischievous action is, doubtless, not attributable to the Christian dogma alone; it is the law of all ideologies: utopian socialism would have produced just as disastrous effects if it had had a lasting influence instead of being swept away by the surge of capitalism."[29]

The social coöperation and spiritual unity of the old city-state was, as has already been explained, based on militant qualities having their origin in common necessities of defence. Any force that affected these relationships or modified the ideals of the family, their chief bulwark, must have been a threat to those qualities toward whose attainment the whole system worked. Christianity, the chief rival of the old forms, with its doctrines of immortality, judgment, and personal communion with God, soon became more than a match for the city-state in obtaining the allegiance of the common people.

The result of the conflict could hardly have been otherwise: the main issues had been decided when individualism became a dominant force in Western culture, and now it was a question only of what would take the place of the moribund sentiment of ancient patriotism. "One cannot maintain," says Sorel, "that Christianity ruined the Roman military spirit; but it was certainly hostile to the ancient conception of the Heroic City and its success was possible only on the day when this conception should have disappeared: it simply happened to draw the conclusion of the peaceful and bourgeois evolution of the Empire."[30]

Christianity was a natural outcome of the new individualism; it was an attempt to solve the difficulties of a new point of view by principles inherent in that point of view. Sorel was not immediately concerned with the success or failure of the solution for Hellenistic minds; he looked rather to the long-term effect on subsequent civilization. Although he was far from denying the grandeur of certain great Christian figures or the nobility of much of the Christian creed, he felt, nonetheless, that its ultimate effect on the development of social conceptions was harmful and destructive in certain important respects. It risked everything—politics, economics, morals—for a belief; it preached that man must abandon the present world if he is to obtain the Kingdom of Heaven; it made renunciation a great virtue and it would suffer no rivals for the allegiance of man: but if that allegiance were challenged and the belief doubted, it left the world without its former human basis for society and left man deprived even of the privilege of working in the common cause of Christian salvation.

If the principles of Christianity were sincerely carried out by every individual, the world might be nearer Heaven, but certainly the complicated structure of civilization, as the Western world has known it, could hardly remain intact. The Church has consciously and unconsciously recognized this fact from its earliest beginnings; aside from rules for certain selected individuals, it has not attempted to interfere unduly with secular life. The great struggle of state and Church has resulted not so much in the spiritualizing of the temporal as in the secularizing of the spiritual. The Christian Church is a perfect example of Hegelian synthesis, and this has made it powerful; but unfortunately its original importance and function depended on absolutes, and these absolutes are now largely lost. When its original function as a bridge between the individual and the universe became obscured in the mechanics of ritual and organization, the Church became a great obstructionist force in the way of new developments that were attempting to bring back a harmony between man and the world. Voltaire and his fellows of the eighteenth century were right in regarding the Church of their time as an outworn institution. It had succeeded in freeing many individuals from the world for God; but when it could no longer give them God, the next step, the inevitable step, must be for someone to recognize the fact of the situation and to claim that the individual was completely free and sufficient in himself.

Voltaire was wrong, however, in regarding the history of Christianity as a history of the repression of individualism: the whole basis of this religion was the fostering of individualism and he was right only in the sense that the Church refused to recognize the ultimate consequences of its teaching, to recognize that the individual no longer stood before Jehovah in judgment but before Nature, or God who was Nature. The transition from Christianity to Deism or the Cult of Reason may be great, but it is nothing like as great as the transition from the patriotism of the city-state to Christianity. The eighteenth century in this as in other respects was really only the culmination of a long development. From a conception of God's judgment of personal merits and defects, the Church itself had come to place great importance on individual achievement in the world. "The Church," says Sorel, "has, then, been the great fosterer of the prejudices which have allowed talents to assume so great an importance in the world. Often, even, it is praised for having raised men of intelligence above men occupied with purely industrial tasks."[31]

Sorel could forgive neither the eighteenth century, nor the Church that lay back of it, for its preoccupation with *genius*. The very word "genius" implies a detachment from the ordinary process of the world. To place a special value on talents is to reward those individuals farthest removed from the experience and understanding of society arrived at through some effort in common. It is to encourage a narcissistic tendency toward an attitude that places its emphasis on personal rights, on private satisfactions, on introspective fantasies rather than on the responsibilities and duties and satisfactions of social participation. It does not represent a mature adjustment to the world; it is an attempt to find security in personal and arbitrary solutions to problems; it is a flight from reality.

Although Sorel attacked the claims of genius to a reward for special talent, he did not intend to deny the contribution great abilities can make to civilization. What he is concerned with is the problem of the relationship of the individual to society and to the world around him rather than with the differences in the qualities and capacities possessed by the individual. He is asserting that it is false to try to detach the individual from the great universal process in which human experience lies and that any attempt to frame a proposal for action on such a basis must also be false because it is not in touch with reality. The danger in the overvaluation of genius does not lie in the simple recognition of great abilities but in the delusion that an understanding of the world can be achieved by an individual who depends on inspiration or fantasy instead of on an immediate contact with the actual forces that support the structure of the society in which he lives. Here again is to be seen the error of intellectualism, of the intolerant use of abstractions.

The definitions men have given to freedom are a direct reflection of the history of moral development. This history represents a slow and painful evolution of individual self-consciousness not dissimilar to the gradual recognition by a child of self-identity. A consciousness of individual separateness is very little evident in primitive societies; so freedom to them, as it was essentially with the Greeks, is defined in terms of tribal or group privilege. It was not until later that the individualism of the Hellenistic age evolved to the extent that it sought an avenue of expression in Christianity. Freedom now meant a break with the old loyalties and obligations of the state; it meant the right of demonstrating a faith in the rule of God. In the sixteenth and seventeenth centuries freedom once more was redefined as this faith became altered or displaced by the natural explanations of the world growing out of the application of the scientific method. The age that had so great a success in explaining natural phenomena through a system of mathematical and quantitative hypotheses produced inevitably a definition of freedom based on an idea of man as an entity, a quantity, subject to forces around him in the same way that an atom is. The atom is completely free only when no external forces affect it: the individual is free when he is emancipated from all demands of his environment. Freedom now came to imply detachment, separateness, isolation. Men found themselves so fascinated by their individuality, by their differences, that they readily accepted implications in the ideas of the physical sciences that postulated a universe composed of material particles held in relationships by mysterious forces of attraction or gravity. They came to regard man as a kind of atom and they were inclined to treat him as if he were a self-contained particle that could be observed and manipulated in isolation from the environment. If a change was noted in this particle they sought the cause in some force acting on it.

To Sorel this whole idea was highly artificial. He did not deny the many pragmatic successes of the quantitative method in the physical sciences, but he saw clearly many limitations of this system of useful hypotheses as a valid means of describing reality. Most particularly he was concerned with the unwarranted assumptions that might be made about the nature of man and society. As he says with a certain acidity: "Epicurus was obliged to introduce a certain liberty among atoms; today men go much further into the matter under the name of *cause*. If they define *cause* as a principle of movement they are unable to escape an anthropomorphic conception. Causes are genii armed with powerful levers which they apply to an atom in order to move it from its neighbors. Such notions take us back to mythology, but modern materialism has none of the gaiety of the ancient fables."[32]

Sorel was a pluralist in his epistemology: he welcomed any method for arriving at workable solutions to the problems of knowledge. He did not, for example, reject the quantitative method as a tool useful for controlling some areas of human experience. For certain kinds of problems it most obviously produced strikingly successful answers. Nonetheless, it seemed to him that many of the experiences of the world cannot be represented quantitatively, that many phenomena are not susceptible of dissociation from their environment for the purpose of analytic study. A more fundamental conception than is to be found in the quantitative approach is the idea of the universe as process, as a great ever-changing flow of consequences in which all experiences and phenomena are bound. Sorel was much impressed by the lectures of Bergson in which he stated such an organic and unitary view of reality. His own ideas had long been running in that direction so he welcomed a confirmation of them. He had always inclined toward the school of Heraclitus rather than toward the more static philosophies that have dominated scientific thinking into the twentieth century. His attitude on these questions, in fact, is an anticipation of the position taken by the modernists in physics who have followed the path leading from Max Planck into quantum mechanics. Here the classical concepts of free will and determinism and of cause and effect have become so altered as to be hardly recognizable. Fundamental reality is no longer conceived of as fixed and disparate matter held together in a system of forces, but rather as an unbroken flow of energy through time. All is change and truth is relative.

The idea of man as an entity free or unfree depending on the presence or absence of external restraining forces is a characteristic expression of an age that saw the triumphs of a static and quantitative science. The nineteenth century was strongly inclined towards the view that the freedom of man could only be secured by emancipating him from irrational—and therefore undesirable—restraints. Condorcet denounced the remnants of feudalism, of traditional institutions for standing, a Bastille, in the way of a progress toward individual liberty. Jeremy Bentham and Adam Smith based their hope of such a progress on the assumption that individual man is the measure of all things and that his attempts to satisfy his will would ultimately benefit the whole of society. Sorel felt that the abstraction of the individual from the claims of his environment would have an outcome quite different from that envisaged by its supporters. He contends: "The more man believes himself raised above his kind, the more confidence he has in his internal voice, the more chances there are that he may be dangerous. The young are urged every day to develop the feeling of the I; but the fundamental vice of our present society already appears from this improper teaching."[38] Reduce the world to the individual and the individual quite logically assumes that the dictates of his reason must apply to the world. Seeing, as he must see, that the world does not conduct itself according to his ideas, he blames the disparity on the folly of the ignorant and the plotting of the wicked. "The optimist in politics," says Sorel, "is an inconstant and even dangerous man because he takes no account of the great difficulties presented by his projects. . . If he possesses an exalted temperament, and if unhappily he finds himself armed with great power, permitting him to realize the ideal he has fashioned, the optimist may lead his country into the worst disasters. He is not long in finding out that social transformations are not brought about with the ease that

he had counted on; he then supposes that this is the fault
of his contemporaries, instead of explaining what actually
happens by historical necessities; he is tempted to get rid
of people whose obstinacy seems to him to be so dangerous
to the happiness of all. During the Terror, the men who
spilled the most blood were precisely those who had the
greatest desire to let their equals enjoy the golden age they
had dreamed of, and who had the most sympathy with
human wretchedness: optimists, idealists, and sensitive
men, the greater desire they had for universal happiness
the more inexorable they showed themselves."[34]

Sorel believed, moreover, that a state of detachment from
the concerns and obligations and traditions of a society
leads to an enervating kind of skepticism so painful, often,
that the individual will permit or perhaps even himself
actively seek a return to the bonds of an irksome authority.
In this sense he quotes a passage from the work of Gaston
Boissier: "I suppose that since the time of Cicero this indecision of beliefs, which leaves all his liberty to the learned
man, has been looked on as a great benefit. . . It was the
hey-day of the free-thinkers, but such times did not last.
In the same way that at certain moments people aspire to
despotism so as to escape disorder, so thinkers come to experience a like desire for certitude, to satisfy which they
are ready to sacrifice anything. Then they demand a return
of the yoke with the same eagerness that they ordinarily
long for independence."[35]

Man's wish to find an adequate expression of himself
in the world is not likely to be served by the negative process
of contriving an environment where few demands are made
of him and where he lives detached from the ordinary preoccupations and concerns of his fellows. On the one hand
he may become, Sorel thought, like the optimistic dreamer
in politics, a ruthless and fanatical tyrant; on the other
he may fall into a state of spineless indecision that makes

him the ready dupe and tool of unscrupulous and ambitious men. These are not successful adjustments of the individual to society: they are not successful for the individual and they are not successful for society. A definition of real freedom must start with an abandonment of the false assumption that led the nineteenth century into its hopeless dilemma of seeking a reconciliation of the rights of the individual and the rights of society. This false assumption is that the individual has an existence apart from society. In fact, man is inextricably a part of the organism that is mankind and of the total organism that is the universe. In so far as he fulfills his function in the organism he feels free. The measure of his success is the degree to which he achieves a balanced expression of the many needs he feels as a component of that organism. An abstract possibility of doing something he has no wish or capacity for has nothing to do with his sense of freedom. Real freedom is positive: it is a feeling that ensues on the effort of expressing a need; it is not a consequence of passive acceptance. Real freedom is something that happens within the individual; it is not something actually that can be granted by the institutions of society. As Sorel says, quoting Talamo: "Economic, civil, political liberties are only words, pure illusions, without that complete internal freedom which is moral freedom."[36]

A free society can exist only when the individuals comprising it are themselves free, when they have grown out of the narcissism and dependencies of the child and have become mature beings capable of recognizing and satisfying their needs within the framework of the realities around them. This was the moral idea Sorel had in mind when he viewed the societies of the past; it was the ideal that gave him a standard to judge the present; it was his hope for the future. According to Sorel: "No writer has defined more forcibly than Proudhon the principles of that morality

which modern times have in vain sought to realize. 'To feel
and assert the dignity of man,' he says, 'first in everything
in connection with ourselves, then in the person of our
neighbor, and that without a shadow of egoism, without
any consideration either of divine or communal sanction—
therein lies *right*. To be ready to defend that dignity in
every circumstance with energy, and, if necessary, against
oneself, that is Justice. . . To feel himself in others to the
extent of sacrificing every other interest to this sentiment,
to demand for others the same respect as for himself, and to
be angry with the unworthy creature who suffers others to
be lacking in respect for him, as if the care of his dignity
did not concern himself alone, such a faculty at first seems
a strange one. . . There is a tendency in every man to
develop and force the acceptance of that which is essentially
himself—which is, in fact, his own dignity. It results from
this that the essential in man being identical and one for all
humanity, each of us is aware of himself at the same time as
individual and as species; and that an insult is felt by a
third party and by the offender himself as well as by the
injured person, that in consequence the protest is common.
This is precisely what is meant by Justice.' "[37]

CHAPTER IV

IDEOLOGY OF THE MIDDLE CLASS

Progress, liberty, economy, technique, science are myths, in so far as they are looked upon as agents external to the facts. They are myths no less than God and the Devil, Mars and Venus, Jove and Baal, or any other cruder forms of divinity.

—*Benedetto Croce*, History, Its Theory and Practice

IN SOREL'S OPINION the greatest danger to the development of a purely proletarian ideology was the possibility of corruption by the ethical teachings of bourgeois philosophy;[1] therefore the proletariat, if it were to succeed in creating a new system of social relationships, had first of all to free itself from this outworn philosophy of progress. As he says: "Democracy succeeds in confusing the mind, preventing many intelligent people from seeing things as they are, because it is served by advocates clever in the art of confusing questions, thanks to a cunning speech, to a subtle sophistry, to an enormous display of scientific declamation. It is above all of democratic times that one is able to say that humanity is governed by the magical power of great words rather than by ideas, by formulas rather than by reasons, by dogmas of which no one thinks to seek the origin, rather than by doctrines founded on observation."[2] Since this democratic ideology depended on the acceptance of a point of view based on intellectualist postulates, the struggle that Sorel envisaged between the proletariat and the bourgeoisie was in certain important respects a struggle between two value systems, between a new and an old metaphysic, between a pluralist and a monistic view of the universe. "Every day," he writes, "sees a continued advance of irrationalism, that is to say of metaphysics that does not agree to the simplification of experiential reality in order to reduce it to mechanical, geometric, or logical relations. Neither the unity that pleased the Greeks, nor the physico-Christian dualism that disturbed Kant, could any longer satisfy modern minds that have recognized the right of life to appear in the foreground of metaphysics."[8] The fundamental weakness of the bourgeois principles of democracy and liberalism and of the eighteenth-century methodology on which they were based lay in their attempt to make such simplifications by the reduction of the complex data of social experience to a logically unified system; it was this tendency, Sorel thought, that vitiated the reality of their conclusions, that led them into so many fallacies and into utopian hopes for the future that experience was to show were only illusions of progress.

The basis of most of the illusions arising out of the philosophy of the eighteenth century was the belief that the problems of society could be solved by an application of a scientific method, and hence that history was useful principally as a statement of these problems and as a demonstration of the errors and evils of past times regrettably ignorant of the true principles of human conduct and government. The Cartesian science that had had an amazing success in the study of physical phenomena was applied uncritically by theorists to the much more complex field of human behavior; this application, however, resulted only in unreal abstraction because it failed to recognize the very definite limitations of a method that was useful enough for the solution of certain particular problems but that was by no means suited to serve as a dogmatic epistemology of universal validity. When a scientific method of this sort is applied outside its legitimate sphere it not only may lead to conclusions out of touch with reality, but, even more important, these conclusions are very often not subject to the kind of pragmatic verification by the brute facts of experience that generally governs the physical sciences. The danger of such an isolation is to be seen in the fact that long after the hypotheses of Descartes had been supplanted by other conceptions in the physical sciences they continued to dominate the philosophy of the theorists of democracy.[4] In Sorel's opinion this dissociation of democratic theory from reality was the inevitable result of the tendencies towards abstraction inherent in the eighteenth-century outlook, so that if a sounder theory of social action is to be developed, he thought, the logically rigid scientific system popularized by the men of the Enlightenment must be replaced by the more tentative, more pluralist conceptions of modern science.[5]

A characteristic of all great modern utopias, Sorel believed, has been their ambition to reduce the complex phenomena of the world to a principle of unity;[6] it was this ambition that led the theorists of the eighteenth century to accept with so much enthusiasm the methodology of Descartes; but in seeking to understand the principle of the whole they misrepresented or ignored many of the particular facts of experience. Recognizing the serious limitations of human understanding, Sorel advocated a more modest and more practical methodology, one which would concern itself not with universal laws but with the peculiar significance of particular phenomena or groups of phenomena. "Social philosophy," he says, "in order to follow the most considerable phenomena of history, is obliged to proceed by a *diremption*, to examine certain parts without taking account of all the ties that connect them to the whole, to determine, in some way, the type of their activity by pushing them towards independence. When it has thus reached the fullest understanding, it can no longer attempt to reconstitute the broken unity."[7]

Instead of trying to furnish exact representations, this method seeks to embody in symbols the essential characteristics of complex and indefinable phenomena. Although it can be usefully applied in many fields of knowledge, Sorel believed it is in dealing with those historical facts that lead to the creative impulses of the free spirit that the merits of the method of diremption appear in full light: "This symbolism fills them with life, magnifies in them the psychological qualities that constitute the real cause of the importance accorded by thoughtful men to memorable actions, whereas ordinary rationalism annuls these qualities, in contracting reality within the limits of skeletonized abstractions; art, religion, and philosophy are at their ease, however, only at times when they have contact with an overflowing vitality."[8]

As an illustration of the usefulness of this method, Sorel refers to one of the great problems of Church history, the struggle of Church and state: "Only the method of *diremption* makes it possible to recognize the inner law of the Church; during the periods when the struggle is conducted seriously, the Catholics claim for the Church an independence consistent with this inner law and incompatible with the general order regulated by the state; for the most part, however, ecclesiastical diplomacy arranges accords that conceal from the superficial observer the absolute of the principles. Harmony is only a dream of theorists which corresponds neither to the inner law of the Church, nor to the practical disposition of affairs, and which serves to explain nothing in history.

"At each renaissance of the Church, history has been disturbed by manifestations of the absolute independence demanded by the Catholics; it is these times of renaissance that reveal what constitutes the *essential nature* of the Church; thus the method of diremption finds itself fully justified."[9]

Although the clarity possessed by the symbols obtained through the use of this process may be of great assistance in

understanding many complicated problems of social development, it is a method that must be employed with the
greatest caution; diremption has frequently been used by
philosophers to throw light on particular problems, but
often they have been so charmed with the resulting clarity
that they have entirely forgotten the original assumptions
of the diremption and have attempted to apply their newly
acquired symbols under conditions quite dissimilar to those
in which they were conceived; when thus distorted, as Sorel
says, "their sense becomes vague, their usage arbitrary and,
consequently, their clarity deceptive."[10] It is perfectly legitimate, he thought, for the philosopher to adopt a completely
empirical attitude by looking to the past purely as a record
of accomplished events, or, indeed, to adopt a quite contrary attitude by meditating on the future, by considering
life, imagination, myths, liberty; but only absurdity can
result from the confusion of these two attitudes characteristic of the rationalists who, deluded by their monistic
prejudices, use symbols as points of departure for the logical
elaboration of systems which they then regard as scientific.[11]

This belief that the future can be predicted by a logical
extension of tendencies observed in the present has been one
of the greatest illusions of utopians;[12] by neglecting the
particular conditions that have given their symbols a validity, the modern intellectualists are able to persuade themselves that these symbols are as real as the fundamental
conceptions of the physical sciences, and all their care is
devoted to an attempt to build on them a logically irreproachable structure of deduction. Sorel says:

"Since philosophers are generally very much more interested by the apparatus adopted in the teaching of a
doctrine than by the actual basis of the doctrine taught,
they have often believed that a system deserved an absolute trust if it was susceptible of being presented as an
imitation of ancient geometry, the rigorous objectivity of

which, up to the nineteenth century, no one had seriously questioned. Descartes, for example, has acquired a great deal of fame for his exposition of a metaphysic deduced from postulates that seemed quite comparable to those of Euclid or of Archimedes. Societies, however, do not offer data that one is able to incorporate in such an arrangement; that is why the men of the seventeenth and eighteenth centuries looked on history as a lowly sort of knowledge; as for symbols, so far as they were able to arrange them more or less easily in a dialectical progression analogous to that of the *Elements*, they treated them as profoundly venerated realities. They were thus led to think that if humanity should some day become wise, it would eagerly set itself under the direction of masters of philosophy, so as to be able, in confiding itself to their counsels, to replace the miserable world of history by a world that, adapting itself perfectly to scholarly disciplines, would be regarded as raised to the level of the spirit."[13]

The acceptance of this pseudo-scientific methodology as an integral part of bourgeois ideology was not, Sorel thought, a simple historical accident, nor can the relationship be stated in clear terms of cause and effect. As he says: "I consider that scientific popularization has a very large place in the formation of the new philosophy; but it has not had a direct influence: the taste for popularization has contributed above all in establishing a close bond between the thought of men of the world and Cartesianism."[14] In his opinion, the reason for the peculiar strength of the tie between popular philosophy and the current conceptions of science lay in their common derivation from certain underlying social and economic conditions that had been developing in France for a long period in the past. In order to understand the way these changes operated it would be very useful, he thought, to apply certain methods of the materialist interpretation of history; for this particular purpose he chose a text from the *Communist Manifesto*:

"Is much perspicacity needed to understand that when changes occur in people's mode of life, in their social relations or social system, there will also be changes in their ideas and outlooks and conceptions—in a word, that their consciousness will change?

"What does the history of ideas prove, if not that mental production changes concomitantly with material production? In every epoch the ruling ideas have been the ideas of the ruling class."[15]

Since the bourgeoisie was the dominant class in the eighteenth and nineteenth centuries, Sorel proposed to trace in their history the tendencies that led to the appearance of an ideology suited to their particular functions in society. "The theory of progress," he says, "has been received as a dogma in the epoch when the bourgeoisie was the conquering class; it ought then to be regarded as a bourgeois doctrine: the Marxist historian ought to find out how it depends on the conditions in the midst of which are observed the formation, the rise, and the triumph of the bourgeoisie. It is only in comprehending all of this great social adventure that one can truly account for the place that progress occupies in the philosophy of history... What the historian strives above all to know, and what is moreover the easiest to know, is the ideology of the conquerors. It depends on all the historical adventures of which there happens to be question. It is connected, in different ways, to the instincts, to the habits, to the aspirations of the dominant class. It has also multiple relations with the social conditions of the other classes. The bonds that can be demonstrated between the dominant ideology and all its points of relationship are not capable of complete definition, in so far as there is always charlatanism and puerility in speaking of *historical determinism*; all that one can hope to do is to throw a certain light on the paths that the historian must follow, in order to set a course towards the sources of things."[16]

Although the outward forms of the Bourbon monarchy would seem to show few signs of a dominance of the bourgeois class, Sorel believed that this class, from the beginning of modern times, was in fact asserting a continually growing influence not only on the institutions but on the ideas of the whole country. "In order to understand the ideas that the eighteenth century brought forth," he says, "it is necessary to take as a point of departure the fact that France was conquered, little by little, by a bourgeois oligarchy that the monarchy had created for its service and which was to lead it to its ruin."[17] In this outcome it is interesting to compare the history of the French monarchy with that of the Christian Church, on whose example Sorel thinks it was formed. The Church built up a great organization of functionaries drawn from the unprivileged classes, but, unlike the monarchy, it was wise enough and fortunate enough, under the Gregorian reform, to prevent the reversion of power to the families of a privileged race. Nepotism and modifications of nepotism seem to be a permanent force in the history of institutions; the royal power in its attempt to crush the rivalry of the nobles and privileged towns placed its fate in the hands of a new and unsuspected rival, the hierarchy of administrative families, a group of men that was rapidly solidifying into a wealthy and powerful class claiming almost sovereign rights.[18]

It is a curious fact of historical development that the most extreme claims for an institution are made when that institution is already showing signs of full decay: Plato's *Republic*, Boniface's *Bulls*, the *lits de justice* of Louis XV are all statements of past glory and not of present reality. Never had a French king issued commands so imperious and absolute as those of Louis in 1766; yet never had the opposition been so powerful and so threatening for the future. The *gens de robe*, outriders of a bourgeois oligarchy, gathered to themselves an extraordinary power operating through the *parlements*, and for a number of decades in the eighteenth century were the focal point of opposition to absolutism. Sorel suggests a combination of factors as the reason for this power. The history of the rise of the new monarchies in Europe has long been recognized as dependent on the extension of judicial functions by the royal officials. The line between judicial and political spheres was then not nearly as sharply drawn as in the modern world; as late as the eighteenth century, the Parlement of Paris was able to profit by this lack of distinction. The French kings had never forgotten the *Fronde* and in the last resort they were too dependent on their hierarchy of *commis* for their absolutism ever to be truly absolute.[19]

The second factor in the Parlement's power was the simple inertia that seems to decide such conflicts far more effectively than legal precedent. Louis XV was willful rather than strong willed and his petulant assertion of power, however arbitrary it might appear at the time, was not based on any principle that was worth the interference it caused in his life of pleasure. After stubborn resistances the Parlement was always recalled and the King's haughty and humiliating treatment of the seminoble magistrates only aroused popular sympathy for them and weakened his own position.[20]

Closely connected with this factor was a third which expresses more concretely the social changes back of the disputes. The families whose sons fell heir to positions in the parlements were wealthy and could afford the heavy burdens that a disagreement with constituted authority entailed. Moreover they had a personal interest in opposing the royal edicts, many of which involved fiscal affairs. Whether or not they were legally justified in their stand, at least they embodied the historical demand of representation for taxation; however selfish they may have shown themselves, they formed an essential part of a movement that was soon to assume other and wider forms.[21]

Sorel disagrees with Taine's assertion that the ideology

of the eighteenth century had as its base an "aristocracy, made idle by the intruding monarchy, of men well born, well educated, who, cut off from action, abandoned themselves to conversation and occupied their leisure in sampling all the serious or delicate pleasures of the mind."[22] Instead, Sorel looked on this ideology as growing from the conditions of life of a class of auxiliaries to royalty. In this he finds an explanation for the fact that the radical ideas so eagerly taken up in France had no honor in their native country England, where, unlike the French dependence on a class of bourgeois functionaries, the aristocracy held real administrative responsibility. "A *class of commis*," he says, "is not able to construct its ideology on the same type as that adopted by a *class of masters*; for it does not reason so much on its own affairs as on those of others. Its ideology tends to take the character of consultations given by jurists, by historians, or by scholars on problems that have been proposed to them. In order to accomplish these tasks easily, it is necessary to submit everything to academic procedure; it is in this way that France has evolved the habit of making all opinion depend on abstract formulas, on general theories, on philosophic doctrines. These ways of reasoning hardly belong to men who conduct their own affairs by themselves, and who are, as a result, accustomed to subordinate their conduct to the conditions of prudence that their personal experience has taught them to discover."[23] This abstract attitude became a permanent characteristic of French political writing and shows itself not only in Montesquieu, who can write a whole chapter on English customs without once mentioning England, but even in the works of Benjamin Constant and Tocqueville who had nothing to fear from the censor.[24]

Although the *commis* had to proceed with a certain amount of caution for fear of offending their master, the practical consequences of such an offense in the eighteenth century have been considerably exaggerated. The chief demand of the administration was that immediate questions and practical reforms should not be openly aired. Like the Church, Sorel points out, the monarchy had a great tolerance for the abstract: "It was not afraid of seeing its *commis* manufacture theories on natural law, eulogize enthusiastically republican virtues, or propose that their contemporaries abandon all traditional institutions in order to go live in a utopian state. Books that our contemporaries look on as daring socialist manifestoes, formerly appeared the more inoffensive in proportion that they were the more remote from all reality; it would have been dangerous to criticize the abuses of the *ferme du sel*; but it was of no great moment to extol communism." The apparent inconsistencies and uncertainty of Malesherbes' policy in officially censoring the *Encyclopédie*, while unofficially tolerating it, and in persecuting enemies of the philosophes as well as their friends, can only be explained "when we place ourselves in the point of view held by him, when we consider the philosophy of the eighteenth century as a simple exercise in rhetoric intended for the amusement of men of the world."[25]

Although most of this fine theorizing had very little practical intention, it was very soon to receive a literal and positive interpretation that, had they witnessed it, would undoubtedly have shocked its authors and brought heated disavowals. In Sorel's opinion the reforms of Maupeou, completing the discredit of the government, marked the turning point in the transformation of theorizing by the bourgeois oligarchy to a practical application by the masses. The French Revolution, with its doctrines of Liberty, Equality, Fraternity, was certainly not a conscious creation of a united and militant Third Estate, in the popular conception of Marxian class struggle; but several of the most significant elements of the democratic ideology expressed by the Revolution were directly derived, Sorel thought, from the functions, from the way of life, and from the social relationships of this great middle class that came to power along with the growth of the absolute monarchy.

Some considerable attention has already been given to the class of *commis* auxiliary to royalty that formed the backbone of the institutions of the modern state. From their first appearance as agents of the king up to their eclipse in the upheavals at the end of the eighteenth century, they exercised a function that required a peculiar mixture of legal and political qualities; this function, Sorel thought, was to have a profound effect on the outlook of the nation at large in nearly all spheres of its thought and action. "As soon as one finds jurists capable of applying the rules of Roman law," he says, "the power of the Church is menaced; the emancipation of the West really begins in the courts of law and in the tribunals; I do not believe that one can even yet acquire a wholly complete idea of this strange drama, of this destruction of Christian culture that seemed to have destroyed for ever the ancient world; even today the Church is not able to envisage the *reception of Roman law* without wrath: historians endeavor to show that this return to paganism was a disaster for the Western nations. The ruin of military institutions founded on the German *comradeship*, the development of the absolute power of princes who had armies and created administrations were bound to lead to the consideration of the relations of men in an abstract manner, without taking account of the qualities of individuals: Roman law, furnishing a ready-made system and a very precise language, was bound to seduce minds still incapable of new theories."[26] Sorel believed that the habits of abstraction acquired by these jurists, in their constant preoccupation with legal concepts, led to the extension of this sort of thinking to all the problems presented by a rapidly changing society; it led, as he says, to an exaggerated respect for the virtues of rationalism: "The prestige that social rationalism enjoys, is due, in large part, to the custom that we have of treating certain of the most serious questions concerning the state by procedures borrowed from juridical practice. Jurists, in academic arguments, in the submission of their briefs, in the considering of decisions, pass over the psychological motives that have led to the actions of individuals; they hide the real men under what they call legal persons, types of social categories who, according to the usages fixed in jurisprudence, are supposed to live almost like automatons; for the application of the laws, however, the judges possess a certain discretionary power which permits them to adapt the rigid forms of the theory of law to the circumstances, so that the feelings of equity held by the general public will not be wounded. These rationalist artifices have been carried over into the discussion of social questions."[27]

Dominated by these formalized conceptions, the eighteenth century evolved as the basis of its social theory a completely abstract conception of human nature, a conception that was to be the starting point for nearly all the utopian fancies that have been so plentiful in times since.[28] In itself this diremption was not necessarily reprehensible—in fact, as Sorel says, it may even be useful "as an artifice of our understanding"[29]—but after having made their abstraction, the philosophers of the Enlightenment regarded it as a representation of reality, rather than as a mere symbol, and on it they constructed a system of principles in the manner of a juridical code.[30] This tendency, Sorel thought, was particularly well represented by the theory of the physiocrats who "expressed so well the most widely spread and the most considered opinions of the administrative class, that they often came to believe that the reforms accomplished by the Revolution resulted from their demonstrations, even though they were merely on the outskirts of a great current, to which their systems were attached as a simple ideological accessory."[31] Like the high administrative officials they wished the state to be all-powerful, and however much they might talk of elective systems or of concern for the citizen, their object was, in the words of Tocqueville, "a democratic despotism."[32] The arbitrary proceedings of the *ancien régime* showed very little respect for tradition; similarly these rationalists looked on the past with a boundless scorn and were quite ready to remove any institution, no matter how well founded in history, that stood in their way and spoiled the symmetry of their plans.[33] The Revolution, with its exaggeration of some of the worst features of the administration of the *ancien régime*, brought at its close a reaction to uncertainty and instability; security of property was now the cry of the republican, so that the physiocrats, with their doctrines of centralized power, obtained an authority hitherto lacking. "It was," Sorel says, "the triumph of the physiocrats, a triumph that has lasted a long time and that is due to historical reasons of which they could not have suspected the future existence."[34]

The juristic conception of man as a free agent who enters into relationship with his fellows by means of distinct legal agreements was fundamental to that most famous of abstractions in eighteenth-century political theory—the idea of a social contract. This conception of the relationships of man, Sorel thought, in spite of the theoretical absurdities derived from it by Locke and Rousseau, had a real basis in certain of the institutions and ways of life familiar to the great mass of the Third Estate from which was recruited the oligarchy of thinkers. This class, auxiliary to the monarchy, conducted the rapidly increasing trade and manufacturing in the country and for this reason was fertile ground for theories hostile to the corporations, to the feudal regime, to administrative arbitrariness. Because of its background of production and trading it was to this class that the radical English ideas, particularly the conceptions of liberty, made their strongest appeal. "Our fathers," Sorel points out, "were willing to make the greatest sacrifices in order to introduce clarity into the first representations that serve to materialize principles; it is one of the chief reasons for the success that atomist theories gain. As with physics, one may simplify societies and find there an atomistic clarity, in suppressing national traditions, the genesis of law, and the organization of production, so as to give sole consideration to the men who come to the market to exchange their products and who, outside of accidental encounters, preserve their full liberty of action. These men are, indeed, *social atoms* that are obtained by idealizing *commercial law*. The eighteenth century had so high an idea of commerce that it was induced to think that natural law, thus obtained by an abstraction from commercial law, ought to prevail over the real law, full as it was of traces of historical influences."[35]

It was on the basis of these concepts that Rousseau stated what Sorel considered to be the fundamental principle of the Social Contract: "the complete alienation of each associate, with all his rights, to the community."[36] The source of this conception of the social atom is to be found, Sorel believed, in observations that Rousseau himself describes, of the free artisan who depends only on his work and who has nothing to carry off but his arms if he is dissatisfied with his position. Owing to the nomadic life of such men, the associations that they form for pleasure, for security, or for professional protection are very flexible and informal, so that their conception of all civil groups is equally free from a concern for historical conditions. A further source of this conception of a voluntary contract for a specific purpose is to be found, Sorel thought, in the submission of the individual to the will of the majority that was characteristic of certain sectarian groups such as the Pilgrim Fathers and the Levellers, both of whom had some little influence on the ideas of the lower middle classes. Still another source, he thought, might be found in the example of societies organized for gainful purposes, particularly in the great colonial companies where each associate was free to retire from his contractual obligations, if he so desired, by selling his title on Exchange.[37]

"These practices," Sorel says, "explain quite adequately the theory that Locke expounds in Chapters VII and VIII of the *Civil Government*. Men who are naturally free, equal, and independent, form societies to assure their security and above all that of their goods. The advantages obtained are considerable because, henceforth, society will have positive laws, judges, and a public force capable of instituting order; the contractors abandon the power that they have of acting as they please in the defence of their interests, and particularly the right of avenging themselves; the society that takes in its charge the service of public order is not permitted to override the limits of what it is necessary to do in order to correct the defects presented by the state of nature; the government will, then, concern itself only with the tranquility, the safety and the obvious welfare of the people. The social constitution does not infringe the rights of men who do not accept it and who may remain, if they so desire, in the state of nature."[38]

In the eighteenth century all these elements of the philosophy of the Enlightenment were brought together to form a widely accepted system of dogma whose popularity can only be explained, Sorel thought, by the anomalous positions of both the noble and the bourgeois classes. "The fact is," he explains, "that the nobility at this time no longer had an ideology that was proper to itself; it borrowed from the Third Estate its subjects of discussion and amused itself with projects of social renovation that it looked on as no different from tales of marvelous voyages made to lands of Cockaigne."[39] The bourgeoisie on the other hand, although possessed of an ideology, did not have the privileges and the responsibilities that belong to a ruling class: it still maintained in many aspects of its thought the characteristics it had acquired as a class of functionaries auxiliary to the monarchy; it was fascinated by the manners of an aristocracy to which it aspired. As a consequence of this social maladjustment the nobility adopted, with what now appears to be a reckless frivolity, ideas completely subversive of its own true interests; it extended its patronage to the philosophes and to men of letters and amused itself by encouraging them to indulge their wildest fancies in the theory of government.

This dominance of the salon over the thought of the time prevented, in Sorel's opinion, anything but the most theoretical and superficial generalizations on actual social problems; it debased the men whom it pampered and it corrupted the ideology of the bourgeoisie who in this, as in other things, wished to imitate the fashions set by the nobility.[40] Not only did the situation undermine the position of the nobles, but, even more significant, it prevented a serious development of a way of thought suited to the real position of the rising bourgeois class; it accounts for the unrestrained manifestations of logical abstraction that were to prove so disastrous to them both in practical affairs and in philosophy. "Experience teaches us," says Sorel, "that the critical spirit is always lacking in classes that do not think along the lines of their proper condition of life; it was lacking for this reason to the bourgeois."[41]

The extraordinary naïveté of the enlightened spirits who took it on themselves to guide France on the path to a new era is one of the most striking aspects of their outlook. Quite lacking in a critical and historical appreciation of the immense difficulties and problems of making social changes, they thought the most radical transformations of ancient customs could be effected without danger by the mere use of *reason.*[42] Tocqueville in summing up the demands of the *cahiers* of 1789 realized "with terror that nothing less is demanded than the simultaneous and systematic repeal of all the laws, and abolition of all the customs prevailing in the country."[43]

These signs of middle-class rashness were no sudden outgrowth of a national emergency, but had been taking shape for the past half-century, encouraged by the rise of a bourgeois oligarchy that felt the hour of its triumph was at hand. Nothing, Sorel thought, could be better calculated to give them an exaggerated confidence in their own abilities, for, as he says: "Daily experience shows us with what rapidity politicians are metamorphosed on approaching power; making a modest entry to Parliament, they do not doubt their universal capacities when they are mentioned by the newspapers as possibilities for the cabinet. Similarly, the Third Estate in acquiring the honors of the aristocracy acquired also the frivolity and the presumption of men of quality."[44] The belief of the eighteenth-century philosophers in their ability to solve all the problems of society by the application of abstract principles, is well illustrated in the following passage from the writings of Turgot: "The rights of men are not founded on their history, but on their nature. . . The greatest of all power is a pure and enlightened conscience in those to whom Providence has entrusted authority."[45]

Much of the driving force of the Enlightenment can be found in the formula *écrasez l'infame* that some of its members used as a cry against the Church. "We can now understand," Sorel states, "why our fathers regarded institutions as being responsible for all evil and why they supposed it was so easy to transform them: the reason is that since, for them, the whole world of the past depended on the Church, which had lost almost all its force, it is possible to hope that, with a little good will and energy, a radical transformation could be effected in a short time. Since we no longer attribute so much importance to the Church and since we have seen it rise again from the ruins, we have difficulty in understanding the boldness of the eighteenth century."[46] In many ways, however, the boasted rationalism of the Enlightenment did not represent a genuine abandonment of the theological point of view, but resulted simply in the replacement of one system of dogmas by another; in these new dogmas, Sorel believed, it is even possible to find a number of obvious derivations from those of the Church that they attacked so bitterly. Rousseau's mystical conceptions of Nature, which showed themselves so clearly in Turgot's statement of the rights of men, are based on an idea of primitive virtue derived from a curious mixture of the Golden Age and the Garden of Eden; his Return to Nature was almost an equivalent of baptism, possessing like that sacrament the power of cleansing the believer of impeding sin. Even the idea of the noble savage that played so large a part in his theories, was little more than a reflection of the enthusiasm shown by missionaries in their accounts of the docility of primitive man to whom they looked for a rejuvenation of the Church. Like the Jesuits, too, the philosophes realized the importance of indoctrination, or, as they called it, of education; Condorcet and Turgot, indeed, speak in almost evangelical terms of the necessity of propagating their doctrines of civic virtue and loyalty.[47]

A further reason for the boldness of the Third Estate is to be found, Sorel thought, in the improvement of economic conditions that showed itself toward the middle of the eighteenth century. Recognition of this improvement was wide-spread and sometimes even in advance of a realization by the philosophes, who in this respect were not always the leaders of thought. The possibilities of progress

seemed unlimited and there occurred an extraordinary development of interest by the administrative officials in state
encouragement of all the industries.[48] Along with this improvement, and, in Sorel's view, as a result of it, there
appeared a general dissatisfaction and a movement for reform: "Economic necessity has disappeared and it was
thought the moment had come to make bold ventures in
social affairs as well as in technology; the reformers and
the inventors brought forth their projects; the politicians
and the heads of industry allowed themselves to be easily
persuaded, because they believed that the profits of the
immediate future would be so great that mistakes would
have no great importance." Optimism is easy in times of
expansion; but to the optimist nothing is quite as good as
it might easily be made. "The breakneck speed with which
progress became accelerated," says Sorel, "was indeed calculated to promote the belief that in the future everything
was possible, so long as one followed the instincts of human
nature."[49]

However much they may have talked of reform, the
philosophes had hardly anticipated the actual course taken
by the events of the French Revolution; the violence and
the oppression that accompanied this profession of liberal
principles left a profound impression on the minds of all
men, whether they agreed or disagreed with the justice of
the movement as a whole. On its conclusion it was no longer
possible to talk in completely abstract terms of Natural
Man and of Natural Rights; it had now become necessary
for the victorious bourgeoisie to adapt its principles to the
practical exigencies of government, and the results of that
adaptation were hardly of the sort to inspire men with
the feeling that the promised millennium had arrived. The
petty politics and lack of inspiration that have impressed
so many writers on the Restoration were not very different,
perhaps, from the normal conduct of government in the

country; but following as they did the idealistic plans and noble sentiments of the Revolutionary period, they seemed a very prosaic outcome for the expenditure of so much energy. If this result would tend to discount the significance of the Revolution in its positive political and social effects, it had, for this very reason, a great influence on the development of the concept of progress. The ideas of the philosophes had been tried, and in large part had been found impractical—or at least impractical in an immediate sense. The acceptance of theis pragmatic conclusion was remarkably prompt, and by 1820 the bourgeoisie had cast off its false skin of aristocratic pretensions and was beginning to develop its own outlook: "The *frivolity* of the *century of the enlightened*," says Sorel, "is opposed by the *seriousness* of the *historical schools*. The doctrine of progress can only survive by borrowing a great deal from that of evolution."[50] The important thing now was slowness and regularity of movement; the naïve hope of the revolutionaries that the world could be reformed in a day began to be looked on with pity. Madame de Staël did much to point out the idea of *historical necessity* and the perils of attempting to oppose it. No longer was there quite the same apostolic zeal; institutions were now regarded as living organisms with dominant characteristics whose variations could be followed in history.

In 1835 a remarkable application of this point of view appeared in Tocqueville's *Democracy in America*, which had as its object to discover, from a study of the people farthest advanced on the new road, the experiences that are capable of guiding the legislator who seeks to facilitate the passage from the past to the future.[51] Proudhon was influenced by these ideas and gave to them a moral form. Progress to him consisted in the justification or the improvement of humanity by itself;[52] but such ideas only appealed to the liberals while they were still obliged to justify their rights to power. When democracy became firmly seated, a philosophy of history was no longer as necessary and the parliamentary heroes found that the masses, on whose support their position depended, were easily pandered to with idealistic bombast and vague references to the conquests of science.[53]

With this decline to demagogy, Sorel thought, the ideology of the bourgeoisie had run its course:

"At the beginning of our researches we found a petty philosophy of men of the world who pretended to enjoy their riches joyously and who no longer wished to speak with the prudence long imposed on their fathers; the contemporaries of Louis XIV boasted of the marvels of their century and became enthusiastic at the thought of the fine things that were about to be spontaneously born to assure a greater and greater happiness to mankind.—Later appeared a philosophy of history that took its definitive form at the time of the liberal bourgeoisie and that had for its object to demonstrate that the changes sought by the champions of the modern state possess a character of necessity.—Today we have descended to the electioneering humbug that permits demagogues to direct their army unhampered and assures them of a happy life. Occasionally upright republicans seek to conceal the horror of this system of politics under philosophical trappings, but the veil is always easy to tear aside.

"All these ideas relative to progress are mixed together in a singular and sometimes fantastic manner, because democracy has very few ideas that it can properly call its own, living as it does almost solely on the heritage of the *ancien régime*. One of the tasks that is laid on contemporary socialism is to demolish this whole scaffolding of conventional falsehoods and to ruin the prestige still enjoyed by those who vulgarize the vulgarization of the eighteenth century."[54]

CHAPTER V

PRAGMATISM AND A PLURALIST WORLD

Am Anfang war die Tat.
—*Goethe*, Faust

ALTHOUGH SOREL never spared his criticism of eighteenth-century thought and of the later vulgarizers of this vulgarization, his opposition was not factious nor was it ever a mere personal polemic. He saw that the conflict involved a fundamental difference of point of view, a difference that had its implications in all the most immediate and practical decisions taken by man in the course of social action; to him the science of the philosophes was a vicious obscurantism that served only to place a complicated mechanism between man and reality, and their boasted *clarté* no more than a vain abstraction. "I believe," said he, "that the French of the eighteenth century lacked clarity; it is alone with particular terms, the only ones capable of evoking images, that one can truly express a thought without deceiving one's reader and without deceiving one's self."[1]

Cartesian philosophy, however, could not be satisfied with such a limitation of knowledge to particular terms, and in its attempts to reach universal explanations of phenomena it used the new method of mathematical reason to elaborate a system of abstractions that had little or no regard for reality, for the fundamental diversity of things and for their fundamental interdependences. It was not until after the Restoration that men generally began to realize the limitations of such scientific abstraction and felt the need of a more constant reference to experience as a check on rationalization. One aspect of this new demand for empirical verification was an awakened interest in the study of the past: a new and more chastened attitude was adopted towards the writing of history; it was no longer a kind of archeological research useful chiefly in unearthing examples of the operations of scientific law, but became instead a positive criterion, a pragmatic means for judging the validity of ideas. From a science cold and aloof, history became an art and as such demanded the full exercise of imagination and of all the emotions.[2]

The new historical outlook can be traced as far back as the Italian philosopher Vico, but it was not until the middle of the nineteenth century that it attained any general significance in the world at large. Along with this changed outlook on the past there appeared a new way of thinking known as pragmatism—a way of thinking in some respects as old as philosophy itself but new, nonetheless, in its influence and in its effects. It is with these pragmatic weapons, with an intuitive realization of the immediate data of consciousness and with a constant reference to history, that Sorel assaulted the logical synthesis and deductive reason of the philosophes and their followers.

The eighteenth-century intellectualists had a naïve faith in the power of reason to control the actions of men; this conviction caused them, as has been noted, to take over from the Church its system of proselytizing through schools and missions and to transform it into their own powerful concept of popular education, in the expectation that all men, if shown, would be led by reason to accept their theories. The change was by no means difficult to effect since the Jesuits had already produced a highly developed system of indoctrination, which, by a simple shift of divinities, served admirably as a model for the university.[3] This system was based very strictly on a classical education removed as far as possible from actual reality; in this respect it resembled the method of the Greek Sophists that Socrates had so strongly condemned for its emphasis on argumentation rather than reasoning, on conviction rather than on the demonstration of truth. Sorel saw a grave danger in such a mixing of artificial idealism and casuistry, for it provided men with the means of justifying with irrelevant reasons any action that their interests might lead them to take; he has aptly described its result as "a state of ideological dissociation," a state that brings about a cleavage between the rules of practical life and spiritual aspirations.[4]

One effect of this dissociation is that the individual is encouraged to explain his actions by arbitrary theories that are not based on reality and consequently lack the checks and restraint that such a reference would give them. By an odd paradox, the cultivation of man's intellectual faculties often results in providing a greater leverage for his prejudices, which become only the more dangerous when they are covered by the deceptive veil of intellectualization. As Sorel says: "The justification of acts is always easy for a man having a certain amount of education; the theses of the old casuistry were pernicious above all, because they facilitated this *inversion of functions* that I am pointing out here: they allow every decision to be clothed in sophistical motives."[5] The real motives, or what Pareto has called the *residues*, are often very different from the supposititious explanations, the *derivations*, and as a result, conduct that would not be condoned by society, or even by the individual, if its *residues* were openly recognized, is under the form of a *derivation* not only accepted but often even commended. "Ideological dissociation," Sorel states, "not only renders sophisms easily acceptable but prevents the operation of all criticism on our intellectual operations; it is thus very favorable to this inversion of elective functions that permits us to justify our acts. It develops a monstrous egoism that subordinates every consideration to the desires of our appetite and that causes us to value the resources set at our disposal as merely a feeble tribute rendered to our talent. In the economic sphere, we are able to lay claim to a share socially equal to our *work*; but, by ideological dissociation we abandon the economic sphere: we lay claim to a share in proportion to our *talent*, that is to say, we pretend to levy on production an amount that we consider to be in proportion to the dignity of our intellect."[6]

When realistic standards based on economics, law, and social customs are abandoned, and when the individual claims the right of private judgment and demands reward for talents as such, then the way is opened for purely arbitrary action, for the indulgence of personal whims and desires without regard for social consequences. Character-istics that ordinarily appear harmless enough, and even well-intentioned, become social vices of the first order when unrestrained. Proudhon has pointed out that: "In former days Nero was an artist, a lyrical and dramatic artist, a passionate lover of the ideal, an adorer of the antique, a collector of medals, tourist, poet, orator, disputant, sophist, a Don Juan, a Lovelace, a gentleman full of wit, of fantasy, of sympathy, in whom life and voluptuousness overflowed. That is why he was Nero."[7] Similarly other idealists and men of talent are likely to conduct themselves in the most reckless and arbitrary manner if they come into a position of power; to Sorel they appeared as the most dangerous sort of persons to be entrusted with political responsibility, because, convinced of their own virtue, they feel it their duty to punish all divagations from it. "I have always been very impressed," says Sorel, "with the ferocity of idealistic revolutions. . . It is not the first time that I have called attention to the bloody character that would mark a revolu-tion conducted by intellectuals craving for vengeance and domination. I believe that a revolution of workers, con-ducted after Marxist ideas, resulting from the action of the organized proletariat, would have a great chance of being produced without terror and without proscriptions. This peaceful character, is, doubtless, only a hypothesis; but the ferocity of the idealists is a certitude."[8]

One of the most remarkable phenomena of political history in the nineteenth century is the ease with which the humanitarians, the socialists, the uplifters of all kinds have so often managed to reconcile their high ideals with their personal interest. It would be superficial to think that all these Millerands, Clemenceaus, Briands deliberately and cynically advocated their theories for the sole purpose of hoisting themselves to power; and Sorel's explanation, through the conception of ideological dissociation, is more profound than this in its psychological analysis. All human beings live not only in the world of actuality but also in a world of fantasy, a fact that psychologists recognize in describing schizoid tendencies. Some men immerse themselves so deeply in their fantasies, in the attempt to escape reality, that they become incapable of making necessary adjustments to life and cannot live in society. Most men, however, are able to achieve some sort of a balance between the two parts of their personality, so that these parts can exist together even though intrinsically unreconciled. This compromise must always be to some extent an evasion and involve self-deception: even when the fantasy construction is pushed to extremes the resulting split from reality is much more obvious to an observer than to the subject himself. In this lack of personal insight lies the grave danger of utopians to society. They themselves are unable to distinguish the motives of their actions; but their divine visions, like those of Loyola, very often seem to guide them to those actions that turn out to be the most expedient to the advancement of their own interests and power. In this sense they are truly rationalists. "No scientist," says Sorel, "uses Cartesian rules; but the glory of Descartes has never ceased to be celebrated clamorously right up to our own day by those writers who, under the pompous title of *rationalists*, have pretended to impose the multiple fantasies of their imagination on modern men in the name of the sacred laws of the Intelligence, laws that are a superior sort of artifice for dissimulating the real, emotional reasons of their systems."[9]

Sorel recognized these artifices as unreal representations of true motives, but he was far from dismissing them as insignificant in their effect on action. "We do not," he says, "live in a material and measurable reality, as thinkers who seek to make of sociology a mechanical science often imagine; the present world alone would, in such a case, furnish the causes of our evolution. But as soon as man is somewhat elevated above animal life, the present and mechanical reality becomes increasingly less important. Man adapts himself to a kind of ideal atmosphere, fashions for himself a world and a future in which he takes refuge by fleeing from the anguish of the past: and this region of the imagined future is the true sphere of humanity."[10] Although .man's spiritual ideals may at times be very significant, they must not be thought of as providing a complete or true explanation of the ordinary conduct of life; hence Sorel's insistence that any theory built on intellectualizations, rather than on the actual emotional bases, could never be more than a logical systematization of half-truths or untruths. This conception, which was later developed by Pareto in his theory of residues and derivations, is clearly stated by Sorel in the following passage:

"Not enough attention has generally been given to the predominating power of emotions in present life; one reasons as if the passions, as if love, were pathological phenomena, foreign to the laws of normal life! One can follow, however, the applications of such principles in all the circumstances of existence.

"What obscures the true character of emotional action

to the eyes of inexperienced persons, is that we fancy our- selves reasoning very logically, when, in fact, our reason- ings are only justifications *a posteriori* of a decision already taken."[11]

A true understanding of the motives of social action can only be had by a recognition of this inversion of functions: "One effect of emotion being to deceive us as to the true nature of things and to prevent us from observing reality in a scientific manner, it follows that the system of accepted opinion always constitutes an artificial construction that does not correspond exactly to the truth of things. A certain time is required before the opinion forms and before a thing that exists comes to be recognized, and, when the original reason for a judgment has disappeared, this judgment still persists for a certain time."[12]

The basic error of the fabricators of utopias is in mis- taking such artificial constructions for reality;[13] they fall into this error because "Utopians are all more or less intel- lectualists; in a manner more or less apparent they all suppress the element of emotion in social life." They pro- ceed by a method of abstraction and logic and end by con- fusing dialectical ingenuity with practical truth. As Sorel says: "To them pure logic has the value of a science of society. They look on the abstract feelings of an epoch as the decisive explanation of history and act as if the world were created by their will; they are led always to give the first place in their thought to considerations corresponding to demonstrations, and end by taking for granted that a system is according to the fundamental laws of the spirit and ought to bring about the happiness of all humanity if it is well protected with syllogisms in such a way that it appears impossible to prove it wrong. The great point, indeed, is not to know the facts, but to satisfy the needs of a rigorous logic: it is a kind of scholastic aesthetics that serves to judge the value of the utopia; if this aesthetics is satisfying and if the construction is irreproachable, happiness ought to be the result."[14]

The theories of the utopians are particularly interesting in the study of modern thought because they present the most highly developed illustration of the intolerant use of abstractions to be found in the political sphere. If they were isolated phenomena, pipe dreams of cabinet philosophers, they might easily be dismissed as mere fanciful and quixotic idylls that had no practical effect; but they are not isolated: they are very closely connected to the movement that attained striking successes in the physical sciences and that, through the so-called scientific method, attempted a similar transformation in the social sciences. Many of the essential elements of the *modern* point of view are based on this method; as has already been shown, the whole doctrine of progress and enlightenment and perfectibility was a development of the dogmas of scientific utility as stated by the eighteenth century. The belief of the utopians that the true way to scientific knowledge had been discovered, once and for all, led to an unwarranted optimism, due, so Sorel thought, to their failure to realize "that what they call science is a way of inventing nature in the manner of Descartes and has no connection with the fathoming of the problems that true science, founded on prosaic reality, poses for itself. The cosmological hypotheses of Spencer or of Haeckel amuse educated people, as mythological tales have amused ancient aristocracies: but the consequences of the enthusiasm provoked by the modern tales are considerable, because their readers like to fancy that their mind is capable of resolving all the difficulties presented by daily life, after having resolved all those that exist in cosmology. From this springs that insane confidence in the decision of enlightened men that has remained one of the ideological bases of the superstition of the modern state."[15]

The most outstanding political theorist of these new

scientific tendencies was undoubtedly Auguste Comte. Although his doctrine is far from being a clear and consistent whole, particularly in the apparent contradictions of the *Cours de philosophie positive* and the later *Système de politique positive*, yet these very contradictions are in themselves representative of the uncertainty and mixed motives that lay back of the current attempt to rule society by science. Positivism pretended, in its early stages at least, to operate without the aid of religion or metaphysics. Its purpose was to take the decisions of government out of the hands of politicians and the ignorant masses and to give them over to experts. The prospect of living under the rule of men who would try to fit the diversity and disjunctiveness of human existence into a rigid scientific system was not one that appealed to Sorel; he thought such a scheme as ridiculous in theory as it was dangerous in practice: "The regrets that one may have in observing the sad effects of the electoral regime ought to be a little mitigated when one reflects on what a government of scientists would be. The Positivist school has very strongly combatted the sophism of equality; it pretends to organize society by science. But what more horrible government could there be than that of academicians?"[16]

Comte, after having denied that religion and philosophy had any place in a world governed by enlightened principles, was himself forced to recognize the necessity of emotion as the means of bridging the gap between conception and action. Boutroux for this reason says that Comte "is not exactly an intellectualist or an apostle of science."[17] This may be true if the intellectualists' pretensions that they deal only with the rational and the logical be admitted; but if intellectualism be considered in a more pragmatic sense, as the *actual* way of thought of its professors, then Comte's position appears not only as the typical but even as the inevitable result of ideological dissociation. If there is a difference between Comte and men like Condorcet and Bentham, who fondly thought that they had produced workable social systems with pure Reason as their only guide, it is that he finally came to admit, as they did not, the importance of the nonrational as a necessary instrument for the realization of the rational. It is important to note, however, that this admission did not affect the dogmatism of his system, except in reënforcing its abstract and unreal assumptions, which still remained as far as ever from a factual verification. It is because of this inversion of functions that Sorel says Comte is not representative of the nineteenth century but entirely of the eighteenth[18] and that he looks on his appeal to feelings as both dangerous and deceptive: "There are still some enlightened people who imagine that the *heart* is able to *suggest* solutions to the man surfeited with rationalism. This illusion troubled the brain of A. Comte in the last years of his life. One can hardly protest too much against these dangerous doctrines, which reveal in their apostles a profound hypocrisy or an encephalic lesion." The danger and hypocrisy of this illusion lay in an intellectualization of emotion and of religion that is an exaggerated development of the scientific outlook, rather than a departure from it. Sorel has aptly described this process as "neo-fetishism": "To turn back the modern world to a neo-fetishism, is to prevent the imagination from seizing, by poetry, anything of the mysteries of life and, in consequence, it is to raise a barrier against art and against philosophy; nothing is less likely to develop the ideas left by Christianity than the cult of the Earth, of Space and of Humanity and, consequently, nothing is less religious than the pretended religion of A. Comte."[19] Comte by introducing Spirit into Positivism did not for that reason make it any the less positive. He thought that the great sphere of the emotions was capable of systematization just as was that of the intellect; consequently he refused to recognize the possibility of any incomprehensible force eternally escaping the methods of scientific inquiry.

Such an attitude was, as Sorel contends, merely a manifestation of the optimism provoked by the triumphs of technological discovery which ignored obscurities and difficulties by regarding them as mere remainder problems sure of eventual solution on the progress of knowledge. "The great discoveries of the last two centuries," he says, "have exerted a considerable influence on the development of the utopian spirit: mechanical inventions possess the faculty of exciting a sometimes very singular enthusiasm that strongly resembles that which seems to have animated the mysterious metallurgists of high antiquity. Men are not far from admitting that although ignorance exists in the philosophy of nature, the mind, nonetheless, has come to realize in an infallible manner all the combinations of which it has serious need. It is precisely this state of mind that is suited to the formation of the utopia. The complete purgation of social systems, the elimination of all that is obscure, imperfect, unintelligible, such is the work that has seemed possible for the past two centuries, during which time man has never ceased admiring the products of his mind and the victories that he has won over matter. One can say then that scientific education has exerted a great influence on the development of the utopia."[20]

While the utopians were engaged in using the methods of rationalism and science as a foundation for plans of a perfect future, this foundation itself was in process of a radical change which not only invalidated their present proposals, but made a sincere belief in the possibility of future utopias much more difficult. This change, which took place largely in the latter half of the nineteenth century, may be called radical not because it represents a complete departure from the ways of eighteenth-century thought— there are, in fact, many vestiges of these ways still re-

maining—but because it represents a profound transformation in the outlook of almost every branch of human activity
from science to politics. "The historians of our century have
not made sufficiently clear the great separation that exists
between the times before 1848 and the times after; in my
opinion, the French Revolution is very much more remarkable for the continuity that it shows in its ideas, than for the
destruction that it has effected; the eighteenth century
traverses it and is prolonged up to 1848. During the first
half of the nineteenth century men continue to believe in
the goodness of man, they construct utopias to make humanity happy, they are at once rationalists and men of
feeling; although a great deal of blood had by then been
spilt, our fathers believed themselves to be profoundly
humane. After 1848 begins the *century of the men of iron*,
the era of hard men who scoff at philanthropy and boast of
their force; the reign of Rousseau which began towards
1762 (the date of the publication of the *Emile*) lasted almost
a hundred years."[21] This revolution in point of view did
not mean that the theorists necessarily gave up their abstractions, or the utopians their fancies; but their ideas
were inevitably modified to meet the new conditions, and
even when modified no longer commanded the same inner
respect of men of action: aspirations for the perfect state
gave way to practical politics and science became increasingly judged by its industrial utility.

The prophets of the Enlightenment had promised that
man, by accepting Reason, would be washed free of past
sin and raised to a new life. But the great conversion had
not come about and the millennium now seemed very far off
indeed; so the world returned somewhat sadly to work in a
present that no longer appeared very different from the
imperfect past. The great contempt of the eighteenth century for gothic times was now replaced by a lively interest
in former ages and in history, as showing the background

of human experience and the slow development by which the world had advanced to its present position. The conceptions of Savigny and Darwin, fundamentally opposed as they were to those that had immediately preceded them, were regarded by Sorel as two of the most important evidences of this great revolution in ideas. "Hereafter," he says, "evolution will be opposed to progress, tradition to creation, historical necessity to universal reason. This is not to say however, as the admirers of the eighteenth century have sometimes maintained, that the defenders of these new ideas pretended to immobilize the world; but they wished to show that in changes, there is a *local historical law*, and they consider as very essential that governments respect it."[22]

This new appeal to experience was no isolated phenomenon; not only did it apply to the writing of history or the study of biology but with equal force to the methods employed in all fields of knowledge—even of physics whose axioms had appeared as the secure standard of scientific truth. "Many people," says Sorel, "would be quite willing to accord to all science a place apart, because they fancy that science is a discovery of laws that, in a perfectly objective way, exercise some function in the world, and that, confined in a holy of holies, may be found out by the erudite. This is an old Platonic conception. More and more another conception of science makes its way in philosophy. It no longer tends to consider science as a system natural, complete, unrelated to man, but as a building that every generation adds to, that has, in consequence, a history and that could have been constructed otherwise."[23]

The idealist epistemology that has dominated Western thought since its classical exposition by Plato, and that has led men always to seek the idea, the essence of phenomena, received a formal and fundamental criticism at the hands of William James. Although he was one of the first to elevate the pragmatic method to the dignity of a philosophy, his work was based on tendencies already quite widespread in the world. Long before he knew of James, Sorel had said: "Science has not for object the determination of essences, of natures, but the determination of relations"; and again: "Science is a means of verifying the possibility of acting in a certain manner."[24] These conceptions go to the root of the pragmatic method and anticipate with remarkable exactitude the ideas that James was later to develop. For example in his essays on *The Meaning of Truth*, James says: "The full reality of a truth for him [the pragmatist] is always some process of verification, in which the abstract property of connecting ideas with objects truly is workingly embodied"; or further: "For the pragmatist . . . all discarnate truth is static, impotent, and relatively spectral, full truth being the truth that energizes and does battle."[25]

Already well on the road to a pragmatic outlook, Sorel enthusiastically welcomed the appearance of James's works in France and was encouraged to push on his own studies in the same direction; although, as always in his reception of other men's ideas, with an independence and originality that preserved him from dogmatic discipleship. The main principles he agreed with: as has just been shown, he foreshadowed the attack that James launched on the "absolute-idealistic" concept of truth as a quality "ante rem" or an "independent prior entity," and he concurred fully in the essential doctrine that "realities are not *true*, they are; and beliefs are true of them";[26] but he found many gaps in James's theory, particularly in the insignificant use he made of reference to historical development as a test for revealing the fruitfulness of ideas.[27] There were also, he thought, a number of inconsistencies in James's application of the fundamental doctrines of the pragmatic method; the most important of these being James's failure to apply his pluralist method to the theory of knowledge. "Instead of examining, in his own way, how modern scientific doctrines are formed," says Sorel, "he blindly accepted the conclusion of metaphysics constructed by the fantasy of illustrious European mathematicians who wished to show the layman that their works lead to extremely surprising results. We cannot too greatly deplore the fact that he should have been dazzled by the scientific reputations of these amateur philosophers, in somewhat the same way that the rich heiresses of New York are dazzled by the noble titles of our ruined gentlemen."[28]

Although he regarded them as being merely approximations, James accepted the useful conclusions of scientific thought as a sort of "conceptual shorthand"; but in spite of his announced skepticism of the abstract validity of systems to which they belonged, he never undertook the task of uncovering the pragmatic reasons for what he himself calls "the curious congruence between the world and the mind."[29] Sorel says of him: "Like almost all the classical authors who have preceded him, he believed that the theory of knowledge has for object above all to provide an understanding of how far the power of knowing can go."[30] Starting with this conception, James came to agree with such men as Henri Poincaré in doubting the reality of all science. Although this attitude appeared to be a salutary attack on Platonic idealism, it followed, as a matter of fact, an inverse order to the true pragmatic approach. It assumed that to be real, a scientific fact must fit a system and since obviously many facts did not fit systems it came to doubt the possibility of any scientific reality. However negative they may be, monistic assumptions are still involved; the appeal is still to universal conceptions rather than to a frank acceptance of pluralism. "In working as they have," says Sorel, "these scientists [such as Poincaré] have been faithful to Platonic recollections; they cannot come to understand that history is able to explain itself historically."[31] In order to provide such a historical explanation Sorel turned to the philosophy of Vico, from which he developed a theory of major importance in extending the scope of the pragmatic method.

According to Vico, man can *know* only what he *does* or *makes*. There is no such thing as abstract understanding without the prerequisite of personal creation and the living knowledge acquired by experience. For this reason, Vico says, "God knows everything because he contains in himself the elements from which he has made everything; man divides them without knowing them; thus human science is like an anatomy of the works of nature."[32] Man, therefore, can never hope to attain or even approach absolute knowledge of the law of the universe; but his failure in this does not prevent the possibility of success in other aspects of knowledge. As Sorel interprets Vico: "Man is able to know in an absolute manner geometry and arithmetic, because these are works of his intelligence, but not nature, which is a work of God; we have in ourselves the elements of mathematical truths whose demonstrative arrangement constitutes creative operations; the sciences are so much the less certain in that they are further engaged in matter."[33]

These ideas of Vico led Sorel to make a distinction between what he called *artificial nature* and *natural nature*. Artificial nature is the body of knowledge that is known to man through his own creative effort, and in this category Sorel includes certain geometrical representations that are as much a construction of man's own mind as his creation of apparatus for experimental studies. "Thanks to the concurrence of these two instrumentalities of the same family," he says, "we arrive at the organization of an *artificial nature*, to which the formulas of our science adapt themselves perfectly. One ought to regard industrial mechanics, whose methods become daily more scientific, as a sort of offspring of this creation; so that the workshop could very well be looked on as a somewhat informalized laboratory; the former furnishes economic utilities under the hand of skilled workers, whilst the latter uncovers laws to those who know how to put the questions; but this difference of social employment is not sufficient to hide from us the systematic identity of these two means of work."[34]

Natural nature—or what Reuleaux hinted at in distinguishing *cosmic* from *mechanical systems*[35]—is, as Vico would say, the idea that God would have of a universe that he had created. The presumptuous desire of man to attain to this knowledge has prompted him to fabricate many cosmologies and, when these attempts failed to explain experience, has led him to fall back on a skeptical subjectivism; or at least to look on science as merely an approximation of reality. All of these attitudes depend on the belief that there can be no truth apart from some monistic or dualistic cosmological explanation, a fetish, Sorel believes, that must be denied by the true principles of pragmatism: "The pragmatist declares that *artificial nature* interests our life at least as much as *natural nature*; he admires its fecundity which appears to him as bound to increase indefinitely; he asks himself how man can have such senseless ambitions as to believe that *artificial nature* is not enough to occupy his genius."[36]

It is true that in accepting this pluralism he will shock both the spiritualists, with their conception of an all powerful God, and the materialists, with their equally dogmatic belief in immanent reason; but, in order to establish a verification of his views, he has only to point out the absurd positions into which theorists have been led by their attempts to find solutions for present problems in the *natural* institutions of primitive society, or their equally vain attempts to solve technological problems by following the models given by nature. "Whatever the region may be

on which we bring our investigation to bear," Sorel writes,
"we shall always come to see that it is an error to continue
to attribute, as in the past, the role of a teaching power to
nature; we use the resources of which, by a process of
experimentation in the given world, we have suspected the
possible advantage; the inventions that we thus form, are
the more independent of models furnished by nature as our
intelligence is more developed."[37]

The distinction between these two realms is not merely a
matter of degree of approximation as some mathematicians
like to picture it, but is, according to Sorel, a definitive one
because of the indeterminate element of passive resistances
that vitiates all attempts of scientists to reduce the phenomena of the world to a system of mathematical law.
Encouraged by the apparent success of Newtonian physics
in astronomy, scientists since then have more and more
complicated artificial nature in terrestrial science in order
to bring it closer to natural nature. "But," as Sorel points
out, "there is a great difference between the planetary
world, where passive resistances are so inconsiderable that
no account need to be taken of them in the ephemerides,
and the terrestrial world, where they intervene with an
importance that so often appears troublesome to us; . . .
natural nature which surrounds us, would then be separated
from *artificial nature*, completely geometric, by a zone rebellious to the law of mathematics; the first ought to be
looked on as contaminated by indetermination, whilst the
natural nature of the planetary spaces and *artificial nature*
are entirely determined."[38]

Sorel attributed great importance to the conception of
passive resistances, which he looked on not only as a major
problem for physics but, even more significant, as the key to
a proper understanding of man's ability to deal with reality.
"It ought now to be considered as certain," he says, "that
passive resistances, passed over by rational mechanics, are

called on to play a very considerable role in the philosophy of nature; it may even be presumed that their study will lead to the adoption of views belonging to categories completely different from those that the classical doctrines depend on, because the phenomena where energy transforms itself into heat are probably not subject to the determinism that our fathers believed applicable to the whole of physics." Recent experiments on friction have resulted in completely upsetting the old laws in favor of the hypothesis of indeterminism and "it is then very probable that the phenomena of friction are more analogous to those of meteorology than to those of normal physics." It is true that modern engineering has had a great pragmatic success in its construction of machines; but the rules that it uses are far from having the exactitude found in astronomical calculations. As Sorel says: "If then industrial mechanics resembles rational mechanics in its didactic aspect, it differs from it profoundly in practice, since it presumes a liberty of judgment comparable to that of an art. This liberty of industrial mechanics is one of the fundamental elements of which the pragmatists must take account, because it is one of the conditions of the progress of modern technology."[39]

To Sorel the facts of artificial nature constitute a realm of positive knowledge that man has created for himself out of the great flux of the experimental world. This knowledge is real in a truly pragmatic sense and does not depend, as in Poincaré's conception, on some mere subjective convenience: "Instead of having an empirical mass," he says, "one has a mathematical nucleus encompassed by a floating envelope."[40] This floating envelope is the indeterminate element of passive resistance that always stands between a practical, pluralist knowledge of the world and any attempt to discover absolute and fundamental laws of nature. It announces its irreversible and fatal force in the second law of thermodynamics; it is the stubborn obstacle of man in his attempts to give an order and meaning to what Heraclitus called the "whirl," what Bergson called the "flux" of cosmic process.

Sorel accepted Bergson's belief that the meaning of this process is not comprehensible by intellectual means, but, unlike Bergson, he did not believe that truth for man could be discovered by immersion in the stream of duration. To him natural nature is a mysterious and even malignant Fate, an arbitrary and meaningless force that constantly threatens to overwhelm the spheres conquered by human reason. As he says: "Nature, moreover, does not let herself be reduced to the role of servant of humanity without protest. Passive resistances warn us that we shall never be able to submit phenomena completely to mathematical laws, that is to say, in short, to our intelligence; it is necessary for us to destroy an enormous mass of accumulated forces in order to succeed in the creation of new forces that we organize for our profit; nature never ceases working, with a cunning slowness, for the ruin of all our works. We purchase the power of commanding in *artificial nature* by an incessant labor; let us pause a single moment and everything tends to return to the former state; it can be said that matter imposes its laws from which the mind stands back. The true doctrine is that which opposes *natural nature* to *artificial nature*."[41]

By "true" Sorel here means pragmatically true: "I believe that there cannot be too much importance attached to the critical method that consists in reascending to the historical titles of theses whose true value one wishes to know."[42] Systems of philosophy are based on social and economic conceptions current at the time of their formation; so, from a point of view analogous to his theory of the *inversion of functions*, Sorel declares that an accurate judgment of cosmological ideas must deal with their background, rather than with the mere logical worth of their abstract systematization. The first task of the truly scientific thinker is to trace these hidden motives of ideas, and then, after having uncovered them, to judge them by their utility and permanent significance to the work of man in the world. Sorel believed that the most exact way of accomplishing the first of these tasks was through a study of a people's art forms; and of the second through observation of the degree of historical success that these ideas have had in giving man a greater control over things, in extending the range of his own created knowledge, of artificial nature.[43]

The culture of ancient Greece succeeded better than that of any other great civilization in establishing human society as a self-sufficient entity, free from the arbitrary forces of a fatalistic cosmic flux. It did not, of course, succeed completely, but its conquests have been the indispensable basis of modern knowledge and technical development in the West. For this reason, the pragmatist must make the study of the origins of Greek rationalism a matter of first importance if he is to understand the tendencies and meaning of present day thought; the development of this rationalism, in its turn, can best be explained, so Sorel thought, by a consideration of the essential forms of Greek aesthetic expression, of architecture and of sculpture which, among all the arts, best express spatiality and hence the power of intellect. The Greeks, he thought, "were invincibly urged to prefer what could be hewn out by the sculptor to that which vacillated in nebulous forms, what gives the impression of having been inspired by the laws of canonical proportions to that which proclaims chance, what suggests the feeling of a harmony to that which is judged to be a chaos of accidents."[44] Greek culture was based on the tangible, on the practical; it was the product of a race of artisans[45] whose great desire was to circumscribe nature and to control it for purely human purposes: "The Greeks," he says, "received from the East mythologies, heroic legends, models of plastic art which were the products of imaginations that were rich, but too often also eccentric and sometimes even incoherent; not having, like their predecessors, the ambition of entering into competition with an exuberant nature, they proceeded by simplifications, by corrections, by alterations, with a view to making the marks of human intelligence very easy to discern; they succeeded thus in creating works so remarkable for their wisdom of expression, for their art of imparting a sense of the existence of rules, for their harmony of parts that they will, perhaps, be eternally considered worthy of serving to form the judgment of youth."[46]

What Sorel particularly admires in Greek art is its sanity and stability and concreteness, its triumph over the superhuman and the arbitrary. It was these qualities in their aesthetic production, he thought, that gave rise to the subsequent mathematical and scientific achievements and that explain the peculiar form, limitations and practical success of these intellectual creations:

"Geometry is not given to us by nature, but was introduced into Greek culture through the requirements of construction by means of which man has affirmed his creative power.

"Space ought no longer to be compared to a net that rational mechanics has caused to descend from heaven in order to give scientific reality to everything it enmeshes on the earth. It was woven, among the ancient Greeks, by incomparable artists to whose genius we owe the monuments that most honor the human species. This Hellenic conception ought to be modified today in order to relate space to our machines."[47]

As long as the Greeks maintained the original relation between geometry and the art forms that they created, they were eminently successful in their "siege of reality"; but when they sought to extend the scope of the mathematical method so as to present a monistic explanation of the universe, they fell into fallacies that to this day trouble the world of philosophy:[48] "A very useful sort of experimentation in ideas is found in the submission of the theories of knowledge to an analysis, inspired by the principles of pragmatism, of the extreme phases of the development of Greek geometry. On the one hand, the study of its origins puts us in a position to discern that this system, regarded for so long as the most authentic product of reason exercising its discursive activity free of all constraint from the material world, has been able to establish itself thanks to the concurrence of numerous historical accidents. On the other hand, the comparison of the period of this geometry's growth with the period of its diminishing life is suited to show how a great science comes to be stricken with sterility, although it is still cultivated by distinguished men, even if unfortunately these men do not demand more of it than to furnish satisfactions of a purely spiritual kind. It appears to me particularly useful to insist on these conclusions with the idea of demonstrating that they are ruinous for intellectualist philosophies."[49]

Although they appeared quite opposite in their intentions to the Greek tendency to overextend the proper field of rationalism and logic, Sorel thought that modern biological theories tended to emphasize the attainment of spiritual satisfactions without sufficient regard for the pragmatic human validity of their postulates. "Every philosophy," he says, "that is predisposed by its temperament to adopt a pragmatic outlook, will establish instinctively a profound difference between the systems of socio-biological images that the zoologists have often fruitfully employed, and the *artificial nature* of the physicists, the principal characteristics of which I recall. It consists of geometric combinations, perfectly adapted to the fundamental tendencies of our intelligence; we seek to realize them materially, with more precision than is possible to obtain, in the machinery of modern factories and in laboratories; the legitimacy of their substitution for the data of *natural nature* derives from the fact that they assist us to procure means of existence and to discover the mathematical laws of the inorganic world. Socio-biological images are only destined to permit us to describe, be it well or ill, the organic phenomena that are radically rebellious to scientific impress; they are suggested by examples on whose operation the intelligence of the individual has only a very small action, but which provoke in our soul very lively feelings of approbation or of disapprobation, and which, in consequence, we like to take as subjects of speculation; we apply, in short, to the facts of life a language fashioned with the object of expressing our opinions on social facts."[50]

These socio-biological images are useful, and in fact often indispensable, but they are after all only derivations of previous derivations, and so are that much more open to the errors of intellectualization unchecked by the immediacy of brute facts. In judging their usefulness and validity, the pragmatist must refer them to the social doctrines from which they derive and then judge the success that these doctrines have had for man: "Biological facts," Sorel points out, "ought never to be expounded by means of images that have inspired hypotheses that ill apply to the explanation of social facts; the school of Cuvier was quite mistaken in treating as related the zoological idea of species and physical ideas to which one is not able to have recourse, in order to give a reasoned description of human acts." There can be no hope, moreover, of man ever attaining a universal systemization of life through the development of such socio-biological conceptions because society itself, as seen in history, is incapable of being reduced to unity. "Thus history has provided an important illustration for pluralism," says Sorel, "since it shows itself rebellious to all reduction to unity." It was on this ground that he laid one of his chief criticisms of Bergson's philosophy: Bergson, lacking the conception of an artificial nature, denied the possibility of a true understanding of entities separated from the eternal flux or duration that expresses itself in creation through an *élan vital*: "He seems to believe, in effect," comments Sorel, "that the theses of biological philosophy contain more reality than the laws found by the physicists in their experimentation; the pragmatist should say, on the contrary, that these theses are products of the imagination whilst the laws express the behavior of *artificial nature*, which, although a human application of brute matter, nonetheless has the most complete reality."[51]

Although he rejected Bergson's epistemology, Sorel did not hesitate to profit by certain of his intuitive theories and to give his approval to many of the scientific methods of this man whose genius he greatly respected. He speaks of the *Creative Evolution* as "this great monument of contemporary reflection"; and says that "in no book, so well as in that of Bergson, is it possible to grasp the metaphysical bases of the systems proposed by our contemporaries."[52] But his quarrel with it is on these very grounds: it expresses the aspirations of contemporary thought and Sorel disliked these aspirations; he disliked them not only in the thought of men about him but, first of all, he disliked them in himself. These aspirations represented a denial of man's role as a conscious creator exerting his will on the world about him; they were an abnegation of man's duty to maintain the hard-won conquests of civilization over chaos; they were a surrender to the arbitrary and the unrestrained. Sorel himself felt the enervating influence of what Hartmann has expounded as the Philosophy of the Unconscious; his whole life, in fact, was a struggle against it, his whole philosophy of history an attempt to show that man has become human only through such a struggle. It is for this reason that he disliked music, which he regarded as properly only a minor art, and that he distrusted the Bergsonian philosophy, based as it was on this "capricious" medium.[53] There is, indeed, nothing fortuitious in Sorel's agreement with the judgment of the Greeks that: "The most perfect type of reality was furnished by the cut stone";[54] it is of the deepest significance to his whole system of thought and to his interpretation of history, which without this conception would be inexplicable. Man's purpose in life is to do and to struggle, not to accept and to be; but Bergson's philosophy rejected the possibility of human willful creation apart from the flux of nature. Consequently it was to the Greeks whom he loved so well that Sorel turned for inspiration, to their profound belief that man can carve his own reality from the welter of experiences that flow around him. "The sculptor who attacks the stone with great blows of the mallet," he says, "knows very well that his work rigorously separates the statue that he fashions from all the rest of the world; the instruments that the musician handles are not able to give him any such suggestion as this; in the argumentation that Bergson directs, with a passionate ardor, against the Greek traditions conserved by vulgar knowledge, I sometimes think to see a little of the ill nature with which men who cultivate the minor arts, speak almost always of the major arts."[55]

CHAPTER VI

MARXISM AND A PLURALIST WORLD

It is not consciousness that determines life but life that determines consciousness.
—*Karl Marx*, The German Ideology

ONE OF THE MOST INTERESTING applications that Sorel made of his theories of pragmatism was in the interpretation and revision of the Marxian doctrines of historical materialism. Although he admired Marx's genius and was profoundly influenced by his thought, he saw no reason why this admiration should stand in the way of recognizing errors and insufficiencies of his theories. To him Marx's work was significant not as a sacred and definitive exposition of dogma, but as a series of hypotheses, of varying usefulness and validity, that might serve as an excellent basis for future developments in the study of social phenomena; many of the difficulties and contradictions that appear in Marx's theory, and in that of his disciples, might be overcome, for example, by an application of the principles of modern pragmatism, a doctrine, he thought, that "is in accord with the historical materialism of Marx."[1] The chief task of Sorel's revisionism was to show that many of Marx's most important theories can be understood only in the light of these principles.

Many of his friends as well as his enemies have interpreted Marx's claim to a *scientific socialism* as a claim to the knowledge of social causation; consequently they have made him out to be either a utopian idealist or the fabricator of a rigid dialectical system admitting of no fortuitous changes or developments. Such a misconception of the word "scientific," Sorel thought, has been one of the most serious obstacles to an understanding of the materialist interpretation of history. Very often critics have assumed that the interpretation was based, as were most previous socialist systems, on a definitive and logical theory of a future society; so that in order to discredit the theory as a whole it would only be necessary to point out its inconsistencies or failures of prophecy. It is true, as Sorel admits, that certain tendencies of Marxist doctrine are purely utopian;[2] but their impracticability does not vitiate the method any more than the corrections made necessary by the quantum theory have destroyed the validity of mathematical physics: in both cases the methods are of far more significance than the tentative conclusions that a Marx or a Newton may have drawn from them or even the very systems that these conclusions may have given rise to.

His disciples have greatly exaggerated the significance of some of Marx's aphorisms, many of which in themselves are little more than truisms of doubtful merit, so that his whole work has quite unjustifiably been judged by them alone.[3] As Sorel says: "Whatever part of Marx's work may be chosen for examination, it appears evident that he does not seek to constitute a doctrine, but that he has conceived the work of philosophy as a means of throwing light on certain questions."[4] Although many of his ideas are untenable, his works are, nonetheless, extraordinarily fruitful in forcing the consideration of things from new points of view, a quality of them that interested and stimulated Sorel:

"Moreover, when one studies the history of philosophy, one very quickly comes to recognize that doctrines have played a part in the world very much less important than that which at first may appear.

"The formulas that have served to sum up systems do not tell why a system has triumphed in a given period nor the reason why it had an influence on institutions. What is most important in the history of philosophy is not what is found in dogmatic theses, it is the attitude taken by each school towards real life. . . The dogmatic side of the system is truly interesting only when considered as a simple means of exposition, as a collection of examples adapted to show that it is possible to make use of it as a means of explanation or better still as an adaptation of myths intended to give an understanding of what can only be expressed by figurative means."⁵

Sorel did not regard Marx's work as a complete or scientific explanation of economic principles of the kind so common in the academic world, but instead preferred to compare him to such a thinker as Plato in that "he has the faculty of divining more than he demonstrates, that he throws light on a problem, but without treating it thoroughly."⁶

The critical judgment and qualified acceptance that Sorel brought to his study of Marxism were bitterly denounced by the official Marxians; this critical attitude, however, is one that is today generally accepted in all fields of scientific inquiry; aside, therefore, from considerations of party politics, the question as to whether he was or was not orthodox is a purely academic one, having no more practical significance than the question whether Einstein is or is not an Aristotelian. Sorel rejected in whole or in part many of the best known doctrines of the Marxians; but this rejection was often based on the method laid down by Marx himself, the chief object of his revisionism being simply to remove the adventitious growths that obscured the essential statement of this method in the materialist interpretation of history. Few conceptions, indeed, have been so deformed by controversy and so generally misunderstood; its significance as a part of Marx's work is still disputed, and there is no agreement even on what doctrines ought to be included as essential to its proper statement. This confusion is due in part to the failure of Marx and Engels to formulate a definite and systematic theory in any of their works. It is futile for disciples to seek an orthodox doctrine when their master himself was sometimes contradictory and often obscure in his statement of it—an obscurity, moreover, that was not reduced by the ill-proportions, stylistic peculiarities, and Hegelian phraseology of the main source, *Das Kapital.*[7]

Another very serious difficulty is a result of the vulgarization of Marxian phraseology. Terms like the "economic interpretation of history" have been popularly interpreted with a simplicity and a dogmatism quite foreign to Marx himself, in much the same way as the technical language of modern psychology has been adopted by the layman with little regard for the complex meaning behind the catch-phrases so glibly used. It is assumed by some critics, for example, that Marx used the word "economic" in a sense even narrower than that given it by Adam Smith, and that the whole essence of the doctrine of economic determinism is to be found in some sort of a close causal relationship between technological changes and corresponding changes in the juridical and political superstructure. This assumption is made partly in a mistaken attempt to clarify and rationalize the obscurity of Marx, and partly for the purpose of setting up a convenient straw man easily overturned by any academic economist. Sorel was not interested in the logical juggling of words and phrases; instead of attempting to force Marx's conceptions into neat and consistent definitions, he was anxious to discover the meaning in each particular use of a given term. Although he admitted that sometimes Marx did seem to say that the means of production are the basis of all society, yet this conception, he thought, was only a part of a much broader one in which the word "economic" is not confined to technological forces but corresponds to what today might be called socio-economic forces—forces that were called by Marx the "relations of production," a term much more general than the relatively tangible "forces of production."[8]

Many of the more obvious misunderstandings and disagreements over the materialist conception of history can be traced to varying interpretations of the complex meaning and significance of this term, "relations of production." Sorel identifies it with what he calls quite simply "civil society" or the "economic structure of society," using the word "economic" in the broad sense just described; or, in the realm of law, with what the jurists know as "property relations."[9] Hegel used the term "civil society" to describe the second moment of social life, the first being the family and the third the state, but Marx never brought the family into his system, so that for him civil society is the ground in which the state is rooted: in it alone is to be found the origin of the legal relations and the form of the state.[10] This conception, according to Sorel, recognized the place and importance of a great variety of forces other than the narrowly mechanical economic causes usually attributed to Marx. "In civil society," says Sorel, "we find: (*a*) the system of needs, in which are distinguished: the production of goods of exchange, in accordance with determined property relationships,—the division of labor along with corresponding professional education,—the division of social status; (*b*) the administration of justice, which assures the protection of property according to legal formulas; (*c*) the police of the state or manifestation of the *ausserliche Staat*, which regulates human activity according to some general aim,—the corporation which reunites the citizens by helping them to go out of the exclusive sphere of their own particular interests."[11] The recognition of these many complex factors as a part of economic determinism removes the grounds for many of the usual criticisms, but it also destroys the delightful clarity of the doctrine in the form of its popular comprehension as a simple cause-and-effect relationship between two entities. As a matter of fact Marx himself had no single formula to be used under all circumstances, and Sorel distinguishes at least three main systems employed as the occasion demanded. They were all of them dynamic, or as the socialist would say, revolutionary, and they range from highly abstract simplicity to the most concrete complexity.

The first of them is the best known and, according to Sorel, the least satisfactory for general purposes: it describes social dynamics as a conflict between productive forces and juridical forms, or in some similar way as an abstract opposition between the means of production and those of appropriation. The second, the familiar class struggle, is almost equally well known. The third, however, involving as it does the antagonisms that produce the progressive decomposition of the civil society already described, is at once the most complete and the most difficult to apply.[12] These three systems obviously represent quite distinct approaches to social problems and so cannot be reconciled in any neat scientific formula. Sorel, however, did not attempt such a task nor did he reject any of them as false or valueless, but instead believed that each must justify itself in a purely pragmatic way, and by its usefulness establish the extent of its own validity.

This solution of the difficulty was by no means an evasion, a simple cutting of the Gordian knot, but was based on the pluralist conceptions inherent in the pragmatic method that formed so important a part of his thought. In a conception analogous to his distinction between natural nature and artificial nature, Sorel opposes to the complexity of social relationships the institutional developments created by man: "Human society, in consequence of the extreme intricacy of its activity, presents a spectacle analogous to that of nature; it too is a reign of necessity; but we are able to use the mechanical means, offered by it, to create freely; we are artists in institutions as we are in the construction of monuments. We are thus obliged to make of society a work of art and to treat it as an entity whose harmony concerns our aesthetic judgment."[13] In the same way that natural nature was conceived of by him as a vast arbitrary flux that must forever escape the apprehension and control of man, so he looked on economics as a mechanistic force unamenable to the will because, in the Vician sense of the word, it cannot be *known* by creation. However, just as man has made scientific systems that assist him to uncover certain practical, if limited, truths in technology, so he has created systems of law and politics that have had a pragmatic validity for certain times and certain situations, but that, like science, must not be thought of as a part or even an approximation of the unknown forces of nature behind them. Man's knowledge is limited and particular: both science[14] and politics[15] are merely an anatomy of great universal forces that they can divide but cannot know. The only sort of truth that human beings can attain is a working truth, a pragmatic usefulness, in the creation of forms that are meaningful to them and that strengthen their hand in the struggle against the unknown and the unrestrained; it is only through this sort of creation that they can be said to free themselves from utter subjection to the determinism of a superior Fate. For this reason it is false to say that civil society determines, in a strictly causal sense, the forms of law, politics and thought, although it is the underlying basis of all these forms. As Sorel says: "Passing from economics to law and to politics, our spirit realizes its own freedom in a certain measure; and we feel perfectly that it would be impossible to deduce law and politics from economics. We always consider as *matter* or *basis* that which escapes, in a more or less complete way, from our will; the form is what corresponds more to our freedom."[16]

It is obvious from this theory that an anatomical dissection of society will not disclose universal laws or divine truth, and in this sense it is wrong to make a distinct separation of economics (in the narrow sense), law, and politics. Human science, however, can only proceed by such diremptions and it is on this ground that Sorel justifies Marx's first two systems, that of the conflict between productive forces and juridical forms, and that of the class struggle. Neither of these must be looked on as possessing universal significance and neither is in fact or intention an approximation of the real action of forces in civil society. Just as the physicist finds it convenient to use varying theories of matter in approaching various problems, so Marx adapted his method to his end; far from seeking abstract validity he was quite content if his method in any way aided in throwing light on a particular problem. At times he seems to have stated a quite definite causal relationship between means of production and ideology; at other times his method seems to be based on an *as if* hypothesis; and yet again he speaks of economic forces as being the real basis or foundation in which social forms are rooted.[17] In this last instance the basis is regarded as passive and not in the strict causal sense as actively determining,[18] since the forms of society and the instruments of production themselves are a human creation that might have been made differently and that, consequently, are in some degree free.[19]

Although Sorel considered that the legitimate sphere of science was strictly limited, although he looked on the ultimate forces of life as an insoluble mystery, yet he did not believe that man is entirely helpless before Chance, that King Whirl reigns. The fact that man can construct monuments after his own wishes, can make machines for his own uses, and can even invent laws that have more than a particular validity must stand as a pragmatic refutation of such a view. These positive achievements, however, do not prove that Chance is merely the residual Unknown that must eventually yield to scientific progress. Various hypotheses have been invented to explain the ideal form and purpose of the vital force, but their interest is purely speculative and can have no practical application. None of them gives to man the ability to control the seeming anarchy that nature presents in its impingement on human activities.

"In actual society," says Sorel, "in the midst of its antagonisms, the influence of the will is trifling; we find ourselves dragged along in the general movement that, although born of chance, seems still no less imperious than if it were derived from a physical law.

"Thus anarchy presents itself before our understanding in the form of necessity. We are free; but we are able to carry out hardly anything of what our minds conceive as desirable."[20]

In understanding physical phenomena man has been able to build up quite broad and comprehensive systems based on formulas that have a general, if not universal application; but since economics is much less amenable to law than is physical science, Sorel insists that it must be treated with that much the more caution:

"Economics is in reality subjected to chance; the regular laws that it seems to furnish are only so in appearance, they have a value only for our use and, above all, only for certain determinate uses. One can represent economic facts schematically by means of points marked on a piece of paper, and in the midst of these one may trace a regular line that represents the general course. Nature, on the contrary, presents us with fixed principles; today if one could analyse phenomena exactly, one would discover in every particular case the realization of a principle.

"Economic laws cover up the fundamental element of chance, whereas physical laws are similarly disguised under an apparent chance; the first do not apply to isolated cases, whereas the second apply to any case whatever. The former can only serve within the limits in which the observations were made, whereas the latter are valid for all times and all places."[21]

By this statement Sorel did not mean to say that economic formulas have no validity or that their use should be avoided. His object was merely to emphasize that they are diremptions with a more or less limited application and so cannot be legitimately used to formulate general theories of freedom or determinism that seek to bring all phenomena under one great system. "An empirical formula," he says, "is made for the purpose of representing in a convenient way the central part of a group of facts; but toward the extremities it gives not very exact results and leads to absurdity when one pretends to apply it outside of certain limits."[22]

To Sorel the only real truth of economics lies in the successful attempts of man to bend the forces of nature to his own use. He knows and controls the world around him by the contact of his hand and by the tools and implements that extend and strengthen the scope of his perception and power. Logical systematizations, in departing from practical and empirical questions, depart also from reality and from usefulness. "Idealism and determinism fabricate a fictitious and deceptive continuity; Marx teaches us to seek historical continuity in what is truly real, that is, in men armed with their means of acting on nature. Men are 'the authors and the actors in their own drama' and 'social relationships are the products of men in the same way as are cloth, flax, etc.'[23] The continuity of history manifests itself in two ways: by means of the development of productive forces[24] which grow one from another, and by means of the development of men whose spirit transforms itself according to psychological laws. This psychological part is still quite neglected by the Marxists, who in general have held themselves outside of the contemporary philosophical movement."[25]

Metaphysical demonstrations that prove the logical incompatibility of free will and determinism did not interest Sorel any more than the equally logical demonstrations of the schoolmen to prove the existence or the nonexistence of God. The impossible dilemmas that resulted in each instance were sufficient evidence to him that the methods used were unsuitable to the issues, that abstractions had been used intolerantly. It may be that an omniscient God or an all-embracing Nature sees the necessary reason for every action, but man in his imperfect state cannot realize such an order and very often he legitimately acts as if he were free agent, or at least as if he could choose between necessities. The theories that he makes in order to explain and control the phenomena of experience are a human creation and might have been made differently. They have no necessary existence or universal validity and that is why Sorel says reality could never be compressed within their limits: "If condensed, formulas of history conceal the true nature of phenomena in the eyes of an inattentive observer and disguise the fundamental element of chance under an apparent social physics, reality none the less comes to light from time to time and shows itself quite evidently. Revolutions, accumulations of decisive facts, great men, free themselves from all determinism; literature reproduces the embarrassment in which writers find themselves when they appeal to providence, to the destiny of the people, to the mysteries of genius: these are political expressions of what is prosaically called Chance."[26]

An excellent example of the abuse of abstractions is provided by the Marxists who, in their attempts to give universal explanations, attribute to technology the determining force of history without explaining how technology itself developed. Marx himself recognized extraneous forces in industrial development; particularly, according to Sorel, the influence of "factory legislation and strike laws, that is to say, of force and chance"; but in spite of the obvious weakness of their doctrine the Marxists have clung to it with the greatest tenacity because they have feared that without it they could not justify Marxism as scientific. Sorel thinks, however, that this fear is based on a misconception of the methods and purpose of science: "I believe that the fatalist prejudice arises in great part from the false idea that the socialists have of science; they imagine that science is like a mill in which problems are dumped and out of which solutions emerge. The office of science is infinitely more modest; it applies itself to understanding and perfecting the attempts and trials of the empiricists. Its own point of departure may be an invention required by the particular circumstances since man does not yet possess any complete inventory of all the possible combinations that can serve as instruments of work; I do not suppose that such an inventory can ever exist; hence chance would seem to be at the base of technical invention."[27]

This ability of man to extemporize for the occasion, to project his personality by means of the products of technology or the products of intellect on the arbitrary flux of natural forces, represents to Sorel his victory over determinism: "In so far as we leave behind us this region of economics where chance produces a kind of necessity the spirit recovers its own freedom and once more appears able in a greater or less degree to realize its own ends."[28] In an immediate sense this freedom is an escape from the fatalism of arbitrary chance, but in a wider sense individual freedom once more introduces the element of chance into the artificial system of human judgment. However the effect on human behavior is quite different: in the first case the individual feels bound by the arbitrary forces of fate, whereas in the second he feels himself the master of his environment. Although his choice of action may be limited by the conditions of nature or society, there still remains, nonetheless, the possibility of human free choice. There was no determinate reason, for example, why a new prophet should preach in Judea or why an inspired disciple should have spread his doctrine through the Hellenistic world. It may be that the world was ripe for it, and it may be that some other faith might equally well have risen in its place, but that does not explain the necessity of the particular manifestation.

In a human sense man creates the forms of his life and in that creation he is free. Through art, science, law, he asserts his will in conceiving structures that are useful to him and that strengthen his hand and add to his power over nature; but they must not be mistaken for systems of universal validity having in their turn a completely determining influence on human affairs. They are merely useful generalizations that are subject in a greater or less degree to reservations and to the exceptions that show themselves in history as chance. It is in this light that Sorel interprets the claims of Marx to the use of a scientific method in his socialism— an interpretation for which he finds support in the similar ideas of Benedetto Croce: "Historical materialism, if it is to express something critically acceptable," says Croce, "can . . . be neither a new *a priori* notion of the philosophy of history, nor a new method of historical thought; it must be simply a canon of historical interpretation. This canon recommends that attention be directed to the so-called economic basis of society, in order that the forms and mutations of the latter may be better understood."[29]

The result of this analysis of Marxian determinism leads almost entirely to the abandonment of the orthodox cause-and-effect relationship between the relations of production and the ideological superstructure. The economic basis is regarded as *passive*[30] and, in Sorel's opinion, a careful reading of Marx's phraseology shows the caution with which he himself has stated the relationship: "The means of production of material life," said Marx, "furnishes the general conditions for the process of social, political and spiritual life."[31] According to Sorel, the more dogmatic statements of a stricter relationship that are customary among Marxists, and at times even with Marx himself, are "counsels of prudence" to impatient men, to utopians who seek to bring about vast social changes without a proper regard for underlying conditions: "In order to discourage the dreamers, deluded by the possibility of changing the world in accordance with the caprices of their minds, they [the Marxists] were justified in affirming that the economic moment is a preponderant consideration. Marx, very much preoccupied with pointing out the powerlessness of a legislative revolution, rendered a great service to his contemporaries in showing them that there is a *resistant economic matter* and that the artist is not able to work it according to his own desire or caprice." Without a suitable economic preparation there can be no emancipation of the proletariat. "In order to express this restrictive rule," says Sorel, "in order to act on his conviction in a efficacious way, Marx gave to his counsel the form of an absolute law governing history. There was nothing reprehensible in his too absolute way of expressing himself on this subject, because counsels of prudence are rarely followed to the letter."[32]

Sorel regarded the extraordinary facility with which Marx changed his method of exposition to fit varying circumstances not as a fault in scientific procedure but as a virtue, and as a necessity of common sense for the explanation of the complexity of concrete reality: "Common sense mixes up all these things: it anthropomorphizes physics and mechanizes sociology, extending to everything that it touches the mixed processes that we employ in daily life, processes that have a considerable psychological value, but that ought not to be taken for scientific processes. In this region everything is intermingled; formulas are true and false, real and symbolic, excellent in one sense and absurd in another; everything depends on the use that is made of them. But, whatever may be their validity, the formulas of common sense are indispensable, since science is too abstract to be able to guide action." Since the so-called laws of Marx are really such formulas of common sense they must, he thought, be interpreted with caution: "Like all the notions of common sense, the idea of historical dependence is contradictory: on the one hand it gives rise to the theory of the coördination of functions and of their harmony; whereas on the other it leads to the study of their contradictions and their antagonisms. Marx, who so vividly set in relief the chronological agreement has also emphasized the disagreement."[33]

If the means of production determines ideology in a strictly causal sense, there is no apparent explanation of the lack of agreement that shows itself in society not only as direct antagonisms between the two, but also as a time-lag in adjustment that may culminate in sudden and violent revolutions having their causes far in the past, or having as a precipitating cause, some extraneous event.[34] The impossibility of explaining the relation between *organic* and *critical* periods is to Sorel a fundamental defect in orthodox Marxism, one that he himself is able to avoid through his pragmatic interpretation. "Historical dependence," he says, "thus shows itself at the same time as both attraction and repulsion; productive forces determine social relations and are at the same time in contradiction to them, they give rise to them and at the same time coöperate in destroying them. All this offers no difficulty to him who sets himself in the point of view indicated above; for him, that is to say, who does not seek to find in the formulas of Marx prophetic indications of the mysteries of history, but only some concise descriptions, made by means of common sense, in view of determining practical conclusions, without any pretension to scientific rigidity."[35]

The three systems that Sorel finds in Marx's interpretation of history are considered by him to be nothing more than explanatory hypotheses, and, as such, rich in possibilities of throwing light on social problems, but by no means universal in their significance or closed to the operation of chance. Their object is to bring man in closer touch with reality and to give him the approach to his experiences most useful for each particular case. Since problems vary both in themselves and in the sort of solution demanded from them, there is no rule that can be applied in all cases under all circumstances. Instead, therefore, of considering the validity of *rules* it is much more profitable to consider the validity of *results*; that is to say, truth does not lie in abstract formulations but in pragmatic usefulness. For this reason it is false to confine the Marxian interpretation to any single doctrine or method since each has a specific purpose that it justifies by its actual success in the siege of reality. It is equally false, however, to extend any one of these methods beyond its proper scope, or to expect to find in a limited hypothesis an invariable and complete account of the behavior of the phenomena to which it is applied; examples of some of these limitations are given by Sorel in his discussion of Marx's three systems of interpretation.

The first system, that involving the relationship between the means of production and the state of economic development, is merely a convenient hypothesis that is useful as a general scale for measuring the extent and character of social change, but that does not comprehend such exceptions as the possibility of greater production through a more rational subdivision of individual tasks. The words of Marx himself show the caution and lack of dogmatism with which he advanced this hypothesis: "What distinguishes one economic epoch from another ought to be sought in the means of production and the means of labor employed rather than in the goods produced."[36]

The second system of interpretation is based on the idea of the class struggle; in Chapter IV it has been shown how Sorel was able to apply this hypothesis in certain ways for the solution of practical problems. In order to explain the outlook, the morals, the typical reactions of any given epoch in history, it is necessary to speak of general ideas that are presumed to be an active part of the life in that period. These ideas, which are not the property of any individual and which have no material existence of their own, can best be understood, so Sorel thought, as the expression of a group of people bound together by socio-economic interests: "Dominant ideas considered apart from classes constitute something quite as chimerical as was the abstract man whom Joseph de Maistre declared never to have met in the flesh, and for whom, nonetheless, the legislators of the Revolution pretended to have made their laws."[37] There is, however, nothing inevitable in the ideology of any particular class, nor for that matter in the existence of a class-consciousness itself. In a certain sense this consciousness is an artificial, a willed creation, and Marx's widely known dichotomous theory of class struggle is not only an explanatory hypothesis but also a myth whose dynamic significance will be explained more fully in a succeeding chapter. As a hypothesis, however, it was not given by Marx the universal and rigid definition that has been assumed by many commentators; although he was chiefly concerned with the opposition of the proletariat and the bourgeoisie, he by no means confined his recognition to these two classes alone. An examination of his description of the various classes in Germany, and those in France, shows that his method is purely empirical and follows no fixed rule or system.[38]

Marx's third system—the most comprehensive of all—finds the essential reason for social change in the antagonisms produced by the progressive decomposition and renewal of civil society. These antagonisms develop in an exceedingly complex way and involve such influences as the spread of popular education, the introduction of new methods of subdivision of work, and innumerable other factors of greater or less significance. These elements of friction, however, do not in themselves produce changes in the social structure; such changes depend on the degree of development of underlying conditions, and are determined in a negative sense by the limits of the possible. Drawing from Marx a statement of these conditions, Sorel presents them in the form of three explanatory hypotheses that are meant to lay down the prerequisites of social change:

"1. Every period of formation that is a preparation of future society, lasts as long as all the productive forces that it can contain are not yet created, and until it exhausts all the possibilities of them. —This judgment of Marx is very important, since it tends to caution the revolutionaries to be prudent: it is the rule of the *maturity of productivity.*

"2. New and more perfect relations of production (in accord with the scale of the preparation) may not be established before the material conditions of their existence are formed, through a process of incubation, in the depths of the old society (*bevor die materiellen Existenzbedingungen derselben im Schoss der alten Gesellschaft selbst ausgebrütet werden sind*).—This can be called the rule of the fermentation of change, using here an expression of Marx himself; it concerns the maturity of civil society as the preceding one concerns the maturity of productive forces.

"3. Humanity propounds only those problems that it can solve; and problems are enunciated only when the material conditions of their solution already exist or, at least, are on the road to realization (*die Aufgabe selbst nur entspringt wo die materiellen Bedingungen ihrer Loesung schon verhanden oder wenigstens im Prozess ihres Werdens begriffen sind*). —Hence the third rule that reflects the *maturity of social questions*; these questions do not truly exist—outside of the fancies of dreamers—and are not worthy of examination by philosophers, if they are not practical."[39]

It is apparent that Sorel's analysis of economic determinism leaves to it little more than a negative influence, and the transformation of men's minds in accordance with psychological laws is a factor of the greatest significance, since it admits the influence of human will in the development of society. This human factor must always prevent socialism from being a science in the strictest meaning of the term; it is for this reason that Sorel speaks of it as *"a philosophy of the history of contemporary institutions."* The value of the materialist interpretation of history does not lie in its ability to explain the necessary operation of Nature or of God, or in its efficacy as a way of forecasting the future: its purpose is the more modest one of attempting to explain the development of present phenomena so that the experience of the past may be used in dealing with them. Since history is an art, it can have no pretension to being a scientific or objective ordering of reality: rather, Sorel thought, it is the creation of a particular moment and must be understood from the point of view of that moment. In this light, he says, history "is never reduced to being an investigation by the erudite; it is always lived in view of present conflicts." Marx has been upbraided for making of history only a justification for his revolutionary hopes, but a purely speculative philosophy of history can have no more than an abstract interest, and Marxism at least was always leading back to the reality of action: "History offers a considerable interest," says Sorel, "when it is considered as a means of understanding the rules that given groups of men will probably follow in their life; but it ought not to have as its object the forecasting of future facts from past facts. History is then, in the last analysis, a psychological collection that allows us to reason on projected undertakings, on legislative reforms, and on the tactics that a particular class ought to follow in order to attain a determined object of improvement."[40]

To Sorel the economic future is "the mystery of mysteries,"[41] so that he thought any attempt to prophesy the course of events was quite beyond the proper scope of socialism. The Marxists, and even Marx himself at times, so far neglected the fundamental nature of the materialist interpretation as to assume that social development is a constant mechanical force that will proceed in the future as it proceeds in the present. Sorel points out, however, that the social mechanism is variable because of the rapid transformation that takes place in modern industry and that psychological factors, which cannot be predicted, are also constantly being modified.[42] He believes that Marx's statement, "centuries belong to principles, rather than principles to centuries," was not in accord with the materialist interpretation of history; that, through implications of dialectical determinism,[43] it opened the door to utopian fancies: "There is no need of allowing ourselves to be mystified by sonorous words; there exists no process for *seeing*, as with the eyes of a soothsayer, *the future in the present*, nor any process for computing the future. All that the utopians have been able to do is confined to the expression of vows and regrets that can still be found in the works of contemporary socialists: these men can cleverly accumulate barbarous and abstract terms; they do not produce a science as long as they do not limit their ambition to meeting determinate problems with the means of scientific method, and do not clearly define materially attainable solutions."[44]

Marx's emphasis on the importance of objective economic conditions was meant as an assault on utopian socialism; but the fact that it in turn should be exaggerated into a new form of utopianism is an illustration of the dangers inherent in all abstraction. This emphasis, moreover, led to a still further paradox. Concerned as he was with the factor of economic determinism. Marx very largely neglected the study of the psychological factors that must be the groundwork for the necessary preparation of the proletariat. He neglected the element of human will in social dynamics and the possibility that a revolution of the proletariat, instead of automatically creating new forces, might be purely destructive; he was so concerned with the restrictions that economic conditions laid on man that he seems to have assumed, in a way very similar to the assumption of the eighteenth century which he ridiculed, that once these restrictions were removed human nature would provide sufficient resources for an easy and rapid reconstruction.[45]

A Marxist might regard this odd mixture of idealism and materialism as the natural product of a dialectic synthesis; but, whatever its explanation, it shows very clearly the futility of trying to assign the thought of a man like Marx to any abstract and formal category. Although his system was primarily pragmatic, there was, nonetheless, a certain tendency to intellectualism that shows itself here as a utopian faith in the necessary progress of mankind to some superior system of classless society in which the fundamental antagonisms and restrictions of the present world would disappear. This intellectualist tendency, however, does not impair the usefulness of the materialist conception as a whole and the impulse for Sorel's further development of that method in the syndicalist philosophy was the result of his desire to repair the deficiency with a more pragmatic conception of the dynamics of social development.

CHAPTER VII

THE PHILOSOPHY OF SYNDICALISM

Les sentiments ont leur valeur indépendement de la réalité de l'objet qui les excite, et on peut douter que l'humanité partage jamais les scrupules de l'érudit, qui ne veut admirer qu'à coup sûr.

—*Ernest Renan*, Etudes de l'histoire religieuse

THE THEORY OF REVOLUTIONARY syndicalism, for which the work of Sorel is most famous, was not a program for the future or even a definitely formulated plan of action for the present; in fact Sorel did not intend it to be a plan at all: to him it was simply a description and an analysis of certain trends of social relationships that were already taking form in the proletariat.[1] Although he has been called the foremost theorist and even the father of syndicalism, it must not be thought that he looked on it as a private invention of his own or even that he elevated it into a dogmatic system which had to be accepted with unquestioning faith. It is true that there are certain striking resemblances between the intransigence of his outlook and that of such early Church fathers as Tertullian and Augustine, but there are also some very essential differences: Sorel had much of their zeal and their passionate desire for conviction, but, unlike the great Christian saints, he was never able to abandon himself to the demands of any one system or belief and to undergo the spiritual revolution that is necessarily implied in the experience of conversion. The very qualities of analysis and criticism that led him to find in the proletariat the hope of a new spiritual movement for society also prevented him from accepting the beliefs necessary for an active participation in that movement.

Sorel always considered himself to be a historian and, in spite of the many polemical allusions and digressions that fill his work, he did maintain an almost constant aloofness, which he himself explained when he said: "It is necessary to remain outside in order to see within."[2] Syndicalism to him was not a system of rules for future happiness; it was a historical phenomenon to be observed in the same light as the patriotism of the Greek city-state, or Christianity, or the ideals of the French Revolution. He did not expect that syndicalism would by some miracle be exempt from the modifying and restricting influences that have had so great an effect on the development of other profound spiritual movements; indeed, the great contribution that he made to socialism was his insistence that it should be studied in the light of historical experience, as a product of social forces rather than as an abstract intellectual theory.

So many writers on socialism have been intellectualists or utopians, with a claim to assured solutions for the problems of social organization, that it is difficult to understand the relatively reserved and detached attitude of a man like Sorel. He has been called a mystic and, by Jaurès in a moment of asperity, "the metaphysician of syndicalism," because he refused to give a specific picture of the society of the future or even to say by what steps that society might be attained. To such criticism he replied quite simply: "I am neither professor, nor popularizer, nor aspiring head of a party; I am a self-taught man who offers to a few people the notes that have served in his own instruction."[3] Sorel did not expect that this attitude would be understood by the socialist politicians, who, he felt, made a profession of the exploitation of thought.[4] Thinking always in terms of political advantage, they could not be expected to comprehend the motives of a man who did not aspire to power, who did not even claim credit for the invention of his theory, and most reprehensible of all, who denied the right of intellectuals to lead the socialist movement. "But we have invented nothing at all," Sorel says of the New School, "and we even maintain that there is nothing to invent: we have limited ourselves to recognizing the historical import of the idea of the general strike; we have sought to show that a new culture could emerge from the struggles carried on by the revolutionary syndicats against the employer and against the state; our greatest originality consists in having maintained that the proletariat is able to emancipate itself without having need of recourse to the teachings of the bourgeois professionals of thought. We are thus led to regard as essential in contemporary phenomena that which was formerly considered as accessory: that which is truly educative for a revolutionary proletariat acquiring its apprenticeship in struggle. We have no ability to exert a direct influence on such a task of formation."[5]

Sorel never subordinated himself to syndicalism because he always regarded himself, in a certain sense, as an onlooker rather than as a participant. For this reason it possessed for him no peculiar validity or abstract truth apart from the possibility of its pragmatic usefulness in meeting the practical needs of men. Unlike utopian socialism, which aimed at a world radically different from the imperfect society of the past, syndicalism offered no promises of specific social reform or of assured material satisfactions in the future. Instead it limited its aspirations to hopes of attaining a kind of social ethics analogous to that which had served as an inspiring force in the great days of the Christian Church and in the early political organization of the Greek city-state; but appropriate—as they no longer are—to conditions of the modern world.[6] Far from being an optimistic promise of universal happiness it was a doctrine filled with a deep pessimistic recognition of human limitations and with a kind of fatalism not very different from that induced by the spiritual feeling of many past religions.

Optimists have always been inclined to look on pessimism as sterile, if not in fact as an attitude definitely dangerous to the good of the world and to progress. Sorel's whole work was a refutation of this idea, one of his most fundamental conceptions being a belief in the fruitfulness of pessimism as the source of all great achievement; as he says, "without it nothing very elevated is accomplished in the world."[7] This true pessimism, however, is often confused with a quite different point of view, that of the disappointed optimist;[8] consequently it has been charged with being no more than the soured expression of the unsuccessful, a weak submission to circumstances that the strong and the confident could have dominated. In Sorel's opinion such criticism showed a complete misconception of the basis and historical significance of pessimism, which is, on the contrary, essentially "heroic by nature."[9] Far from expressing an acknowledgement of defeat and a withdrawal before the responsibility of action, it was, he thought, a point of view that could be held only by the strongest spirits, by men who were willing to face unpleasant reality and to accept the limitations and disappointments that the forces of the world imposed on their hopes and plans. It is, in fact, not the pessimist but the optimist who, like Condorcet, seeks refuge from reality in a utopian world of fancy, and it is to men such as him that Sorel refers in expressing his scorn of "the deceptive hopes in which feeble souls delight."[10]

The experience of many of the great religions in the past has shown that there is nothing necessarily negative in the attitude of pessimism and that it can in fact be the basis of the most profound spiritual striving. It is, thought Sorel, simply a way of action and not a plan of action. "It is a metaphysic of morals rather than a theory of the world; it is a conception of a *way to deliverance*, limited strictly on the one hand by the experimental knowledge that we have acquired of the obstacles that are opposed to the satisfaction of our fancies (or, if one prefers, limited by the feeling of a social determinism), on the other limited by the profound conviction of our natural weakness."[11]

The determining force of these limitations has already received considerable attention in Chapter VI, in which was discussed Sorel's conception of society as a reign of necessity. The apparent determination of human activities by socio-economic forces was considered there as a result of the inability of man to understand the total meaning of these forces, and consequently of his inability to control them. This determinism was described by Sorel as passive, and by that he meant that it limited the possibilities of man's ability to create his own *artificial* systems of pragmatic usefulness. The pessimist recognizes these conditions, and when he finds plans unworkable or hopes mistaken, he is not led to attribute responsibility for the ills of society to the plotting of the wicked; not being under the spell of deceptive illusions he has not, as Sorel says, "the sanguinary frenzies of the optimist maddened by the unexpected resistances that his plans encounter; he does not dream of creating the happiness of future generations by butchering the egoists of the present."[12]

Although man is restricted to certain possibilities by the basis of civil society, it does not follow, in Sorel's theory, that his conduct is absolutely determined by it: within these bounds he has a certain real freedom in creating forms of a validity peculiar to himself. In the primitive Christian Church the way was left open for such a conception of freedom by the doctrine of deliverance, and the later development of this doctrine in Augustine's theory of salvation through grace was an expression of true religious pessimism. "What is most profound in pessimism," says Sorel, "is its manner of conceiving the way to deliverance. Man would not proceed very far in the investigation, either of the laws governing his wretchedness or of the laws of fate that are so shocking to the ingenuousness of our pride, if he did not have hope in overcoming these tyrannies by an effort made in common with a group of his fellows. The Christians would not have reasoned so much on original sin if they had not felt the necessity of justifying the deliverance (which was expected to result from the death of Jesus) by supposing that this sacrifice had been made necessary by a frightful crime for which humanity was responsible. If Occidentals have been very much more occupied with original sin than Orientals, that is due not only, as Taine thought, to the influence of Roman law, but also to the fact that the Latins, having a more elevated feeling of the majesty of empire than the Greeks, looked on the sacrifice of the Son of God as having realized an extraordinarily miraculous deliverance; in this conception originated the necessity of fathoming the mysteries of human wretchedness and of destiny."[13]

Although the early Christians firmly believed in this doctrine of deliverance as a way of escape from the bondage of earthly sin, the nonbeliever might very well say that the doctrine was entirely a matter of faith and that, as a matter of fact, no human being had ever succeeded in conquering the devil nor had the promised millennium arrived. Such a criticism would not, however, invalidate Sorel's contention that man has asserted himself freely even though he may not have attained his objective. The ideals that Christianity set up were an example of what he called a "myth," and their significance to the historian lies not in their pretensions but in their achievements. The historian is not concerned with the validity of the Church's belief that Christ would return to rescue the world from the rule of Satan; but he cannot overlook the very real effects that this belief has had in the lives of men: "The whole of this Christian life," says Sorel, "was dominated by the necessity of forming part of the holy army, constantly exposed to the snares set by the minions of the devil; this conception excited many heroic acts, engendered a fearless propaganda and produced a substantial moral progress. The deliverance has not taken place; but we know through innumerable indications from this period how much of greatness can be produced by the attempted advance to deliverance."[14]

The strict Calvinism of the sixteenth century, with its essentially medieval dogmas of sin and predestination, pushed these tendencies of pessimism to their extreme and was able to maintain an extraordinary unity of purpose through its militant assault on the Renaissance paganism of the Catholic world. However this early pessimism and dynamic force of Protestantism lasted only as long as its intolerant apostolic zeal remained untouched by compromise and as long as it remained willing "to establish the Kingdom of God by force." When Protestantism abandoned its stiff and narrow doctrines, when it accepted the tolerance and compromise of the Renaissance spirit, it lost its vital force and became "simply an easy-going Christianity." In expanding from a fanatical cult to a great popular religion, it lost most of its early dogmatism; instead of preserving the original purity of its myth it became increasingly ready to sacrifice perfection in the future to the possible in the present; instead of demanding all or nothing it accepted partial attainment; but by such a policy it emasculated the myth of its virtue and turned it into a simple utopia. Sorel insisted that the spiritual aspiration that forms a myth cannot be divided into a series of steps towards an actual realization, but must be considered as a driving force whose meaning and value lie in itself: "The experience of this great epoch shows very clearly how the man of spirit finds, in the feeling of struggle that accompanies this *will to deliverance*, a satisfaction sufficient to sustain his ardor. Because of this phenomenon I believe that one can draw from this history excellent illustrations in support of the idea . . . that the legend of the Wandering Jew is the symbol of the highest aspirations of humanity, condemned always to press on without knowing repose."[15]

Sorel's conception of the term "myth" is entirely a dynamic one: unlike utopian ideals, it is not affected by criticism of detail or even by the apparent failure of its believers to attain their aspirations. The Catholics have never been discouraged by the most disheartening trials, each new difficulty being only a fresh challenge to action because, as Sorel says, like all men who participate in great social movements, they "conceive their coming action under the form of images of battle assuring the triumph of their cause." These "myths" may never be fulfilled, but they provide, nonetheless, an indispensable incentive to action since, as he thought, "man would probably never abandon his inertia if he had a perfectly clear view of the future, and if he could calculate exactly the difficulties in the midst of which he ventures."[16]

Although it is easy to show how primitive Christianity and the Protestant Reformation were based on an elaborate myth structure, it must not be thought that the myth is necessarily confined to religious uses. All great spiritual movements have had similar constructions: they can be clearly seen in the French Revolution, in the Risorgimento, and, during recent times, most clearly in the dynamics of socialism. The recognition by Sorel of the importance of these myths, and more particularly of the myth of the general strike in syndicalism, was his most original contribution to the interpretation of history and to the theory of socialism. It was largely through this conception that he attempted to replace the utopianism of early socialism by a pragmatic social theory that would give a genuine recognition to historical tradition and that would complete Marx's doctrine of economic determinism by a theory of man's creative freedom in moral development. Just as the utopia is a typical development of intellectualist procedure, so the myth is an anti-intellectualist construction and consequently is not amenable to criticism by the ordinary rationalist methods of analysis. Sorel points out how futile have been the attempts to refute dogmas of faith by producing rational objections founded on scientific method; all such attempts are, he thinks, inevitably doomed to failure since they are based on a complete misconception of the basis of faith.[17] The systems of images that give a dynamic force to great spiritual movements cannot be decomposed into elements: they must be taken *en bloc* as historical forces, since their significance does not lie in what they promise to do but in their actual effect on the world. For this reason, he says, "It is necessary above all to beware of comparing the accomplished facts with the representations that had been accepted before action." The usual explanations of the motives of action do nothing, he thought, to show its real creative basis. All they do is "to project our accomplished acts on the field of judgments that society has drawn up in advance for the various types of action that are the most common in contemporary life."[18] In Bergson's terminology this is merely the external projection, the spatial, or in other words, the social representation of a creative consciousness that has a much more profound manifestation in those rare moments of intuition when the individual catches brief glimpses of living states in process of ceaseless formation within himself. It is only at such times that the individual is free, that he acts rather than is acted upon by external forces; for, as Bergson says, "To act freely is to regain possession of oneself; it is to replace oneself in pure duration."[19]

The qualities of indivisibility, of unlimited extension, by which Sorel distinguished the myth from the utopia were based on a conception of movement derived directly from Bergson's celebrated idea of duration. Unlike the utopia, the value of the myth does not depend on an actual attainment of professed ends but rather on the movement in itself which may, in fact, never even approach those objectives. "It seems to me," Sorel says, "that in conceiving a profound psychology one must abandon the idea that the spirit is like a machine that responds to the various incentives provided by nature in accord with a more or less mechanical law. When we act, it is because we have created an entirely artificial world, placed in advance of the present, formed of movements that depend on ourselves. Thus our freedom becomes perfectly intelligible. . . These artificial worlds generally disappear from our mind without leaving any recollections; but when masses of people become aroused, then a representation is formed that constitutes a social myth."[20]

Since the myth represents an artificial world, expressed in terms of movement, the validity of its purpose cannot be judged by a scale of reference based on spatial concepts of social actuality; consequently it is placed beyond the reach of the simple tests of experience ordinarily applicable to utopias. Although it is true that myths are rarely free of all utopian admixture, yet this utopian element is purely subsidiary: it is in itself completely powerless to arouse mass action and a criticism of it has no effect on the creative consciousness that gives it life. In Sorel's opinion, however, "the present revolutionary myths are almost pure; they allow us to understand the activity, the feelings, and the ideas of the common masses preparing themselves to enter into a decisive struggle; they are not descriptions of things but expressions of wills. The utopia is, on the contrary, the product of an intellectual process; it is the work of theorists who, after having observed and discussed the facts, seek to establish a model to which one may compare existing societies, in order to measure the good and the evil that they contain. . . Whilst our present myths lead men to prepare themselves for a battle to destroy what exists, the utopia has always had the effect of directing men's energies toward reforms that could be effected by taking the system piecemeal; it is not, then, a matter for surprise that so many utopians were able to become skillful statesmen when they had acquired a greater experience of political life."[21]

This difference in tactics between the myth and the utopia is a vital one to social theory. In the early days of socialism, complicated and detailed plans were made to show how happiness in the future would result from certain specific changes in the present social system. These utopian conceptions were clearly derived from a typically eighteenth-century belief in the natural goodness of man, and their aim was primarily to reform the evils of an oppressive society that prevented this goodness from showing itself. Sorel's conception, on the contrary, assumed that man was naturally amoral or perhaps even bad and that he could obtain virtue and freedom only through a continuous struggle—a struggle that would mean not only an advance toward a new social order, but would also provide a severe training in those high moral qualities without which the new society could not hope to succeed. The myth of the general strike was important to him chiefly as a means of fostering such a "revolutionary apprenticeship of the proletariat"; for this reason he looked on the Marxian doctrine of class struggle as having been particularly valuable in changing the direction of socialism from emphasis on plans for future happiness to an emphasis on the means of preparing the proletariat. The significance of the change was that Marx, instead of attempting to construct a neatly logical theory of his own, turned to a study of the proletariat itself for an understanding of the forces that were actually in process of changing society. Sorel, with a greater social experience behind him, felt able to carry this study still further, and in the proletarian hope of a general strike he thought to find a myth that would provide that revolutionary apprenticeship so essential to the success of social change and so lacking in the theories of utopian socialism. "Thus," he says, "the utopia tends to disappear completely from socialism, which does not have to try to organize work since capital is already organizing it. I believe to have shown, moreover, that the general strike corresponds to feelings very intimately connected with those that are necessary to secure production in a very progressive industrial regime, and that the revolutionary apprenticeship can also be an apprenticeship of the producer."[22]

An essential difference between the operation of the myth, with its quality of infinity, and the utopia, whose finite aspirations might be achieved by gradual reform, is that the myth, through its emphasis on class war as the most essential principle of socialist tactics, offered a much greater possibility of preserving a purely proletarian ideology. The significance of such a myth appeared peculiarly great to Sorel because it gave an entirely new meaning to the very ancient phenomenon of the factional struggle between rich and poor. He thought, in fact, that much of the corruption introduced into socialism by the nominal followers of Marx could be traced to their failure to recognize the significance of this principle. Instead of treating the class struggle as a means by which the proletariat would consolidate and prepare itself for an eventual dominance of society, many of the socialist politicians look on it simply as a convenient instrument of political tactics that they may use on appropriate occasions as a threat to the bourgeoisie for the purpose of securing party advantage or personal advancement. Such an attitude, Sorel thought, is very little different from that of the demagogues of ancient Greece: "The parliamentary socialists very much resemble the demagogues who constantly demanded the abolition of debts, the partition of the lands, who imposed on the rich all the public charges, who invented conspiracies in order to be able to bring about the confiscation of the large fortunes."[23] Although such tactics certainly represented a struggle of classes, they were not, in Sorel's view, at all similar to the struggle that Marx conceived as the essence of socialism. As Sorel points out: "The ferocious jealousy of the impoverished intellectual who would like to see the wealthy merchant guillotined is a vicious feeling that is not in the least socialist."[24]

A further confusion of the true Marxian doctrine was provided by the spectacle of dissension and bloodshed that the Commune presented during the brief but terrible period of its existence. This experience served only to confirm the worst fears of the propertied classes that the real object of the labor movement was to dispossess them and to seek revenge. Sorel, however, denied that the Commune was a true class struggle in the syndicalist sense of the term: "Blanquism is, at bottom, only the revolt of the poor led by a revolutionary staff; such a revolt can occur in any epoch whatever; it is independent of the regime of production. Marx, on the contrary, contemplated a revolution made by a proletariat of producers who had acquired an economic capacity, a knowledge of work and a juridical sense under the influence of the conditions of production. . . From *discipline* one proceeds toward *organization*, that is to say toward a juridical constitution; without this juridical constitution one could hardly be justified in saying that there may be such a thing as a fully developed class."[25] The methods of parliamentary socialism seldom got beyond this conception of civil strife since they depended not on a genuine spirit of class unity and purpose but on an appeal to all the discontented elements in the complex life of modern society.[26] Sorel considered such methods to be useful only for the attainment of parliamentary majorities: they did nothing to further the development of truly proletarian ideals or to produce a genuine revolution in the forms of society. As he says: "Marxism differs notably from Blanquism in that it dismisses the *idea of party*, which was fundamental in the conception of the classical revolutionaries, in order to return to the *idea of class*. . . It is no longer a question of leading the people, but of bringing the producers to think for themselves, without the aid of a bourgeois tradition."[27]

Despite a certain outward adoption of Marxian phraseology, the political conception of socialism in France has, in fact, been based almost entirely on an idea of party rather than on the idea of class. One of the enduring legacies of the Revolutionary wars has been a strong feeling that the state must present a united front to her enemies. Firm in the conviction that it had restored their natural rights to the citizens of France, the Republic felt obliged to treat the dissenting Vendeans as infamous traitors who must be suppressed since they refused to accept the rule of justice and virtue that had been offered them. The Declaration of the Rights of Man was supposed to abolish all distinctions of classes before the Law; consequently good republicans still retain something of the belief that attempts to arouse class-consciousness are malicious and treasonable attacks on justice and right. Force of circumstances has dimmed their original faith in the possibility of a perfect government, but it has not destroyed their belief that the state still remains the proper organ for the expression of a higher right, which, they maintain, is capable of reconciling the claims of the separate parties within it. This view is particularly appealing to the politician, based, as it is, on the rather oversimple belief that men at bottom all want the same things and that their interests can always be reconciled by judicious compromise. The obligation of each faction in a dispute to come to such a compromise is conceived of as a duty to society, but it has never been shown how the extent of this duty is to be determined. It certainly does not rest on any law of economics: "In the world of economics, each limits his duty by the dislike that he feels in abandoning certain profits; if the employer estimates that he has done his full duty, the worker will be of a contrary opinion, and no reason will be able to decide the issue: the first will believe that he has been heroic, and the second will treat this pretended heroism as shameful exploitation."[28]

Since no one can define social duty or apply it to any particular dispute, it is absurd to expect that arbitration will be any more efficacious in deciding the duty of either side than a throw of the dice. The employer may be induced to give way in order not to lose the goodwill of the politicians who wish to obtain the glory of having ended the conflict, and sometimes the leaders of the strikers are won over by hopes of advancing into the bourgeois world to which they may secretly aspire. However the usual outcome of such tactics is to convince the workers that conciliation and arbitration rest on no real economico-juridical basis, and consequently they do not hesitate to make all sorts of exaggerations, to introduce irrelevant claims, and even to fabricate additional demands on the spur of the moment in order to impress the arbitrators with the social iniquity of their opponents. Such tactics are the stock-in-trade of social diplomacy; they differ very little from the tortuous maneuverings familiar to international diplomacy: in both cases it is found after a settlement that concessions have been made that were once declared impossible and so the workers are given the impression that their employers are either ignorant or liars. As Sorel says, "There is no more a social duty than there is an international duty."[29]

The politicians of the modern state have taken particular delight in conceiving for themselves a sort of paternalistic role in the development of economic life. They pretend to assume great responsibility in seeing that the various productive groups and industries are protected against unfair competition and that the interests of the producers and the consumers are properly harmonized. It is this attitude, in Sorel's opinion, that explains the politicians' approach to labor problems: "One can see, first of all, that today the workers *count* in the world in the same capacity as the various productive groups who demand to be protected; they ought to be treated with solicitude in quite the same way as the winegrowers or the sugar makers."[30]

It does not require a wide experience of modern politics to realize that the decisions of tariff commissions are based very little on science and very much on the demands of pressure groups. The protectionists are able to assert their power by subventioning party leaders or supporting party journals, but the workers have a weapon even stronger than money: they are able to create fear and, in spite of the frequent assertions by the government that it could not be intimidated, this weapon has been remarkably efficacious in turning "bourgeois cowardice" to profit. Sorel thought, however, that such a policy of concession could have no other than fatal consequences for the class that practiced it: "A social policy founded on bourgeois cowardice, which consists in always ceding before the menace of violence, cannot fail to engender the idea that the bourgeoisie is condemned to death and that its disappearance is no more than a matter of time. Every conflict that gives place to violent acts thus becomes an advance-guard action, and no one can foresee what may issue from such engagements; the great battle has, indeed, always seemed to recede just when it appeared within grasp: it is the great *Napoleonic battle* (by which the conquered are definitely overwhelmed) that the strikers hope to see begin; in this way, by the practice of strikes, is to be engendered the idea of a catastrophic revolution."[31]

The policy of wringing concessions from the bourgeoisie by threats of violence has been characteristic of almost all socialist movements in recent times, but the purpose and significance of such a policy has differed widely. The parliamentary socialists have looked on it as a highly important element in party tactics, although one that must be carefully controlled by experienced political leaders, who, according to Sorel, have consequently come to regard themselves as the only competent custodians of proletarian action: "An agitation, wisely canalized, is extremely useful to the parliamentary socialists who plume themselves, before the government and the rich bourgeoisie, on knowing how to moderate the revolution; they are thus able to insure the success of the financial affairs in which they are interested, to insure obtaining small favors from many influential electors, and to insure the voting of social legislation for the purpose of giving themselves some importance in the eyes of the simpletons who fancy that these socialists are great reformers of law. It is necessary, in order that all this may succeed, that there should always be a little movement and that one should be able to give the bourgeois a fright."[32]

All socialist politics—whether compromising like that of Jaurès or uncompromising like that of Vaillant—depends, Sorel thought, on the weakening of the capitalist economy and on a consequent enfeeblement of the bourgeois class ideology. Although such a prospect filled the politicians with joy and happy hopes, it presented itself to him as one of the gravest dangers facing socialism.[33] Marx, it will be recalled, did not condemn capitalism as bad or unnatural in itself; on the contrary he looked to it for the development of a new organization of labor that would be the necessary basis of the socialist state. He had expected capitalism to end in a short decisive revolution of the proletariat—a revolution that he regarded as an inherent part of the development of capitalism just as much as was the heritage of economic forms that would be conserved by socialism.[34] All of Marx's revolutionary theory rested on this supposition that capitalism would be struck down in its full vitality when it had brought to maturity all the necessary conditions for change and when the proletariat had similarly reached a peak of self-conscious opposition and autonomy; so that if the revolution should be postponed until after a decay had set in and the sharp distinction between the classes should be clouded over with a vague mist of mutual compromise, then, in Sorel's opinion, the future would be completely indeterminate and conceptions of the role of socialism in society would have to be revised in the light of such radically different conditions.[35] Sorel sought to throw some light on these two possibilities for the future of socialism by an analysis of two great revolutionary movements in the past, the rise of Christianity and the French Revolution.

The Revolution was a surprisingly successful movement, both in transforming society and in preserving the acquisitions of the *ancien régime*. Various writers have been at pains to emphasize either one or the other of these accomplishments, but Sorel felt there was no need of treating them as inconsistent or opposed tendencies. In his opinion the success of each depended on a remarkable progress in the economic productivity of the time, a progress that not only provided a firm foundation for the construction of a new state, but which also engendered that supreme confidence in an unlimited progress of man that was the basis of the audacity of the eighteenth-century reformer in France. "The triumph of the Revolution," Sorel says, "astonished almost all its contemporaries, and it seems that those who were most intelligent, most thoughtful, and most conversant with political affairs were the most surprised; this is accounted for by the fact that reasons drawn from the ideology are not able to explain such a paradoxical success. It seems to me that today the question is hardly less obscure for historians than it was for our fathers. The primary cause of this triumph must be sought in the economic system: it is because the *ancien régime* was attacked by rapid blows, at a time when production was on the road to great progress, that the contemporary world has had a relatively easy birth and has been able to be assured so quickly of a lusty life."[36]

The other great movement, the rise of Christianity, appeared to Sorel an alarming example of what happens when a fundamental transformation takes place in times of economic decline. The high hopes of the new religion that it would put an end to the corruption and oppression of the decadent Roman Empire not only proved to be completely illusory, but, even more disappointing, the Church itself fell into the same evil customs that it had denounced in paganism. Even the conversion of the barbarians, from which so much had been hoped, did not check the downward trend: unfortunately they were just as easily converted to the corrupt practices of Roman life as they were to Christianity, and it was not until the political decline continued for many centuries that a progressive movement again showed itself in Europe.

Sorel did not deny that the future of socialism might resemble this experience of Christianity, but he thought it possible only on condition that the revolution should take place in an era of economic decline and that there should exist an agency, such as a party governed by politics, that would conserve not only the economic forms but also the outworn ideology of a decadent civilization. "Many times," he says, "the *civilized* socialism of our official doctors has been presented as a safeguard for civilization: I believe that it would produce the same effect that was produced by the classical instruction given by the Church to the barbarian kings: the proletariat would be corrupted and brutalized as were the Merovingians and the economic decline would be only the more certain under the action of these pretended civilizers."[37] However, this sad outcome might be avoided,

Sorel thought, if the division of the classes were reconsolidated and the bourgeoisie were to regain something of their former energy so that the revolution might take place at the height of social and economic development. The purpose of proletarian violence was to bring about just this result and that is why he considered it an indispensable instrument in the development of civilization: "Proletarian violence, practiced as a pure and simple manifestation of the feeling of class struggle, thus appears as a very beautiful and very heroic thing; it is at the service of the primordial interests of civilization; it is not perhaps the most appropriate method for obtaining immediate material advantages, but it may save the world from barbarism."[38]

The significance that Sorel attributes to violence may at first appear paradoxial, but much of the widespread misunderstanding of the role that it plays in syndicalist theory is due to the common error of attributing to an abstract term qualities and meanings which can belong only to concrete applications of it. Violence is not a thing in itself but merely the expression in action of the interests or ideals that give it life; it is therefore futile to attempt to draw universal conclusions from its particular manifestations in any given situation. Since the syndicalists have called themselves revolutionaries and have openly advocated the use of force rather than the ballot box as the proper instrument of social change, many people, according to Sorel, have assumed that their tactics must necessarily lead to the sort of terrorism witnessed by France in 1793 and 1871 and on this assumption have condemned them. After the subsidence of the great national enthusiasm aroused by the Revolutionary wars, the other aspects of political life in that period were subjected to a colder and more critical scrutiny; the resulting picture of the arbitrary activities of police, of brutal proscriptions, and of servile tribunals was not one to encourage sympathy with any policy that might bring about a return of similar conditions in the future. The parliamentary socialists have been well aware of this tendency and they have not hesitated to turn it to their profit. "One is not at a loss to understand," says Sorel, "why the parliamentary socialists make such great efforts to persuade the public that they have the souls of tender shepherds, that their heart is filled to overflowing with sentiments of kindness, and that they have only one passion: *hatred for violence.*"[39] As the self-appointed guardians of social peace, the socialist deputies have pretended to be governed only by good reason, by considerations of humanitarian justice, and they have accused the syndicalists of following the practices of the men of blood that so discredited former revolutions. Sorel felt, on the contrary, that syndicalist violence was a very different phenomenon from such terrorism and, in fact, offered the only possibility of avoiding it. He points out that the terrorists of the French Revolution were not members of the laboring classes or even of the productive bourgeoisie: of the 577 deputies to the Third Estate in the Constituent Assembly, 373 were lawyers of various kinds. The administrative ability of these men was of the greatest assistance in preserving the governing framework of the country through many years of crisis, but along with this quality came another more doubtful heritage from the *ancien régime*, an almost superstitious reverence for law as a means of advancing the ends of the state rather than as a system concerned primarily with private justice. Under the influence of procedure copied from the Inquisition, the French monarchy extended its power by treating cases against the king in an exceptional, extralegal manner; by the reference of cases both of administrative discipline and of ordinary crime to the same judges it was able to use criminal procedure as a means of destroying all powers standing in the way of its expansion. These practices, however, in obscuring the proper sphere of law, tended to produce a blind veneration for the state at the expense of individual rights—a veneration, according to Sorel, that was inherited by certain of the leaders of the Revolution who showed so many scruples of legality in the exercise of their arbitrary power. Robespierre's famous Law of the 22 Prairial was, Sorel thought, no more than a logical application of these legal procedures to the revolutionary situation, and his fanatical attempt to set up a Republic of Virtue by force was simply a new expression of the time honored doctrine of *raison d'état*.[40]

Although the nineteenth century saw a very marked reaction to such a worship of the God-State, it was not able to rid itself entirely of this conception; the passions aroused by the Dreyfus case showed how easily the army and the Church could revert to doctrines that they had never really abandoned; in Sorel's opinion even certain of the Dreyfusards themselves, in their moment of triumph, were by no means unwilling to adopt these very practices that they had so bitterly denounced in their opponents.[41] Jaurès, with his blind veneration of success, used arguments in support of his cause that were no different from those of Cavaignac or of Robespierre, and Sorel believed that the parliamentary socialists' pious preoccupation with legal process, and with the safety of the state, held possibilities of brutal terrorism in no way different from that which had been induced by similar preoccupations in the mind of Robespierre: "Up to now," he says, "experience has shown us that our revolutionaries argue from *raison d'état*, that they employ police procedure as soon as they arrive at power, and that they look on justice as a weapon they are entitled to abuse by turning it against their enemies. The parliamentary socialists do not escape from the common rule; they retain the old cult of the state; they are therefore prepared to commit all the crimes of the *ancien régime* and of the Revolution."[42]

In contrast to these other revolutionaries, the proletarians were bound by their doctrine of class struggle to deny the validity of all such conceptions of state justice and national solidarity. Violence to them, according to Sorel, was not a means of executing some sort of "superlatively idealistic mandate of justice" but was properly to be conceived as a struggle and a discipline carried out in the spirit of a well-trained, seasoned army in campaign: "Proletarian violence has no connection with proscriptions: it is purely and simply an act of war, it has the value of military demonstrations and serves to mark the separation of classes. Everything that touches on war manifests itself without hatred and without spirit of vengeance; in war one does not slay the conquered; one does not make inoffensive beings suffer the consequences of the troubles that the armies may have experienced on the fields of battle; force is there displayed in its true light, without ever pretending to borrow anything from the judicial procedure that society enlists against criminals."[43]

The defeat of one army by another in decisive battle, Sorel thought, has nothing in common with the treatment of the accused before a judicial tribunal, because it is not an attempt to enforce abstract principles of justice, but is simply an expression of the will to power: it does not represent the aspiration to an ideal but is a pragmatic manifestation of strength, and as such attains its fulfillment in itself. Such an assertion of superior strength is simply the demonstration of a fact; consequently its dominance does not depend on legal justification or on the exercise of penalties for divagations from some abstract system of law. The end of military tactics is not properly conceived as the inflicting of carefully graduated punishments for the infringement of a criminal code, but is summed up in the single and comprehensive idea of the annihilation of enemy resistance. It is in such a light that Sorel looks on syndicalist violence: its end is the general strike and in this myth is embodied the whole meaning of socialism.[44]

As has already been noted, the essential characteristic of the myth of the general strike is its quality of infinity and indivisibility; it is this uncompromising attribute that has proved so valuable in imparting a unity and discipline to the proletariat, yet it is nonetheless this very quality that is most repugnant to the parliamentary socialists. According to Sorel: "They detest the general strike because all propaganda made on this ground is too socialist to please the philantrophists."[45] There is no way of attenuating the conception of the general strike, as, for example, the politicians have been accustomed to attenuate their professed internationalism by speaking of the sacred duties owed to one's country; for this reason its acceptance by the proletarians as the proper aim of socialist effort would completely undermine the position of the gradualists, of the politicians who seek to combine the most absolute intransigence in theory with the most supple opportunism in practice.[46] These men, according to Sorel, are completely familiar with all the tricks of rhetoric, with all the possibilities of interpreting the formulas of socialism to suit any occasion; consequently, the violence of their denunciation of the syndicalist myth is the measure of their recognition that it is capable of exerting a profound appeal among the workers and that it might actually bring about the catastrophic revolution that they would so much rather talk about than see. In spite of their loud professions of a proletarian ideology, their real ambition is little more than the ousting of the bourgeoisie from positions that they hope to fill themselves. It was, however, just such an outcome that Sorel hoped a syndicalist revolution would prevent, and that was why he looked for a method that would accentuate the class struggle rather than diminish it, and that would sum up the whole meaning of socialism in an idea so powerful and so comprehensive that there could be no escape from the entirety of its implications. As he says: "Language does not possess the means of producing such results with any degree of certainty; it is necessary to make an appeal to *ensembles* of images capable of evoking *en bloc and by intuition alone*, in advance of all reflective analysis, the mass of feelings that correspond to the various manifestations of the war carried on by socialism against modern society. The syndicalists resolve this problem perfectly by concentrating the whole of socialism in the drama of the general strike; there is thus no place for the conciliation of contraries through the nonsensical jargon of *official savants*; everything is clearly marked out in such fashion that there can be only one possible interpretation of socialism."[47]

A paradoxical thing about the syndicalist myth is that it is at once too clear and too obscure for its critics. As has been already shown, its professed end, the catastrophic general strike, appears to them too radical, too uncompromising, too little open to the modifications that political exigencies might demand; on the other hand they find it vague because it does not set forth specific objects of reform, it does not deal with what they are accustomed to call practical problems, with hypotheses that can be compared with other hypotheses and evaluated in advance.[48] Sorel was completely indifferent to all attempts to prove that the general strike was impractical or unscientific.[49] As he says: "Without the use of formulas, which may appear vague or erroneous to the scientist, the man of action will never arrive at lasting results. It is often observed that unintelligible dogmas easily produce heroic acts. It is useless to argue with anyone accustomed to refer everything to great principles that do not evoke any real image, that produce their effects automatically without leading to any act of reflection, and that maintain themselves in the mind with an extraordinary tenacity, sometimes succeeding in dominating it in an absolute manner. It would be puerile to condemn processes that have their roots in the laws of our mind."[50]

The intellectualist is so accustomed to treat the future as

a simple projection of the present, as a series of events arising from a logical development and consequently susceptible to scientific prediction, that he finds it almost impossible to believe in the honesty, much less the validity, of a theory that quite frankly admits the improbability of achieving its professed end. The fact that in the past great ideas have never fulfilled their promises is explained by him as due to a Stupidity or a Maliciousness that Progress will dispel in the future; but the anti-intellectualist, not having the intellectualist's faith in the ability of progress to conquer such abstract and personified forces, must rely on previous experience as the only possible guide to an understanding of the probable outcome of similar aspirations in the future. This experience shows him that, in the words of Sorel, "there is a heterogeneity between the ends realized and the ends given." Just as Christianity, the French Revolution, the Risorgimento were given their dynamic force by faith in elevated ideals, which were themselves never achieved, so might a widespread belief in the general strike lead to a similarly vast transformation of society without actually attaining a catastrophic revolution in the way looked for. A consideration of these phenomena shows that it is a psychological mistake to treat the social myth as a logical demonstration: "In order to appreciate the bearing of the idea of the general strike, it is necessary to abandon entirely the manner of discussion that is current among politicians, sociologists, or men having pretensions to practical science. One can concede to the opponents everything that they endeavor to demonstrate without reducing in any way the value of the thesis that they believe easy to refute; it matters little whether the general strike is a partial reality, or only a product of popular imagination. The only question is to know whether the general strike really contains everything that the socialist doctrine of the revolutionary proletariat expects."[51]

The proper attitude in such an investigation, then, is not to judge the content of the myth on the basis of philosophy, history, or economics, but merely to inquire if the proletarians active in the revolutionary movement find in the general strike a complete representation of their socialist conceptions. Sorel thought that such an inquiry would show that this objective of the general strike is indeed "the *myth* in which socialism is comprehended in its entirety, that is to say, an organization of images capable of evoking instinctively all the sentiments that correspond to the various manifestations of the war engaged by socialism against modern society. Strikes have engendered in the proletariat the most noble, the most profound and the most moving sentiments that it possesses; the general strike groups them all in a harmonious picture and, by their conjunction, gives to each of them its maximum intensity; appealing to very poignant recollections of particular conflicts, it vividly colors every detail of the representation appearing before the understanding. We thus obtain in a perfectly clear manner this intuition of socialism that language is not able to give—and we obtain it in a totality perceived instantaneously."[52]

Although many of the followers of Marx have treated his doctrine as a new scholasticism, he himself, according to Sorel, drew all his best intuitions from a close observation of actual proletarian practice, and the further development of these practices, culminating in the idea of the general strike, has only served to confirm his theory by giving it an integral formulation in the revolutionary myth. One of the most interesting results of this development is the new meaning that is given to the point of departure for all Marxian socialism, the doctrine of class struggle.[53] It has long been pointed out that observation of society shows not two classes but many, and this is quite true if divisions are made by occupations; but Sorel believed that a completely clear dichotomous division would be forced on ideological grounds by the myth of the general strike, which pictures all social progress as a battle waged between opposing armies. As he says: "No philosophical explanation of facts observed in practice could furnish as keen an insight as the completely simple picture that the general strike sets before the eyes." The virtue of the revolutionary myth appeared peculiarly great to Sorel because it effectively disposed of two of the gravest dangers threatening the future of socialism. These dangers were the tendency of the upper levels of the proletariat to desert to the bourgeoisie, and the equally fatal tendency of the masses to fall under the influence of a Caesar. Since both these tendencies depend on the weakening of class lines, he looked to the idea of the general strike as the only bulwark against ideological corruption: "The more the policy of social reforms becomes preponderant, the more socialism will feel the need of opposing to the picture of progress that such a policy endeavors to realize, the picture of the total catastrophe that the general strike furnishes in a truly perfect manner."[54]

Not only does the myth of the general strike provide the most effective means of maintaining a clearly defined class struggle, but, according to Sorel, it also offers the best possibility of accomplishing the revolution under the conditions postulated by Marx—conditions of very considerable importance since they would, in his theory, decide the whole character of the movement. Marx always emphasized the necessity of an adequate preparation of the proletariat in order to give its struggle a meaning quite different from the spontaneous mass uprisings that have swept society in almost all periods of history. If it is to avoid the excesses and futility of such rebellions, the proletariat must be disciplined, must have a clearly developed ideology of its own with which to replace the society that it overturns. According to Sorel, such a class-consciousness can best be developed by syndicalist intransigence, just as Christianity, by a similar rejection of conciliation, was able to maintain its individuality in the Roman world.[55] It is with such present conditions in mind that he says of the early Church: "Most likely it would have been able to obtain toleration, as did many other esoteric cults, as did Judaism; but it sought to isolate itself; in this way it provoked distrust, and even persecution. There were certain intransigent doctors who prevented the new religion from taking a normal place in Roman society; however there were not lacking sage persons who labeled Tertullian and all those who did not wish to accept any conciliation as completely mad. Today we see that it is thanks to this senselessness that Christianity has been able to form its own ideas and become master of the world when its hour arrived."[56]

Coupled with the fulfillment of this condition is the tendency of the general strike idea to preserve the essential principles of capitalism from decadence, and, as has already been pointed out, to bring on a clear-cut struggle of ideologies in the Marxian catastrophic sense, so that the capitalist organization of production may be preserved in all its original vigor. "The workers are accustomed," says Sorel, "to see their revolts against the necessities imposed by capitalism succeed during times of prosperity; as a result one is able to say that the single fact of identifying revolution and general strike banishes all idea of conceiving that an essential transformation of the world could result from economic decadence."[57]

A final condition of the proletarian revolution is that it should not be bound by a preconceived program for the future. As Marx said, "He who composes a program for the future is a reactionary."[58] Sorel felt that the syndicalist myth was the best possible guarantee against the dangers of such doctrinaire utopianism. "Socialism," he declares, "is not a doctrine, a sect, a political system; it is the emancipation of the working classes who organize themselves, instruct themselves, and create new institutions. This is why I ended an article on the socialist future of the syndicats with these words: 'to condense my thought into one formula, I shall say that the whole future of socialism dwells in the autonomous development of the workers' syndicats.' "[59] The utopians and the socialist politicians object strenuously to such an autonomous development because it dispenses with their proposals for directing socialism according to their preconceived plans of an idyllic future. Marx, however, regarded the future proletarian society not as an artificial creation of professional thinkers, but as the determined product of an economic structure that, through a technological continuity, would be derived directly from the capitalist methods of production.[60] For this reason Sorel looked to the workers themselves, rather than to the intellectuals, for proper guidance in the development of socialism. "The just customs of the workshop," he says, "are evidently the source from which the future law will come; socialism will inherit not only the machinery that will have been created by capitalism, and by the science that results from technical development, but also the procedure of cooperation that will be constituted at length in the factories for the purpose of utilizing to the best advantage the time, the strength and the skill of men."[61]

The process by which these forms of capitalism are to to be transformed into a new social organization is one that has never been explicitly described by syndicalists, and Sorel justifies the apparent obscurity on the ground that analysis and rational deduction are completely incompetent to deal with processes of this sort that involve radical changes in the most mysterious of all elements in economics, that of production. The attempt of intellectuals to reduce such complicated relationships to a science, and to give them a logical systematization, has not produced the promised clarity, but has, by its superficiality and abstraction, merely confirmed the fact that the future of socialism is not amenable to scientific analysis and prediction.

In contrast to this approach, Sorel conceived the development of socialism in a purely dynamic sense: like movement in the Bergsonian philosophy it could not be spatialized into a series of stages, but must be grasped by the intuition as an entity, as an uninterrupted flow. The myth of the general strike fulfilled these conditions, he thought, in giving a complete and exact representation of the proletarian movement, but it did so only as long as it should be seized in its entirety: "It must never be forgotten that the perfection of this mode of representation would disappear in a moment if one pretended to resolve the general strike into a sum of historical details; it is necessary *to grasp its undivided whole and to conceive the passage from capitalism to socialism as a catastrophe whose course escapes description.*"[62]

Just as the idea of motion cannot be conveyed by the geometrical conception of a succession of points, so the integral idea of the dynamic myth loses its value if it is analyzed into separate parts; this is the essential difference, Sorel believed, between the proletarian general strike and the political general strike, with which it is often confused. "In the first case," he says, "it is not permissible to consider any detail apart from the rest: in the second, everything depends on the art with which the heterogenous details are combined. It now becomes necessary to consider parts separately, to abandon their importance and to know how to harmonize them."[63] Such a task of judgment and harmonizing requires special talents, the talents of the politician, and its execution leads to results not only very different from those to be expected from syndicalist methods, but also different from the professed aims of its exponents who pretend to be interested only in the practical methods of advancing socialism. The real business of these men is the exploitation of politics and however revolutionary their ideals may appear, their policy is essentially reactionary;[64] in abandoning the pure conception of the syndicalist general strike, Sorel thought, they change at a blow the whole significance of the socialist movement, since, in his words, "Politics leads to the constitution by the intellectuals of an oligarchy of masters who make it their profession to govern the world of labor."[65] The general strike is no longer regarded as a complete statement of the revolutionary movement, but is now become only one of the many factors that must be combined and controlled by what the politicians like to call a "superior intelligence," that is to say, by political committees.[66] Just as absolute monarchs undermined feudalism by the most unscrupulous methods, and, having accomplished their purpose, refused to give up their power without a struggle, so, Sorel thought, the rights of power claimed by the socialist politicians would result only in a new despotism from which they would never voluntarily abdicate. "The men," he says, "who could organize the proletariat in the form of an army, always ready to obey their orders, would be generals who would establish the state of siege in conquered society; we would have then, on the morrow of the revolution, a dictatorship exercised by the group of politicians who have already formed a compact unit in the present world."[67]

The domination of socialism by such political committees involved the use of tactics quite different from those outlined by Sorel as proper to the syndicalist movement; consequently the conditions that he regarded as necessary for a successful social revolution could no longer be fulfilled. Far from checking the decadence of capitalist organization, political methods actively encourage such a decline, depending, in fact, for most of their success on the weakening of assurance and initiative in the capitalist class. The function of the intellectualist politician is necessarily to exploit all such elements of uncertainty and uneasiness by pretending that he, and he alone, possesses the ability to reconcile the discordant interests in the state; but, as a matter of fact, this secret ability consists of nothing more than the age-old technique of playing off one interest against the other. Like the similar maneuvers of diplomats in the international field, however, it can never be successful in providing lasting solutions to fundamental problems.[68] As Sorel says: "Observation of the corruption of philosophers installed in high places proves, better than the finest argumentation, how vain is official wisdom; one might have thought, formerly, that the evils of ancient societies would diminish as soon as they should be governed by moralists; the experiment has been tried and it has turned out to the confusion of the pretended representatives of reason."[69]

One consequence of the claims of these men to a universal competence in social questions is the great significance that they attribute to elaborate plans for the organization of the future, because on such plans depends their whole reputation as the saviors of society. Here again their methods are quite the reverse of those advocated by syndicalism: instead of offering a means for avoiding utopianism, they are led by their position to become the foremost advocates of fantastic and unreal projects for the future; instead of seeking to further the conditions thought of by Marx as essential to the revolution, they place the greatest emphasis on scholastic systematizations, on the "lucubrations of misunderstood geniuses." These utopias, moreover, all depend for their execution on the power of a paternalistic state, so that the Marxian and syndicalist conception of an irreformable revolution is abhorrent to the *wise* socialists, to the men who are looking forward to occupying the seats now held by their parliamentary rivals. Nothing would suit their plans less than to see a self-conscious proletariat actually abolish the state and take the control of production into its own hands. As Sorel says, they anticipate a "society divided into two groups: the one forms an élite organized in political parties that gives itself the mission of thinking in the place of a nonthinking mass and that considers itself admirable because it has no objections to sharing its superior enlightenment with this mass;—the other consists of the whole of the producers. The political élite has no other profession than that of employing its intelligence and it finds it very much in accord with the principles of immanent Justice (of which it is the proprietor), that the proletariat work to feed it and to provide a life for it that does not recall too markedly that of the ascetics."[70]

The idea of a political general strike, with its emphasis on benevolence and a paternalistic state, gives rise to a conception of class struggle very different from that to be found in Marx. Instead of defining classes through the positions occupied by their members in capitalist production, the politician returns to the old distinction of rich and poor; his tactics consist almost entirely of seeking the support of the dispossessed by promising them the riches that an ignorant and selfish society has withheld. Such a definition of class struggle has, however, no relationship with the conception of Marx or of the syndicalists: it represents nothing essentially different from the factional quarrels that have been exploited by demagogues since antiquity and that, in Sorel's view, will continue to be exploited no matter how disinterested and beneficent the professions of the political leaders may be. "The chiefs," he says, "who sustain their men in this charming illusion see the world from a quite different point of view; the present social organization shocks them in proportion as it creates obstacles to their ambition; they are less shocked by the existence of classes than by the impossibility that confronts them of attaining the positions held by their superiors; the day when they have sufficiently penetrated into the sanctuaries

of the state, into the drawing-rooms, into the pleasure re-
sorts, they generally cease to be revolutionaries and talk
wisely of evolution."[71]

Since the main object of the political general strike is to
gain control of the state, rather than to abolish the state
completely, as in the syndicalist general strike, it appeals
to quite different emotions and gives rise to quite different
qualities among its proponents. The socialist politician has
no objection to the power of the state as such: his aim is
merely to discredit the men at present exercising that power
and to harass them by encouraging ideas of jealousy and
vengeance among the workers. To their political leaders
the proletariat is little more than an instrument, so Sorel
thought, to be used as a colonial administrator uses his
forces and to be rewarded with the prizes customarily given
to such troops: "They sustain the ardor of their men, as the
ardor of mercenary troops has always been sustained, by
exhortations to the next pillage, by appeals to hatred, and
also by the petty concessions that permit them already to
dispose of certain political places. However, as Marx put
it in 1873, the proletariat is for them only cannon fodder
and nothing else."[72]

In contrast to such a war of conquest, Sorel described
another form of battle: one in which not plunder is the
objective but glory; one that appeals not to jealousy but
to heroism; in short, one that has its end in itself, that is
truly felt as a test of confident strength in the same way
that the wars of ancient Greece or the Revolutionary wars
in France were a test of strength. The high motives and firm
ideals essential to this form of battle, he thought, could be
found in the contemporary world only in the violence
associated with the syndicalist general strike. "This general
strike," he says, "in affirming that it intends to suppress the
state, marks in a very clear manner its indifference to the
material profits of conquest; the state has been, in effect,

the organizer of the war of conquest, the dispenser of its fruits, and the *raison d'être* of the dominant groups who draw the profit from all these enterprises and who leave the expenses to be supported by the whole of society."[73]

The way that socialists conceive their relationships to the state determines, according to Sorel, the kind of social conflict that the application of their theories will produce; it is on this basis that he makes a useful distinction between *force*, which uses the authority of the state to demand automatic obedience, and *violence*, which seeks above all to shatter that authority. The bourgeois state, he thinks, has relied for its successful development on the use of force; its natural laws of economics are simply the expression of a complicated evolutionary process in which coercion has been used with some skill to produce and maintain the capitalist system.[74] Since it is maintained by force, capitalism may be radically changed or even completely overturned by force, but such an event could mean only the substitution of a new set of masters for the old; it would do nothing to modify the essential methods of the bourgeois state.

In Sorel's opinion, the proper object of the proletarian revolution was not simply to change masters but to change the essential forms of society; a change that could be effected only by violence, by a complete overthrow of the whole conception of the state with its attendant sanctions and its privileges exercised by a ruling minority.[75] To Marx and to Sorel the significance of socialism did not lie in its ability to wring concessions from an all-powerful state, but in the new juridical basis that it offered to society.[76] The utopian theorists look on socialism as a humanitarian movement that must depend for its success on the generosity, the benevolence, or at most, on the enlightened self-interest of the possessing bourgeois class. The true Marxian, however, regards it as simply the objective manifestation of profound changes in the relations of production: when, for example, he speaks of the expropriation of the expropriators, he does not imply an act of brigandage, but is merely describing in concrete terms the assertion of a new ideology more closely related to the economic basis of society and thus more expressive in a positive way of the true juridical principles of the time than is the bourgeois ideology. As Sorel says: "The vindication of the proletarians is not a brutal revolt of men who resort to immediate violence in order to attain a better lot; it is not, consequently, an insurrection of villeins and slaves; it is not even a grievance formulated in the name of a more or less ingenious ideal; but it is a truly juridical vindication, founded on the rights of law drawn from the same sources as those that constitute the law of the bourgeoisie."[77]

Modern society is such a delicately balanced organism that a complicated system of law and regulation has grown up around it, and has become so much a part of modern thought that it is difficult to discuss violence without arousing associations of lawlessness, of arbitrary assertions of individual will. Considerations of material prosperity have assumed so great a place in bourgeois life that peace and progress have come to be looked upon as necessarily connected and acts of violence are thought of instinctively as manifestations of a regression to barbarism.[78] There was, however, nothing anarchical or arbitrary in Sorel's conception of violence: paradoxically enough he was less ready to justify it as an ordinary instrument for the enforcement of ideas than have been many of the most ardent advocates of liberty, equality, and fraternity. At least he recognizes and appreciates, as few of them do, the part that violence has played in history and sets forth without any equivocation the role that he thinks it should properly fill in the present.[79] What is even more unusual he defines the grounds for his advocacy of violence and the specific limitations that he puts on it: these grounds and these limitations are both derived from a Marxian conception of a relatively objective role to be played by the proletariat in the development of society; and they are based on what, in the widest sense of the term, must be called moral considerations. As Sorel says of Marx: "He never failed to set forth the juridical point of view in social wars. In his eyes the modern class struggle has for its objective a transformation of the principles of legislation of a country; it is a right that raises itself against a right; it is not a simple conflict of interests. In order to understand his thought, one must never separate what he says on the struggle of the proletariat against capitalism from the theory of the *mission of the proletariat*, which plays a leading part in his doctrine, a mission whose end is essentially moral."[80]

Some consideration has already been given in the preceding chapters to Sorel's conception of the basis of morals and to the mission that he hoped to see fulfilled in the proletariat. This mission was a moral one in the sense that it concerned the relationships of man with his fellows, and it derived its positive significance from a myth of struggle very similar to previous myths that have provided the indispensable incentive to all great social and moral movements. In Sorel's view, these movements arise and retain their force only under the stimulus of an active struggle, of a war against opposing principles and institutions, and when this stimulus disappears, the social institutions that were based on it lose their meaning and fall into decadence.[81] Civilization has depended, he thought, on a long succession of such struggles, and if the present world must look to the proletariat for the regeneration of humanity, "it is," he says, "merely because this is the only class that at the present time may be animated with a warlike spirit and, consequently, the only one that may have virility and be capable of progress."[82] This progress, however, depends entirely on the role that the proletariat is to play in the struggle with capitalism. If it allows itself to be intimidated or bought off by concessions, even though its leaders should rise to positions of power in the state, it will fulfill no moral purpose because it can acquire moral strength only through the discipline of social war.[83]

Sorel had no faith in the naïve belief of the eighteenth-century sentimentalists that the poor, since they are supposed to have remained closer to nature, are therefore more fitted to a life of virtue; he thought it ridiculous to suppose that these natural men should, by reason of their poverty, possess any moral qualities intrinsically superior to those of the higher classes.[84] In fact no orthodox conservative realized more fully than he the dangers inherent in any uprising of oppressed masses who had not been thoroughly prepared by a rigorous social discipline. Such a revolt could do nothing to advance moral progress since it would be inspired only by feelings of vengeance or hatred: "Hate is able to provoke disorders, to ruin a social organization, to cast a country into a period of bloody revolutions; but it produces nothing." However justified it might be from a humanitarian point of view, Sorel denied that such an act of brigandage could properly be called socialism, because socialism rests on a juridical basis and, as he says: "The activating force of the whole socialist movement is the opposition that is produced between morals and law."[85]

Violence is significant in syndicalist theory chiefly as an exemplification of this opposition, as a means for ensuring that the issues involved shall be clear-cut and the result decisive. It does not necessarily entail a great development of brutality or a general bloodpurge so long as the capitalist class is energetic and willing to help maintain the class division by a frankly reactionary class policy. As Sorel points out, the history of primitive Christianity shows that the actual facts of persecution and martyrdom are so few as to be almost insignificant; their importance lies in their effects, not in their frequency. Although modern research shows that there were very few actual martyrs, yet these few were quite enough to serve as a juridical proof of the truth and triumph of the new religion, and it was on the basis of such rare heroic acts that the militant ideology of the Church was founded.[86] In a similar way the conflicts incidental to the spread of socialism, by being associated with the idea of the general strike, may be amplified and given an epic quality that will serve perfectly to maintain a catastrophic conception and a well-defined separation of the classes. "Thus," says Sorel, "the objection that is often directed at revolutionaries is removed; civilization is not menaced with succumbing to the consequences of a development of brutality, since the idea of the general strike allows the conception of class struggle to be sustained by means of incidents that would appear mediocre to bourgeois historians."[87]

The modern world, with its humanitarian outlook, its horror of the brutalities that have characterized the history of previous eras, is easily led to an uncritical acceptance of the dogma that all violence is bad. Very seldom has any serious attempt been made to understand its significance as a factor in the development of civilization or to understand the social implications of its abandonment.[88] Because of his constant tendency to treat abstractions as things in themselves, the intellectualist looks on the disappearance of violence as a sign of absolute progress: having failed to uncover the underlying motives of violence, he is unable to recognize these motives when they reassert themselves in a different guise, and so falls into the error of thinking that such a change in their manifestation represents a genuine moral advance. Sorel believed that the mysteries of a people's moral conceptions could be penetrated only by a study of the practices of the dangerous classes in society, so he turned to them for an understanding of the widespread changes that have taken place in the social consciousness of various eras.

In modern times one of the most striking of these modifications in criminal practice is the general abandonment of brutal methods by the cleverer and more experienced criminals in favor of trickery, cunning, and fraud. Wealthy societies like that in America, where everyone is watchful of his own interests, are much more indulgent of fraud and deceit than are countries where material success is not as easy and where the economic life is narrow and parsimonious. When money flows freely, it is not a serious affair if politicians and financiers despoil honest industry, but in the more limited societies of former times the whole stability of traditional institutions and family life depended on a strict regard for probity in property relationships. This circumstance explains, Sorel thought, why the eighteenth century inflicted the extreme penalty of death on such offences as fraudulent bankruptcy.[89] Today, in lands of high capitalism, it is so difficult to distinguish banditry and fraud from legitimate commercial enterprise and so difficult to shake the well-protected position of the more distinguished swindlers, that public sentiment has ended by finding it unjust to condemn minor practitioners of fraud for crimes that their more powerful fellows commit with impunity. If this lowering of ethical standards in all phases of social and economic life is preferable to the brutality of former times, it does not, in Sorel's opinion at least, represent a clear gain: the ancient world was certainly not the idyllic place pictured by some of its apologists, but it had, he thought, certain moral qualities that are noticeably lacking in modern civilization. In support of this criticism of the contemporary belief in moral progress he quotes a passage from Eduard von Hartmann, although with reservations as to its idealization of certain aspects of the past:

"When the atrocities and barbarities of former times are pointed to, we should also not forget to take into account, on the one hand, the probity and honesty, the clear feeling of equity, and the reverence for consecrated custom of ancient peoples living in a state of nature, and, on the other, the growing deceit, falsehood, cunning, chicane, non-regardance of property and of the well-founded, but no longer understood, instinctive morality accompanying civilization. Theft, fraud, and forgery increase, despite the penalties annexed to them, more rapidly than the gross and serious crimes (such as robbery, murder, rape, etc.) decrease; the basest self-interest shamelessly rends asunder the most sacred bonds of the family and friendship wherever it comes into collision with them."[90]

One of the most interesting manifestations of the changes in social morality is to be found in the relations that exist between the state and criminal associations. As Sorel points out, such relations have always existed; but in the century following the Revolution, public feeling became so opposed to the open exercise of force in political affairs that such tactics usually alienated popular sympathy from any group trying to use them, and there appeared an increasing tendency to abandon force almost entirely, in favor of trickery. When, for example, the anti-Semites organized paid bands to express patriotic indignation over the attempts of Zola to reopen the Dreyfus case, they aroused a genuine panic among the bourgeois; in Sorel's opinion, the effects of this threat are to be seen in the anticlerical legislation of the twentieth century. The peace-loving bourgeois world refused to tolerate force in politico-criminal associations just as it refused to tolerate brutality in individual criminals; the result has been that the most successful of these associations have been those that exercised their control through stratagems. Organizations like the Société de Saint-Vincent-de-Paul for the Catholics and the Masonic lodges for the

republicans, by their highly efficient surveillance of government officials, provided very useful lessons for the development of this modern type of pressure group; later, in the
Ligue des Droits de l'homme, the possibilities of applying
the principles as an ordinary instrument for the furtherance
of political special interests were for the first time realized
on a large scale. Not all theorists have been as pessimistic
as Rousseau about the threat to democracy of groups possessing a *special will*, but many have recognized the danger
and have sought remedies. Sorel, however, thought their
hopes of ridding democracy of this evil were quite utopian,
since all experience shows that popular government cannot
function in a capitalist country without falling into the
criminal abuses that are today so clearly manifested every-
where.[91]

The modern politician is usually so accustomed to deal
with these politico-criminal associations that he comes to
treat all organized opposition to the state as no more than
a bid for power or special privileges that may quite readily
be satisfied by concessions and compromises within the
existing framework of government. This is the explanation,
Sorel thought, for the attitude of Waldeck-Rousseau in his
apparent tolerance of the syndicalist movement after 1884.
Faced with the menace of a strong conservative and clerical
opposition he felt the need of finding some new support for
the opportunist and rather cynical Republic; in the rising
influence of the syndicalist movement he saw the promise
of such a support, a support that, if brought under his control, might be used like any other politico-criminal association as a threat to his enemies. At first he sought to exercise
his control through the prefects in much the same way
that Napoleon had tried to control the Church; but when
these methods became inadequate he attempted through
Millerand to win over the leaders of the syndicats by social
and political bribery. His success in these maneuvers de-

pended entirely on his ability to maintain a nice balance between the protection of the established order on the one hand and an active connivance with the syndicalists' revolutionary tactics on the other. As Sorel says, he gave to the syndicats a role analogous to that played by the Masonic lodges in bringing pressure to bear on dissentients; but in rewarding them, instead of dispensing decorations and personal favors, he had only to allow the workers to extort wage increases from their employers. The demands of the workers could not exceed certain limits however, and these limits were those that the politician was accustomed to set for the usual gratuity given in return for useful services. So ordinary, in fact, is this political practice of settling difficulties by means of gratuities that the politician can hardly conceive of any affair without them, and it is in this spirit that he regards the arbitration that he is called on to make between the workers and the employer. If the settlement is successful, the employer is assured of a stability in wages for several years at the cost of a gratuity to the workers, and the politician, in his role of public benefactor, receives as his reward the electoral advantages that follow on a successful reconciliation, a reward that is ordinarily more welcome than any direct gratuity could be.[92]

Sorel believed that these practices of political jobbery and corruption were the inevitable result of a policy of social peace and that it would be useless to expect any raising of social ethics, any aspirations toward the sublime, as long as a vicious social system remained that depended for its very existence on the expedients and subterfuges of a class of politicians. As he says: "Participation in politics under any form whatever is, nonetheless, a great misfortune for socialism because this participation leads men to attribute importance only to bargaining; by this process the juridical spirit and the revolutionary spirit are extinguished at one and the same time." These policies, Sorel thought, might bring certain immediate gains to the leaders of the party and even, in a more limited way, to the proletariat as a whole, but such gains could be obtained only at the cost of a degradation of the ethical motives of socialism. "When politicians intervene," he says, "there is, and almost necessarily, a notable lowering of morality, because these men do nothing for nothing and act only on condition that the favored association joins with their clientele. This takes us far from the road to the sublime, instead we are simply on that which leads to the practice of politico-criminal societies."[93]

If socialism is to attain any sublimity, Sorel thought, if it is to free the proletariat from the slave morality imposed by capitalism, it must reject the self-interested leadership of politicians and intellectuals; in fact the whole future of revolutionary syndicalism depends, he believed, on the development in the proletariat of a new ethic based on the qualities demanded by a society of free producers.[94] Consequently the most difficult task of socialist theory is, as he himself states, to show "how it is possible to conceive the transition from the men of today to the state of free producers laboring in a workshop rid of masters."[95] Since there are no political precedents for such a social regime—not even democracy, which depends on external constraints of the same type as capitalism[96]—many socialists have given way to pure utopianism in their solutions of the problem. Such hypotheses, however, were too illusory to satisfy Sorel: he had no faith in the ability of prophets to foresee the future. Accordingly he explicitly confines his task to an investigation of tendencies in the present that might serve, in ways similar to analogous tendencies in great social movements of the past, as the basis of a revolution in social and economic relationships.[97] If some light can be thrown on these tendencies, it would be possible, he thought, to see more clearly the way along which the proletariat may go in developing its own relationships of production; for, "The activating force of the revolutionary movement ought also to be the activating force of the morality of the producers."[98]

Just as Christianity and the French Revolution derived their dynamic force from myths that aroused in their adherents a self-sacrificing enthusiasm capable of transcending the ordinary difficulties standing in the way of coöperation among individuals, so, Sorel thought, the myth of the general strike might offer to the proletariat a similar basis for a common inspiration and purpose arising from needs already manifested among the workers themselves. By giving to these needs an epic character, Sorel believed that the syndicalist myth with its militant conception of a violent class war might very well engender qualities of personal responsibility and personal significance analogous to those, for example, that aroused in the ill-organized soldiers of the Revolutionary armies a will to victory that proved much more effective than the automatic discipline enforced in the royal armies. It is just such qualities of individual initiative and self-discipline that would be demanded by a possible regime of free production; consequently Sorel considers that this is a decisive factor in favor of revolutionary syndicalism.[99]

Aroused to a passionate sense of individualism by the revolutionary myth and disciplined by a struggle with the representatives of the bourgeois state, the proletarians, Sorel thought, would then be capable of developing certain characteristics in relation to production that have in the past reached their full expression only in the lives of some great artists. "The free producer in a highly progressive workshop," he says, "should never measure the work that he furnishes by an external scale; he finds all the models presented to him mediocre and wishes to surpass everything that has been done before him. Production thus finds itself assured of improving always in quantity and in quality; in such a workshop the idea of indefinite progress is realized."[100] Because of the interesting analogy between these requirements of a free producer and the qualities engendered by the zeal of the artist, Sorel is led to state that art is an *anticipation* of the most highly developed production. In the past the relationships of production have not been suited to a widespread manifestation of such qualities, just as in a similar way they were not suited, for example, to the exploitation in Hellenistic times of Hero's steam engine, or to the acceptance in the eighteenth century of Vico's philosophical ideas; but the enthusiastic receptions of Watt's invention in the nineteenth century and the popularity enjoyed by pragmatism today justify the assertion that the attitudes of Hero and Vico were anticipations of contemporary developments. It is in this same sense that Sorel believed it legitimate to regard the relatively isolated examples of artistic individualism in the past as anticipations of certain qualities that are already taking form in the gradual evolution of a self-conscious proletariat and that, under the influence of a stimulus analogous to the inspiration of the artist, might provide the ethical framework for a system of free production.

One of the most obvious characteristics that distinguishes the artist from the common artisan has been his originality and his unwillingness to reproduce accepted types. Such qualities, Sorel thought, are also the mark of the inventor; in the many very considerable improvements made by anonymous workers to the crude machines first offered them by modern industry, he saw a manifestation of what is essentially an artistic urge. Another characteristic of the artist, he believed, is a constant striving for integrity of workmanship, and here again an interesting analogy is to be found, for, despite the pessimistic prophecies of Fourier, the more advanced modern industry has become, the more honest and substantial have been its products. Finally, he states, the production of the artist is not governed by the expectation of a personal, immediate reward in proportion to merit, but is simply the expression of a striving for perfection quite independent of external recognition. It was such an impulse, Sorel thought, that must have animated the architects of the great Gothic cathedrals; for they apparently received very little notice from their contemporaries and possibly, even, may have been the only real admirers of their own masterpieces. Similarly in modern times, the inventor, who has so seldom received the compensation due his labors, is led to his task not by the hope of material reward but simply by a spontaneous urge to make innovations and improvements. The tremendous technological progress of modern industry has depended in large degree on the contributions of ingenious workers to the refinement of machinery and methods; yet, as with the artist, these workers asked for no recompense and as a matter of fact have seldom got any.[101]

Great movements in the history of ideas have never been achieved by men who act only after a rational calculation of the personal advantages and disadvantages of their projected plans. The soldier in the early campaigns of Napoleon, the Huguenot who gave up his home and livelihood, the early Christian martyr—none of these men could have hoped to attain any of the ordinary material advantages that are commonly reckoned as the sole motive of men's activity. Whatever objective judgment may be passed on the wisdom or success of such enthusiasts, it is an undoubted fact that a large number of them did find in the zealous support of certain principles an adequate compensation for the hardships they suffered.[102] The future of socialism, Sorel thought, depends on the possibility of developing in the proletariat a similar moral strength. In the essentially creative and artistic qualities manifested by the skilled worker in countries of high production, he believed, the basis of such an ethic was already to be found—a basis that needed nothing more for its development than the stimulating force of an enthusiasm capable of overcoming the inertia, the prejudices, and the demand for immediate satisfactions of the individual worker.

"There is," he says, "only one force that could today produce this enthusiasm without whose coöperation no morality is possible: this is the force that results from the propaganda in favor of the general strike.

"The preceding explanations have shown that the idea of the general strike, constantly rejuvenated by the feelings that proletarian violence provokes, produces a completely epic state of mind and, at the same time, leads all the powers of the soul toward the conditions that allow the realization of a workshop functioning freely and progressively in a high degree; we have thus recognized that there are very close relationships between the feelings of the general strike and those that are necessary in order to provoke a continued progress in production. Therefore we have the right to maintain that the modern world possesses the prime mover that *is able* to assure a morality of producers."[103]

CHAPTER VIII

CONCLUSION

$$E = mc^2$$
—Albert Einstein

EACH AGE HAS CHARACTERISTIC QUESTIONS to ask of the world it knows. Each thinker within an age has his own way of framing those questions; the fruitfulness of his ideas, in fact, depends directly on the intuitive grasp he may have of the particular concerns of his time and on his ability to realize their implications. It is becoming every day more evident that one such fundamental question that marks our own time is: What is energy? It is precisely this question that is implicit in the life work of Sorel. The inner logic of his work lies in the reiteration of the question through the whole range of his speculations on history, ethics, aesthetics, religion, politics, science. When he speaks of the fall of Rome, or the moral upsurge of the Risorgimento, or the eroticism of modern music, or the militant myth of Christianity, or the images of battle that could produce a violent assertion of will in the general strike, or the dynamic flow that constitutes the reality of the physical world, his language is full of energy words. This preoccupation is not accidental. The work of the physical scientists from the sixteenth century—and most dramatically in the nineteenth and twentieth centuries—has made evident the tremendous potentialities of the universe which may be unlocked by the right key. Man has acquired an entirely new consciousness of the existence of energy; he has been alternately enraptured by the possibilities of its constructive use and ridden by fears that it might be turned destructively against him.

The recognition of these possibilities has had, in turn, a profound effect on his views in every sphere of life. Sorel was particularly sensitive to such influences. He did not need to witness the final dramatic achievement of nuclear fission in order to feel the tremendous responsibilities for good or evil that lie in the hands of modern man.

Power has so multiplied itself through the machine age that the central problem of social life has with increasing obviousness become one of exercising controls over expansive energies. In a past age when a man with an ax could cut a clearing to plant a field of corn, or use the ax as a weapon against his enemy, there needed to be no special concern with the manifestation of energy as such. However when vast metropolises, based on an extraordinarily intricate technological network, spread brick and steel over the fields and exposed their populations to such man-made yet impersonal and largely incomprehensible forces as involuntary unemployment or assembly-line production, then the question, what is energy? was no longer to be confined to the philosopher's study or the physicist's laboratory; it forced itself on the attention of the world at large. The symbol of the tendency that Sorel anticipated is now clear before us: the navel of the universe is no longer a shrine at Delphi tended by the priests of Apollo but the atomic piles at Oak Ridge where the physicists guard the sacred bomb.

Quite obviously energy is not something invented in modern times, nor is the concept that there is a driving force in the universe a realization that has become significant only with the machine age. Our knowledge of man, wherever he is found, shows him as concerned with the explanation in some form of the mysteries of the causation of events, with the dynamics of action. The most primitive peoples have a religious or magical theory that satisfies their wonderings about the change in the order of things that constitutes history as they experience it. Often they attribute to all objects a spirit or *animus* which they think accounts for the way things behave. More sophisticated theories attribute the important powers of life to an appropriate hierarchy of gods or, in still more developed religions such as Christianity, to a single god who is himself the source of all power. Whatever their form these beliefs have comforted men and assuaged their fears in facing the otherwise inexplicable forces that charged their universe.

Primitive man relies primarily on magic formulas or appeals to the gods to determine the course of events—his *fate*. The crops will not grow if the proper fertility ceremonies are not performed; the sun will not rise if it is incorrectly addressed. Even in the most minute details of living he is reconciled to the possibility that ordinary routines based on observed uniformities may be upset at any time by supernatural intervention. The role of science has been to bring about a far-reaching reversal in these expectations of mankind. We are now inclined to believe that sequences of events will remain in their observed order as long as the surrounding conditions are the same; we are also inclined to believe that those sequences can be changed in any desired way by a deliberate change in the conditions. This shift in expectation is not absolute by any means, but it is quantitatively so great as to be qualitative in its effect. A part at least of divine power has now fallen into the hands of man; his astonishing success in binding and loosing the great forces of the universe has radically changed his conception of his relationship to the sources of energy. It is with the consequences of this new conception that the history of the modern age is concerned: since man's activities now take place in a new dimension his speculations in every field must be appropriately redefined.

When the scientific method was introduced in the sixteenth century, it was generally taken as a rival of the Church since it offered, in the realm of abstraction, an explanation of universal truth. It was a rival in this sense but it was far more: to the *words* of traditional philosophy it added *deeds*, and the resulting experimental evidence ultimately became so overwhelming that theoretical abstraction often fell behind or gave way entirely before it. It no longer seemed vital to decide the ultimate truth of all theories before attempting to put them to use. Scientists, for example, have accepted impartially the corpuscular and the wave theories of light, making their choice between the two on the pragmatic grounds of immediate usefulness.

The modern age has sometimes been denounced for its uncritical pragmatism, for its materialistic reference to power dams, internal combustion engines, or electronic bombardments as evidence of its progress; but such denunciations have been entirely futile in changing the course of general opinion. Their main effect, actually, has been to obscure in the philosophic mind itself the clear fact that science and technology have given man not only a wealth of material objects but, much more deeply significant, an altogether new sense of mastery in the physical world: not only his comfort but his whole pattern of security, his existence itself, depends on the skill with which man can exploit the newly realized sources of energy around him. It is no wonder, then, that he looks on his engines with awe and grants to their creators the attributes of priesthood. For better or for worse the genie has been released from the bottle and he must be reckoned with—he cannot be ignored.

Man's feelings about power have always been ambivalent. When it is effectively controlled it induces a special kind of aesthetic satisfaction: the sailing ship throwing the waves to each side, the plow turning an even furrow, the generator humming quietly in the ordered expanse of a hydro installation are objects of unselfconscious beauty—they are characteristic symbols of man's conquest of the arbitrary. However, the serenity induced by these representations can be banished in a moment by the disappearance of the sense of control: a hurricane, an eroding torrent, a high voltage arc will produce feelings of terror to the degree that they appear unrestrained. Human beings have always had a special fear of unpredictable power in the form of the unexpected or the unknown. This kind of fear is intolerable to them for any prolonged time; if it cannot be met physically it will be met psychically; if it cannot be met realistically it will be met by fantasy construction.

The great fact that underlies the modern age is a tremendous acceleration of the tendency to bring area after area of the natural forces of the universe under rule. This might be described in physical terms as a disentropic tendency—a tendency toward order and control and away from randomness and unpredictability. Not only in the conventional sense has power been harnessed by technology but, in expanding circles, the same proliferation of systems of control is to be seen in the organization of economic and social relationships. Archimedes' figure of a lever to move the world is now something more than pure fantasy. Man need no longer approach his daily enterprises in a spirit of submission to the unpredictability of natural forces. He is no longer a child who lacks the physical strength and coördination to manipulate the world around him to his advantage and satisfaction. Now that he has come of age the center of the problem has shifted from the *means* of acquiring power to the *ends* for which that power had best be exercised. The situation of the present day is a new one for civilization but an old one in the experience of the individual: it is the problem of adolescence. The child has acquired the powers of a man, but he doubts his right to exercise them and his ability to exercise them well. The very consciousness of his strength leads him to fear the consequences of its expression. The decisions he may make to resolve his doubts are infinitely varied: he may regress to some previous stage of lesser responsibilities; he may turn with manic ferocity on the world around him; he may retreat from all recognition of unpleasant reality; or he may, and usually does, adjust himself in a working relationship with things as they are. A fortunate few have achieved a degree of harmony and creative expression that stands as a sign that the problem of the control of power is not an insoluble one when maturity is arrived at.

The work of Sorel appears in this midpoint of the growth of our civilization. It is a restless age that he describes. Great new forces are being driven into the consciousness of mankind. He was by no means alone in sensing their presence, but he was one of the few to admit them for what they are without evasion and without feelings of guilt. His place is beside Nietzsche and Freud as one of the great prophets of the modern age. All three of them saw that the system of organization that was giving man an unparalleled power over his environment could at the same time create such an intolerable burden that the individual might well be crushed by it. Whether they set as their ideal the superman, the whole man, or the creatively free workingman, they were seeking in the best tradition of humanism for a set of values that might permit man to express himself in responsible action with his fellows. It is ironic, but not altogether strange, that the popular conception of these men should so misrepresent their purpose as to make them out to be the advocates of the very things they most deplored. Their insistence on power conflict as the base point for definitions of the structure of social organization was too honest—and too brutal—for popular acceptance. The very word "power" carries with it from the history of the race and of the individual so many associations of repression and helplessness that it is still difficult in most circumstances for people to react to it without fear. It is the wish to play safe that has led so many people to assume that the chief end of civilization is to deny expression to power or even to deny its very existence. The parallel to experience in the individual personality is obvious: if the libidinal drives are inacceptable they may be denied expression; if they are considered bad they may not even be recognized. When, as a consequence, the drives turn inward it is customary to speak of the individual as neurotic.

Nietzsche, Freud, and Sorel were all concerned with a sickness of civilization. It was a sickness that showed itself at some times and places as a passive withdrawal from responsibility and, at other times and places, as over-aggressiveness. These symptoms are an indication of a serious disfunction. All three men proposed the same cure: if anxiety is to be replaced by harmony and hatred by love man must regain his self-respect, he must accept the energies at his disposal and use them maturely for his own welfare and for the welfare of others. Much of his aggressiveness can be turned to constructive activity and much of his hostility to fruitful competition. In these terms power is no longer thought of primarily as the ability to deprive but rather as the ability to grant and to do. Liberty is to be defined as participation, not as isolation.

There is one very apparent difference between the process of growing up of the child and the growing up of civilization. The child always has before him the model of adult conduct to which he is expected to conform; but there is no such model of a mature civilization. Who is to say, then, what its characteristics might be? Who is to say, even, that it could actually exist? Answers to these questions must be found by every serious investigator of the prospects of mankind. The claim of Nietzsche, Freud, and Sorel to be prophets of the modern age rests on the kind of answer they found and on its appropriateness to the forces of the world they lived in.

All three thinkers combined a poetic insight with a scientific curiosity. They sought consciously for a full picture of man's experience and in that experience they looked for the vitalizing images that have moved him to action. They sought to understand the process that is life—whether of the individual or of civilization. When put in these terms the difference between the history of the individual and the history of civilization is no longer as marked: individuals have obviously transcended the teachings of their fathers; they have acted not only under the compulsion of conforming to fixed models but also under the much more dynamic compulsion of expressing their potentialities. The intellectualists fix their attention on the static pattern of models to be imitated: anti-intellectualists seek intuitions of process, of things coming into being. The gift of the poet and the prophet is to see the essential structure of life beneath the obscuring forms of the commonplace. By intuition they can complete and correct the imperfect and broken forms that constitute things as they seem. The ideal representations they create are not intolerant of reality since they rise out of it in the most immediate sense. Great prophets of ancient religions and poet-artists like Leonardo da Vinci and Goethe have caught sight of unrealized possibilities in man; they have achieved anticipations, as Sorel so often called them, of things not yet externally formed; they have set before man images or myths toward which he could work in the fulfillment of his own possibilities. A similar imagery is to be found in the prophets of our own time: Zarathustra's vigil on the mountain-top was a preparation for his return to the society of his fellows; the whole man of psychoanalytic theory achieves his harmony by an artful adjustment of tendencies common in a different balance to all humanity; the free producer of the syndicalist workshop brings the creative instincts of an artist to an industrial organization that threatens to enslave the laborer to the machine. All of these images represent the same thing: they show us man freely conscious of his power and exercising it without fear in the control of his environment. They are anticipations of a civilization come to maturity.

Sorel always called himself a pessimist; he spoke with scorn of the optimists. At the same time he obviously demonstrated that his pessimism was a positive attitude, that it led to action and not to passive and fatalistic acceptance. His definition of pessimism is best understood as a part of his attitude toward the relationship of man to energy. In the physical world, he thought, an entropic process underlies all the system-building man may contrive for his momentary satisfaction; in society conflict and struggle are the lot of man and he can never rest; within the individual great emotional forces, the most mysterious and significant of them being sexual forces, dominate the important decisions of the personality. Sorel insisted on looking these facts in the face even though they clearly set limits on man's power to mold the world as he wishes. His fundamental objection to the optimist of his times was that he refused to see these facts; the optimist did not have the courage to admit that man could never be the complete master of energy and must be content, therefore, to play out his role as a part of the unending energy process that is life.

The optimists, disliking the picture of raw power disclosed by the pessimists, turned on them in a natural but illogical reaction of repugnance and fear and accused them of *advocating* these forces or in some way of being *responsible* for them. Nietzsche, Freud, and Sorel all suffered these accusations. The phenomenon is not new: many of the innovators in religion, philosophy, and science have been similarly denounced for outraging the complacency of the fearful and the timid. The uneasy patterns of security that man creates to protect himself from the undefinable dangers of arbitrary power cannot be disturbed with impunity.

Sorel was not without his own fears at what he saw. He had a truly tragic view of man's age-old struggle to survive and fulfill himself in the world of uncomprehending and largely incomprehensible forces that surge around him. The drama, though, was not yet played out: there had been moments of terrifying catastrophe in its course and there had been moments of grandeur. Sorel saw both, but not simply as a spectator removed from action. The best years of his life were given to a search—at times a desperate search—for some principle of organization for society that would stand the stress of the shattering forces now in the hands of men. His claim to a position as prophet of our age lies in the fact that he saw early and saw clearly the terms in which our social problem is put and that he set out to find a solution of the problem in those terms. He had nothing but scorn for the escapists, whether they fled in terror to the banks of the Susquehanna or into the sweet realms of sentimentality where there are no winds to ruffle the calm surface of the pool into which they gazed. He accepted the modern age without evasion of its hard problems. He was an engineer in a world of machines and he accepted them. His principal hopes rested in the operators of those machines, but not because he thought they were by some peculiar grace more virtuous than other men or, on account of poverty and oppression, more deserving. His regard for the workingman was a regard for the man closest to the source of physical energy, for the man whose hands actually controlled the process of production. He thought that the discipline rising out of industrial production— especially as it approaches the creative feeling the artist has for his work—is one of the most important foundation elements of morality. Man can learn from work and from the family, whose structure depends on work, the self-discipline that will enable him to use advantageously the great forces at his disposal without, on the one hand, denying them or, on the other, being shattered by them. Sorel had hoped that the workingman in the syndicat might develop a discipline based on his work that would produce a social and political reorganization able to deal with the problems of the industrial age in a manner that would not suppress the free and creative expression of man's capacities. He was disappointed in that hope, but the basic problem remains as he stated it. If the world is to achieve the freedom and responsibility that maturity implies it must find a way to bridge the gap between production and government—between the making of power and the use of it. Just as envy and destructiveness and hate are the products of fear of power, so coöperation and constructiveness and love are the products of assurance in its use. If man is to learn self-control he must first learn self-respect.

NOTES

I. INTRODUCTION

1. Georges Sorel, "Lettere a Croce" (letter cxxxii, of May 6, 1907), *Critica*, XXVI, 100.

2. Benedetto Croce, Introduction to the Italian translation of Sorel's *Réflexions sur la violence, Considerazioni sulla Violenza* (Bari, 1926), vi.

3. Georges Sorel, *Réflexions sur la violence* (Paris, 1930), 8.

4. Sorel, "Lettere a Croce" (v, June 2, 1897), *Critica*, XXV, 44.

5. Sorel, quoted by René Johannet, *Itinéraires d'intellectuels* (Paris, 1921), 228.

6. *Réflexions*, 9.

7. *Ibid.*, 12.

8. *Ibid.*, 8.

9. Georges Sorel, *Insegnamenti sociali della economia contemporanea: Decadenza capitalista e decadenza socialista* (Palermo, 1906), 89.

10. Georges Sorel, "Avenir socialiste des syndicats," *Matériaux d'une théorie du prolétariat* (Paris, 1929), 127.

11. Georges Sorel, *La Ruine du monde antique* (Paris, 1933), 293, 291–292; *Réflexions*, 43.

12. "Avenir socialiste des syndicats, Note A, Instruction populaire," *Matériaux*, 138, n. 1. See also "Lettere a Croce" (cxxxii, May 6, 1907), *Critica*, XXVI, 102.

13. Georges Sorel, "Grandeur et décadence," *Les illusions du progrès* (Paris, 1927), 318.

14. Max Ascoli, *Georges Sorel*, French translation (Paris, 1921), 43.

15. "Lettere a Croce" (lxxxv, April 28, 1903), *Critica*, XXV, 372.

16. Georges Sorel, *Contribution à l'étude profane de la Bible* (Paris, 1889), vii.

17. "Grandeur et décadence," *Illusions*, 333.

18. "Mes raisons du syndicalisme," *Matériaux*, 240, 248.

19. "Préface pour Colajanni," *Matériaux*, 179, n. 1 (this comment was added in 1914). See also "Mes raisons du syndicalisme," *Matériaux*, 263.

20. "Préface pour Colajanni," *Matériaux*, 179.

21. *Ibid.*, 178–179.

22. "Mes raisons du syndicalisme," *Matériaux*, 264, n. 1.

23. Johannet, *Itinéraires*, 191.

24. See especially his *La Révolution dreyfusienne* (Paris, 1911).

25. "Mes raisons du syndicalisme," *Matériaux*, 268.

26. *Ibid.*, 286 (written in the spring of 1910); also "Lettere a Croce" (cxcv, January 25, 1911), *Critica*, XXVI, 345.

27. "Lettere a Croce" (cxcvii, February 19, 1911), *Critica*, XXVI, 347.

28. See Johannet, *Itinéraires*, 206 ff., for a quotation of the prospectus for the *Cité française* drawn up by Sorel.

29. Georges Sorel, *De l'utilité du pragmatisme* (Paris, 1928), 182, n. 1; see also his essay, "L'Organisation de la démocratie," *Matériaux*, 367, n. 1.

30. Johannet, *Itinéraires*, 206.

31. "Lettere a Croce" (cclxii, September 1, 1915), *Critica*, XXVII, 289.

226 *NOTES*

32. "Pour Lénine," *Réflexions*, 454.

33. *Réflexions*, 110.

34. From a conversation reported by Jean Variot in *Eclair*, September 11, 1922; quoted by Georges Pirou, *Georges Sorel* (Paris, 1927), 53.

35. "Pour Lénine," *Réflexions*, 442.

36. Georges Sorel, *L'Europa sotto la tormenta* (Milan, 1932), 189.

37. "Pour Lénine," *Réflexions*, 451, n. 1.

38. *Ibid.*, 451.

39. "Exégèses proudhoniennes," *Matériaux*, 433–434.

40. "Pour Lénine," *Réflexions*, 453.

41. "Mes raisons du syndicalisme," *Matériaux*, 286.

42. Nikolay Lenin, *Matérialisme et l'empiro-criticisme*, cited by Pirou, *Georges Sorel*, 49.

43. According to M. Philippe Serre as quoted by Pirou, p. 37, n. 1.

44. Vilfredo Pareto, "Georges Sorel," *La Ronda*, September–October 1922, 545.

45. For a statement of some of the conflicting conceptions of Lenin and Sorel on religion, the family, the state, etc., see Michel Freund, *Georges Sorel der revolutionäre Konservatismus* (Frankfurt-am-Main, 1932), 250.

46. See C. A. Avenati, *La Rivoluzione italiana da Alfiere a Benito Mussolini* (Turin, 1934); Herman Finer, *Mussolini's Italy* (London, 1935); Giuseppe Prezzolini, *Fascism* (London, 1926).

47. "Avenir des syndicats," *Matériaux*, p. 128, n. 3.

48. Georges Sorel, *La Décomposition du marxisme* (3rd ed.; Paris, no date), 68.

49. "Lettere a Croce" (cxcv, January 25, 1911), *Critica*, XXVI, 345.

50. *Réflexions*, 387–388.

51. Quoted by E. H. Posse, "Bemerkungen zur Einführung zu G. Sorel's 'Uber die Gewalt' ", *Jahrbücher fur Nationalökonomie und Statistik*, CXXXXXI (1929), 845–846, with a citation to G. H. Bousquet, *V. Pareto, le développement et la signification historique de son oeuvre* (Paris, 1923), 6–7.

52. "Le Caractère religieux du socialisme," *Matériaux*, 357.

53. *Ibid.*, 356.

54. *Ibid.*, 358–359.

55. *Ibid.*, 314.

56. *Ibid.*, 361–363.

57. *Ibid.*, 316–317.

58. Jérome and Jean Tharaud, *Notre cher Péguy* (Paris, 1926), 137–138.

59. See Chapters V and VI.

60. Pirou, *Georges Sorel*, 9.

61. "Lettere a Croce" (cccxlii, July 8, 1921), *Critica*, XXVIII, 195.

II. THE WORLD OF IDEAS

1. Vilfredo Pareto, *The Mind and Society* (New York, 1935), III, 1317.

2. Alfred North Whitehead, *Science and the Modern World* (New York, 1927), 12.

3. *Ibid.*, 26.

4. Max Planck, *Where Is Science Going?* (New York, 1932), 136.

5. For a discussion of this question see Sorel, *Pragmatisme*, 180–182.

6. See Henri Bergson, *L'Evolution créatrice* (Paris, 1930), 163 ff.; William James, *The Meaning of Truth* (New York, 1909), 246–247.

7. James, *Meaning of Truth*, 246, 250; Whitehead, *Science and the Modern World*, 26.

8. Edmund Burke, *Reflections on the Revolution in France* (Boston, 1865), 346, 347.

9. Comte Joseph de Maistre, *Etude sur la souveraineté*, in *Oeuvres complètes* (Lyons, 1884), 357–358; Maistre, *Les soirées de Saint-Pétersbourg* (Brussels, 1838), 100–101.

10. Comte Joseph de Maistre, *Du Pape* (Lyons, 1849), 163.

11. Marquis de Condorcet, *Esquisse d'un tableau historique du progrès de l'esprit humain* (Paris, 1847), 13.

12. *Ibid.*, 223, 176.

13. *Ibid.*, 276.

14. Jeremy Bentham, *An Introduction to the Principles of Morals and Legislation*, Bowring edition of *Works* (Edinburgh, 1843), I, 1.

15. Jeremy Bentham, Preface, *A Fragment on Government*, Bowring edition of *Works* (Edinburgh, 1843), I, 227.

16. Bentham, *Morals and Legislation*, 2.

17. Jeremy Bentham, *Constitutional Code*, Bowring edition of *Works* (Edinburgh, 1843), IX, 24.

18. Sir Henry S. Maine, *Lectures on the Early History of Institutions* (New York, 1875), 396.

19. Leslie Stephen, *The English Utilitarians* (New York, 1900), 235.

20. Karl Marx, *Capital* (London, 1929), 671.

21. Georges Weill, *Histoire du mouvement social en France (1852–1924)* (Paris, 1924), 42.

22. *Ibid.*, 194 ff.

III. THE MORAL CRITERION: SOREL THE MORALIST

1. Georges Sorel, "L'Ancienne et la Nouvelle Métaphysique," *Ere nouvelle*, 1894, 203.

2. *Ibid.*, 66.

3. Georges Sorel, "Nuovi contributi alla teoria Marxistica del valore," *Giornale degli Economisti*, July 1898, 19; *L'Ancienne et la Nouvelle Métaphysique*, 331.

4. Sorel, *Réflexions*, 378–389.

5. *L'Ancienne et la Nouvelle Métaphysique*, 72–73, 75.

6. *Ruine du monde*, 147, 177.

7. *Ibid.*, 272–273.

8. "Avenir socialiste des syndicats," *Matériaux*, 98.

9. Georges Sorel, *Le Procès de Socrate* (Paris, 1889), 85.

10. "Avenir socialiste des syndicats," *Matériaux*, 111.

11. *Ibid.*, 118–119.

12. *Insegnamenti sociale*, 172–173; see also *Ruine du monde*, 295.

13. Georges Sorel, "L'Ethique du socialisme," *Revue de la métaphysique et de la morale* (May 1899), 293.

14. Georges Sorel, "L'influenza della razze," *Saggi di critica del Marxismo* (Palermo, 1902), 107–108.

15. "Préface pour Colajanni," *Matériaux*, 198–199.

16. *L'Ancienne et la Nouvelle Métaphysique*, 59.

17. Georges Sorel, "Une Faute du crime politique," *Archivio di Psichiatria, Scienza Penali ed Antropologia Criminale*, vol. XIV, part V, 1893, 453.

18. *L'Ancienne et la Nouvelle Métaphysique*, 65–66.
19. "Église, évangile et socialisme," *Ruine du monde*, 294–295.
20. *Ibid.*, 290–292.
21. *Réflexions*, 20.
22. *Socrate*, 217.
23. Friedrich Nietzsche, *Généalogie de la morale*, 57–59, 43, quoted in *Réflexions*, 357.
24. *Socrate*, 172.
25. *Ibid.*, 150–151.
26. *Ibid.*, 158.
27. *Ibid.*, 232–233.
28. *Ibid.*, 6–7.
29. *Ruine du monde*, 44.
30. *Ibid.*, 132.
31. *Ibid.*, 89.
32. *Socrate*, 314.
33. Georges Sorel, "La Psychologie du juge," *Archivio di Psichiatria, Scienze Penali ed Antropologia Criminale*, Vol. XV, Part II, 1894, 47.
34. *Réflexions*, 15–17.
35. Gaston Boissier, *La Fin du paganisme: Etude sur les dernières luttes religieuses en Occident au quatrième siècle* (9th ed.; Paris, no date), II, 324, quoted in *Ruine du monde*, 160.
36. "Eglise, évangile et socialisme," *Ruine du monde*, 292.
37. *Réflexions*, 315–318; quotation from Pierre Joseph Proudhon, *Oeuvres complètes*, Vol. IX: *De la justice dans la Révolution et dans l'Eglise* (Paris, 1930), I, 414–415.

IV. THE IDEOLOGY OF THE MIDDLE CLASS

1. Georges Sorel, "La Crise morale et religieuse," *Mouvement socialiste*, July 1907, 36–37.
2. *Illusions*, 10.
3. *Pragmatisme*, 60.
4. *Réflexions*, 220.
5. *Pragmatisme*, 1–2.
6. *Insegnamenti sociali*, 199.
7. "Unité et multiplicité," *Réflexions*, 407.
8. "Avant-propos," *Matériaux*, 7.
9. "Unité et multiplicité," *Réflexions*, 415–416.
10. "Avant-propos," *Matériaux*, 15.
11. *Ibid.*, 24.
12. *Marxisme*, 66, n. 1.
13. "Avant-propos," *Matériaux*, 27–28.
14. *Illusions*, 36.
15. Karl Marx, *The Communist Manifesto* (London, 1930), 50.
16. *Illusions*, 5–9.
17. *Ibid.*, 65–66.
18. *Ibid.*, 69–71.
19. *Ibid.*, 74.
20. *Ibid.*, 76.
21. *Ibid.*, 77.
22. H. A. Taine, "L'Ancien régime," *Origines de la France*, I (Paris, 1876), 241, quoted in *Illusions*, 80.

23. *Illusions*, 80–81.
24. *Ibid.*, 82.
25. *Ibid.*, 83, 85.
26. Georges Sorel, "L'Eglise et l'état," *Revue socialiste*, August, September, October 1901, 138–139.
27. "Avant-propos," *Matériaux*, 28.
28. "Vi e dell'utopia nel Marxismo?" *Saggi del Marxismo*, 146.
29. "Unité et multiplicité," *Réflexions*, 407.
30. *Ibid.*, 403.
31. *Illusions*, 109.
32. Comte Alexis de Tocqueville, *The Old Regime and the Revolution* (New York, 1856), 198, quoted in *Illusions*, 112.
33. "L'Organisation de la démocratie," *Matériaux*, 386–387.
34. *Illusions*, 120.
35. *Ibid.*, 97.
36. *Ibid.*, 95.
37. *Ibid.*, 97–99.
38. *Ibid.*, 100.
39. *Ibid.*, 90.
40. *Ibid.*, 120.
41. *Ibid.*, 134.
42. "Avant-propos," *Matériaux*, 16.
43. Tocqueville, *Old Regime*, 176, quoted in *Illusions*, 174.
44. *Illusions*, 177–178.
45. A. R. J. Turgot, *Oeuvres* (Daire and Dussard edition), II, 503, quoted in *Illusions*, 185.
46. *Illusions*, 193.
47. *Ibid.*, 185–189, 194–196.
48. *Ibid.*, 209–210.
49. *Ibid.*, 211, 214.
50. *Ibid.*, 250.
51. *Ibid.*, 251–253.
52. Proudhon, *Justice dans la Révolution*, III, 511–525, cited in *Illusions*, 262.
53. *Illusions*, 265.
54. *Ibid.*, 275–276.

V. PRAGMATISM AND A PLURALIST WORLD

1. *Illusions*, 52, n. 3.
2. *Ruine du monde*, 1.
3. *Ibid.*, 84–85.
4. *Ibid.*, 84, 63.
5. *Psychologie du juge*, 47.
6. *Ruine du monde*, 87.
7. Pierre Joseph Proudhon, *Représentant du peuple*, April 29, 1848, quoted in *Réflexions*, 251, n. 1.
8. *Ruine du monde*, 315.
9. Georges Sorel, "Vues sur les problèmes de la philosophie," *Revue de la métaphysique et de la morale*, September 1910, 606.
10. Georges Sorel, "Les Aspects juridiques du socialisme," *Revue socialiste*, October 1900, 398.

230 *NOTES*

11. *Ruine du monde,* 52.
12. *Ibid.,* 55–56.
13. *L'Ancienne et la Nouvelle Métaphysique,* 473.
14. "Vi e dell'utopia nel marxismo?" *Saggi del Marxismo,* 162; *Insegnamenti sociali,* 198.
15. *Illusions,* 49–50.
16. *Socrate,* 183.
17. Etienne Boutroux, *Science and Religion in Contemporary Philosophy* (New York, 1911), 72.
18. Georges Sorel, "La Religion d'aujourd'hui," *Revue de la métaphysique et de la morale,* March 1909, 246.
19. *Socrate,* 327; *Religion d'aujourd'hui,* 246–247.
20. Georges Sorel, "La Science dans l'éducation," *Devenir social,* February, 1896, 219.
21. Georges Sorel, "Idées socialistes et faits économiques au XIXᵉ siècle," *Revue socialiste,* March 1902, 386.
22. *Illusions,* 239.
23. *Insegnamenti sociali,* 62.
24. Georges Sorel, "Les Théories de M. Durkheim," *Devenir Social,* April 1895, 3; Sorel, "Storia e scienza sociale," *Rivista italiana di sociologia,* March–June 1902, 224.
25. James, *Meaning of Truth,* 202–203, 204.
26. For James's exposition of these ideas see his *Pragmatism,* 217 ff., and *Meaning of Truth,* 194 ff.
27. Georges Sorel, review of A. Leclerc, *Pragmatisme, modernisme, protestantisme,* in *Indépendance,* 1911, 108.
28. Sorel, *Pragmatisme,* 76–77.
29. James, *Pragmatism,* 56; *Meaning of Truth,* 59.
30. *Pragmatisme,* 71.
31. *Ibid.,* 85, n. 2.
32. Giovanni Battista Vico, *Principes de la philosophie de l'histoire,* French translation and selection by J. Michelet (Brussels, 1835), 218–219, quoted in *Pragmatisme,* 336, n. 2.
33. *Pragmatisme,* 288–289.
34. *Ibid.,* 83–84.
35. *Ibid.,* 42, n. 2.
36. *Ibid.,* 337.
37. *Ibid.,* 338–341.
38. *Ibid.,* 342–343.
39. *Ibid.,* 310, 319, 320–321.
40. *Ibid.,* 335.
41. *Ibid.,* 426–427.
42. *Ibid.,* 342, n. 1.
43. *Ibid.,* 328, 328 n. 2, 342.
44. *Ibid.,* 328–329 and 415, 330.
45. *Ibid.,* 413, n. 2. See also Bergson, *L'Evolution créatrice,* 48–49.
46. *Pragmatisme,* 329.
47. *Ibid.,* 46–47.
48. *Ibid.,* 60–61, 327–331.
49. *Ibid.,* 246–247.
50. *Ibid.,* 376–377.

51. *Ibid.*, 382 (see also 392); 62; 378.
52. *Ibid.*, 358, 444.
53. *Ibid.*, 449, 451.
54. *Ibid.*, 449.
55. *Ibid.*, 449.

VI. MARXISM AND A PLURALIST WORLD

1. *Pragmatisme*, 85, n. 2.
2. "Avant-propos," *Matériaux*, 37–51.
3. "Introduzione," *Saggi del Marxismo*, 16.
4. *Ibid.*, 7.
5. *Ibid.*, 9–10.
6. *Ibid.*, 8.
7. Benedetto Croce, *Historical Materialism and the Economics of Karl Marx* (New York, 1914), 78, 49.
8. "Osservazione intorno alla concezione materialista della storia," *Saggi del Marxismo*, 20–21; "I tre sistema storici di Marx," *Saggi del Marxismo*, 245.
9. "I tre sistema storici di Marx," *Saggi del Marxismo*, 245.
10. *Ibid.*, 243.
11. *Ibid.*, 244.
12. *Ibid.*, 256.
13. "Prefazione al 'Socialismo' di Colajanni," *Saggi del Marxismo*, 395.
14. *Pragmatisme*, 336, n. 2.
15. "I tre sistema storici di Marx," *Saggi del Marxismo*, 244.
16. "Osservazione intorno alla concezione materialista della storia," *Saggi del Marxismo*, 44.
17. "I tre sistema storici di Marx," *Saggi del Marxismo*, 240–243.
18. *Ibid.*, 240, 247.
19. *L'Ancienne et la Nouvelle Métaphysique*, 203.
20. "La necessita e il fatalismo nel marxismo," *Saggi del Marxismo*, 79.
21. *Ibid.*, 84.
22. *Ibid.*, 87.
23. Karl Marx, *La Misère de la philosophie, résponse a la philosophie de la misère de M. Proudhon* (Paris, 1892), 159, 151.
24. *Ibid.*, 169.
25. "La necessita e il fatalismo nel marxismo," *Saggi del Marxismo*, 88–89.
26. *Ibid.*, 89.
27. *Ibid.*, 92, 92–93.
28. *Ibid.*, 83.
29. Croce, *Historical Materialism*, 77, quoted in "I tre sistema storici di Marx," *Saggi del Marxismo*, 227.
30. "I tre sistema storici di Marx," *Saggi del Marxismo*, 240.
31. *Ibid.*, 246, quoting Marx.
32. "Osservazione intorno alla concezione materialista della storia," *Saggi del Marxismo*, 47; "La necessita e il fatalismo nel marxismo," *ibid.*, 63.
33. "La necessita e il fatalismo nel marxismo," *ibid.*, 69, 73.
34. "Le spiegazioni economiche," *Saggi del Marxismo*, 118–120.
35. "La necessita e il fatalismo nel marxismo," *Saggi del Marxismo*, 74.
36. Quoted in "Osservazione intorno alla concezione materialista della storia," *Saggi del Marxismo*, 21.
37. *Illusions*, 10.

38. "I tre sistema storici di Marx," *Saggi del Marxismo*, 227–230.
39. *Ibid.*, 253–254.
40. *Réflexions*, 61; "Introduzione," *Saggi del Marxismo*, 14; "Osservazione intorno alla concezione materialista della storia, *Saggi del Marxismo*, 48.
41. *Insegnamenti sociali*, 151.
42. "Vi e dell'utopia nel marxismo?" *Saggi del Marxismo*, 143, 151.
43. "La necessita e il fatalismo nel marxismo," *Saggi del Marxismo*, 67.
44. "Vi e dell'utopia nel marxismo?" *Saggi del Marxismo*, 151.
45. "Osservazione intorno alla concezione materialista della storia," *Saggi del Marxismo*, 46, 55.

VII. THE PHILOSOPHY OF SYNDICALISM

1. "Avenir socialiste des syndicats, Préface de 1905," *Matériaux*, 60–61.
2. *Réflexions*, 67.
3. *Ibid.*, 7.
4. *Marxisme*, 56.
5. *Réflexions*, 51–52.
6. See Georges Sorel, *Le Système historique de Renan* (Paris, 1905), 2; *Ruine du monde*, 311.
7. *Réflexions*, 13.
8. *Socrate*, 217.
9. Georges Sorel, "La Valeur sociale de l'art," *Revue de la métaphysique et de la morale*, May 1901, 258.
10. *Réflexions*, 12–13.
11. *Ibid.*, 17.
12. *Ibid.*, 18.
13. *Ibid.*, 18–19.
14. *Ibid.*, 21.
15. *Ibid.*, 23, 24.
16. *Réflexions*, 32; *Aspects juridiques*, 397.
17. "Avenir socialiste des syndicats, Préface de 1905," *Matériaux*, 61–64.
18. *Réflexions*, 33, 40.
19. Henri Bergson, *Essai sur les données immédiates de la conscience* (Paris, 1919), 178, quoted in *Réflexions*, 42.
20. *Réflexions*, 43–44.
21. *Ibid.*, 46.
22. *Ibid.*, 48–49.
23. *Ibid.*, 73.
24. "Avenir socialiste des syndicats," *Matériaux*, 98, n. 1.
25. *Marxisme*, 48–49.
26. *Réflexions*, 74.
27. *Marxisme*, 51.
28. *Réflexions*, 83–84.
29. *Ibid.*, 89.
30. *Ibid.*, 90–91.
31. *Ibid.*, 96.
32. *Ibid.*, 102.
33. Georges Sorel, "Socialismes nationaux," *Cahiers de la quinzaine*, 14th cahier, 3rd series, 1902, 55.
34. *Réflexions*, 12.
35. *Ibid.*, 111–112.

36. *Ibid.*, 125–126.
37. *Ibid.*, 130.
38. *Ibid.*, 130.
39. *Ibid.*, 141.
40. *Ibid.*, 145, 149–151.
41. *Ibid.*, 155.
42. *Ibid.*, 156–157.
43. *Ibid.*, 161.
44. *Ibid.*, 168.
45. *Ibid.*, 169.
46. *Ibid.*, 171.
47. *Ibid.*, 173.
48. "Avenir socialiste des syndicats," *Matériaux*, 81–82.
49. *Pragmatisme*, 75, n. 3.
50. "La necessita e il fatalismo nel marxismo," *Saggi del Marxismo*, 70.
51. *Réflexions*, 179, 180–181.
52. *Ibid.*, 182.
53. *Insegnamenti sociali*, 182.
54. *Réflexions*, 191, 195.
55. *Insegnamenti sociali*, 54–55.
56. *Ibid.*, 398.
57. *Réflexions*, 198.
58. According to Professor Brentano, of Munich, who cites a letter written in 1869 by Marx to his friend Beesly. Quoted in *Réflexions*, 199.
59. Georges Sorel, "La Crise du socialisme," *Revue politique et parlementaire*, December 1898, 612.
60. "Avenir socialiste des syndicats," *Matériaux*, 112.
61. "Avenir socialiste des syndicats, Préface de 1905," *Matériaux*, 70.
62. *Réflexions*, 217.
63. *Ibid.*, 232.
64. "Avenir socialiste des syndicats," *Matériaux*, 98.
65. Georges Sorel, "Les Dissensions de la Socialdémocratie en Allemagne," *Revue politique et parlementaire*, July, 1900, 50.
66. "L'Organisation de la démocratie," *Matériaux*, 386–387.
67. *Réflexions*, 253.
68. *Ibid.*, 249.
69. *Système de Renan*, 333.
70. *Réflexions*, 238, 240–241.
71. *Ibid.*, 243.
72. *Ibid.*, 250.
73. *Ibid.*, 249.
74. *Ibid.*, 262–263.
75. "Avenir socialiste des syndicats," *Matériaux*, 123.
76. Georges Sorel, "Quelques mots sur Proudhon," *Cahiers de la quinzaine*, 13th cahier, 2nd series, 1901, 25–26.
77. "Le idee giuridiche nel marxismo," *Saggi del Marxismo*, 202.
78. *Réflexions*, 269.
79. Georges Sorel, "Essai sur la philosophie de Proudhon," *Revue philosophique*, July 1892, 44–45.
80. Georges Sorel, "Morale et socialisme," *Mouvement socialiste*, March 1899, 208–209.

81. "Lettere a Croce" (no. cxcv, January 25, 1911), *Critica*, XXVI, 343.
82. Georges Sorel, review of "Le Caractère religieux du Socialisme," by E. Dolléans, *Mouvement socialiste*, November 1906, 287.
83. "Avenir socialiste des syndicats, Préface de 1905," *Matériaux*, 69.
84. Statements of this point of view may be found in the following: *Insegnamenti sociali*, 52; *Illusions*, 199 ff.; *Marxisme*, 22-23; review of Dolléans' *Caractère religieux du Socialisme*, 287.
85. *Ethique du socialisme*, 288, 290.
86. *Réflexions*, 276.
87. *Ibid.*, 279.
88. Georges Sorel, "Le Crime politique, d'après M. Lombroso," *Revue scientifique*, May 1893, 561.
89. *Réflexions*, 290.
90. Eduard von Hartmann, *Philosophy of the Unconscious* (London, 1893), III, 104, quoted in *Réflexions*, 288-289.
91. *Réflexions*, 298.
92. *Ibid.*, 308, 310.
93. *Insegnamenti sociali*, 341; *Réflexions*, 324-325.
94. *Insegnamenti sociali*, 397-398; "Avenir socialiste des syndicats," *Matériaux*, 128.
95. *Réflexions*, 368.
96. *Ibid.*, 29.
97. *Marxisme*, 66.
98. *Réflexions*, 371.
99. *Ibid.*, 371.
100. *Ibid.*, 377.
101. *Ibid.*, 378, 379-380, 384, 385.
102. *Ruine du monde*, 246.
103. *Réflexions*, 388.

INDEX

Hegel, Georg Wilhelm Friedrich, 30, 33, 38, 86, 146, 147
Heraclitus, 90, 136
Hero, 210
Heroic struggle, Bolshevism as, 23; of Christianity, 15, 170, 203; of Greece, 15, 16, 79, 80, 85, 137–138; monasticism, 29; through myths, 36, 188, 209; and pessimism, 167; of proletariat, 23, 28, 29, 183; syndicalism, 174, 179, 198, 212
Hetaira, 81, 82
Historical Sketch of Progress, 55
Hobbes, Thomas, 60
Homer, 79, 80
Huguenots, 211
Humanitarianism, 61
Humanité, 61

Id, 49, 52, 53, 54
Ideological dissociation, 119–121, 125
Iliad, 79
Indeterminism, 73
Individualism, arbitrary will of, 200; Bentham, 58–61; Burke, 52, 55; of Eastern cults, 81; encouraged by Church, 87; and freedom, 172; history of, 77–79, 84–94, 220; integrity of self, 12, 31; under liberalism, 27; Maistre and, 55; pretensions of, 120, threat to Greece, 81; of Socrates, 83–84; of syndicalists, 209
Intellectualism, abstractness, 57, 60, 88, 99, 165, 203; of Comte, 125–126; dangers, 120, 176, 208; definition, 32, 39–40, 43–49; and dogmatism, 38, 95–96; and Dreyfus Case, 18–19; of early Sorel, 17; limitations of, 76, 122; of Marx, 163; misconceptions, 26–27; in politics, 70–71; pretensions, 24, 68–69, 193–197; rationalism, 118–120, 189, 220; in socialism, 166; of Sorel, 36; and utopia, 123, 172, 173
Intolerance, Christian, 170; of Condorcet, 56; of intellectualism, 32, 44, 46; of liberals, 27; of utopians, 124
Inquisition, 184

Inversion of functions, 119, 123, 126, 136
Irrationalism, 76, 91, 95–96
Italy, betrayal of, 21–22; fascism, 26; Sorel's attitude, 22

Jacobin, 80
James, William, anti-intellectualist, 44; definition of intellectualism, 45–46; influence, 38; pragmatism, 42, 45, 64, 130–131
Jaurès, Jean Léon, 165, 180; Dreyfus Case, 185
Jesuits, as educators, 113, 118
Jesus, 16, 169
Judaism, 192
Judea, 154
Justice, of Condorcet, 56; economic basis, 199–200; family, 4; French Republic, 177; French Revolution, 23, 114; in modern France, 184–186; of politicians, 197; of Proudhon, 18, 94; in the workshop, 193

Kant, Immanuel, 78, 96
Kapital, Das, 146
Koinonia, 81, 83

Labor movement, 17, 18–20
Law, commercial, effect of, 109; Roman, effect of introduction, 106–107, 169
Law of the 22 Prairial, 185
Legion of Honor, 3
Lenin, Nicolay, praise of, 22–23; views on Sorel, 24
Leonardo da Vinci, 220
Le Play, P. G. F., 38
Levellers, 110
Liberalism, of bourgeoisie, 62, 96, 116; of French Revolution, 114; in practice, 115–116; Russian, 22; of Sorel, 27, 38
Libidinal energy, 59, 219
Ligue des Droits de l'homme, 206
Locke, John, 42, 43, 108, 110
Louis XIV, 116
Louis XV, 102, 103
Loyola, Ignatius, 121

Psychoanalysis, 220
Psychological factors, 161
Psychologists, 75, 77
Psychology, 52–53, 74
Puritanism, 15, 72

Quantitative method, 89–93
Quantum mechanics, 90
Quantum theory, 144

Radicalism, 15, 38, 109
Raison d'état, 185
Rationalism, abstraction, 40, 98–99, 117; adulation, 107; anti-intellectualism, 43–49; dogmatism, 108, 113; education of will, 75; of eighteenth century, 40–41; expediency, 122; false freedom, 69; French Revolution, 40; government under, 196; Greek, 137–138; illusions, 112; intellectualists, 125–129; limitations, 172; Positivism, 126; pretensions of, 83; Proudhon, 17; utilitarians, 58
Red Guard, 23
Reflections on Violence, 1, 6, 18, 19, 24, 25, 30
Religion, certitude in, 43, 46; Condorcet, 56; Eastern cults, 81; innovators, 221; Maistre and, 54; pessimism, 166, 167; positivism, 125, 126; pragmatism, 98; primitive peoples, 214–215; role of energy, 213; Socrates, 83–84; of Sorel, 29–35
Renan, Ernest, 15, 38, 39
Republic of Virtue, 185
Residues, 119, 122
Restoration, 114–115, 117
Reuleaux, 133
Revisionism, of Marx, 143, 145
Revolution, proletarian, 179, 180, 181, 182, 183; of 1848, 62
Reybaud, Louis, 62
Ricorso, 16, 19, 27, 28, 31, 36
Rights of Man, Condorcet on, 56
Risorgimento, 36, 171, 189, 213
Robespierre, Maximilien, 185
Romanovs, 24
Rome, decadence, 182; decline, 85;

ethical role, 24; fall, 213; intransigence of Christianity, 192
Rousseau, Jean Jacques, and democracy, 70, 206; influence, 128; natural virtue, 113; social contract, 108, 109
Royalism, 20–21
Russia, 23
Russian Revolution, hope for, 24; victims of, 23

Salon, 111
Savigny, Friedrich Karl von, 129
Schizophrenia, 47–48, 88, 121
Scholasticism, 41, 45, 47, 123, 152
Science, abstraction, 117–118; attitude of Nietzsche, Freud, Sorel, 219–220; Descartes, 121, 122; government by, 125; illusions, 99; industrial basis, 67; influence in education, 127; innovators, 221; law, 118; limitations, 188; modern pluralism, 97; political exploitation through, 116; predictability, 215; proper role, 44, 125–142, 149–157, 161–163; research, 214; role of energy, 213; simplifications, 109; Sorel's qualities, 39; success of, 13, 47, 48, 193, 216
Scientific method, Condorcet's trust in, 56; faith in, 96–97; ideas of freedom, 89; intellectualism, 46; limitations, 40, 89, 123, 149, 162, 172; in Marx, 145, 155, 156–157; misconceptions, 100; revolutionary effects, 41–43; in Sorel, 25, 26–27, 29–36; success of, 48–49, 124
Scientific socialism, Marx's claim to, 143–144
Scriptures, 15
Sculpture, Greek, 137, 142
Second Empire, 62
Sex, emancipation of woman, 81; as entropic, 72–73; ethical role, 71–72, 75; importance in psychology, 73, 122, 221; marriage, 81–82; in music, 213; Sorel's anticipation of Freud, 72
Sixteenth of May, 63
Skepticism, 8–9, 92, 131, 133

170; and proletariat, 28; monism, 97; optimism, 62–63; rashness, 156; rationalism, 127–128; reforms, 166; socialism, 85, 165

Vaillant, Edward, 180
Valois, Georges, 20
Variot, Jean, 20
Vendeans, 177
Vico, Giovanni Battista, 64, 118, 132, 133, 149, 210
Violence, apology for, 26; causes of outbreak, 157; concern with energy, 213; ethical role, 179–212 *passim*, French Revolution, 114; Greek heroes, 79; intellectuals, 120
Voltaire, François Marie Arouet, 41, 86–87

Waldeck-Rousseau, Pierre Marie René, 206

Wandering Jew, 171
War, significance to Greece, 80–81, 84; Sorel's prediction of, 22; and violence, 186
Watt, James, 210
Whitehead, Alfred North, 42; definition of intellectualism, 45–46
Woman, as educator, 71, 75; emancipation, 82
Workingman, as artist, 66; docility, 33; ethical role, 64–71; exploitation of, 179; potentialities, 4; Sorel's trust of, 64, 222
Workshop, ethical role, 67, 68, 193, 208, 209, 210, 220; influence on science, 133

Xenophon, 15

Zarathustra, 220
Zola, Emile, 205